People Get Ready

.

PEOPLE GET READY

Twelve Jesus-Haunted Misfits, Malcontents, and Dreamers in Pursuit of Justice

Edited by

Peter Slade, Shea Tuttle,
and Jacqueline A. Bussie

WILLIAM B. EERDMANS PUBLISHING COMPANY
GRAND RAPIDS, MICHIGAN

Wm. B. Eerdmans Publishing Co.
4035 Park East Court SE, Grand Rapids, Michigan 49546
www.eerdmans.com

29 28 27 26 25 24 23   1 2 3 4 5 6 7

ISBN 978-0-8028-7904-2

Library of Congress Cataloging-in-Publication Data

A catalog record for this book is available from the Library of Congress.

For all the saints,

the misfits, malcontents, and dreamers,

from whom we borrow hope in the present age

Contents

CONTENTS

FOREWORD

Life Stories and the Exemplification of Christian Truth

In a letter from Tegel Prison, written on the occasion of the baptism of the son of Eberhard and Renate Bethge in May 1944, Dietrich Bonhoeffer spoke of the new form that Christian witness would assume in "the revolutionary times ahead"—that period following the German church's complicity in mass death and the mission to create a world without Jews.

Bonhoeffer offered this "first child of a new generation," Dietrich Wilhelm Rüdiger Bethge, a sober assessment of the possibility and future of Christianity. It was not solely intended to gentle him into the faith; the challenges of the coming years would throw everyone back to first convictions. What could be more obvious than that the church had lost its capacity to make real the word of reconciliation and redemption to the world? "We have spent too much time in thinking, supposing that if we weigh in advance the possibilities of any action, it will happen automatically. We have learnt, rather too late, that action comes, not from thought, but from a readiness for responsibility. For your thought and action will enter on a new relationship; your thinking will be confined to your responsibilities in action. With us thought was often the luxury of the onlooker; with you it will be entirely subordinated to action."[1]

What Bonhoeffer was hinting at here was exemplification, "the importance of human example (which has its origin in the humanity of Jesus and is so important in Paul's teaching)," and apart from which it is difficult to see the Christian difference. "It is something that we have almost entirely forgotten."[2]

Exemplification is an idea he would have also encountered in his readings of Nietzsche, who figured prominently in Bonhoeffer's thinking after his *Nachdenken*, if you will, Christianity's historic demurral on worldly passion, and was among the pantheon of such artists and thinkers as Michelangelo, Raphael, Mozart, the Knight of Bamberg, Luther, Cervantes, Rubens, Karl Barth—it's a crowded pantheon—who stuck themselves into their work with a certain audacious confidence that they were giving the world something good, even if the world thought otherwise. A "high-spirited confidence," "a willingness to defy popular opinion" (and if this has you thinking of the plucky Catholic writer from rural Georgia who licensed the secular American literati "a generation of wingless chickens," you're on the right dirt road). "Not a faith, but a course of action," Nietzsche wrote, "above all a course of inaction, non-interference, and a different life."[3]

In his final theological sketch, "Outline for a Book," Bonhoeffer spoke of the importance of exemplification in understanding the truth of the gospel. "It is not abstract argument," he wrote, "but example, that gives its word emphasis and power."[4] "I hope to take up later this subject of 'example' and its place in the New Testament," he told Eberhard, to whom he sent "Outline" in August 1944 (three months after he wrote the baptismal letter). Ten months later he was executed by the Nazis in the concentration camp at Flossenbürg.

In the sketch, Bonhoeffer outlines the possibility and future of Christianity in the aftermath of the war. There is not a hint of ecclesial triumphalism in these paragraphs. Is it even prudent to speak of the God of Jesus Christ to the unbeliever after this period of cataclysmic evil? Even the most provisional yes must come with clear and costly conditions; and after that "revolutionary" period, mentioned in the baptismal letter, the Christian witness would be limited to, nourished through, prayer and righteous action alone.

"The church is the church only when it exists for others." The church will share in "the secular problems of ordinary human life," not by overwhelming others with our cleverness but in being with, through generosity and service, as instruments of peace and steadfastness, taking the field "against the vices of hubris, power-worship, envy, and humbug, as the roots of all evil."[5]

What, or where, is the church for us today? That question preoccupied Bonhoeffer in his last months, and, *mutatis mutandis*, it rightly preoccupies disciples of Jesus Christ today. Jesus Christ remains the same, "yesterday, today, and forever," but Christians will need to discern the form, and the place, of his presence in the world with optimal attention to the present era. What is Christianity, or who is Christ for us now? The question troubled him incessantly, he said: this question of "what Christianity really is, or indeed who Christ really is, for us today."[6] What does it mean to be Christian in a world that through disobedience, and indeed out of apostasy, can no longer hear the miraculous announcement that God so loved the world, so loved, so loved? Are we still of any use?

Bonhoeffer's own life, as much as anything he wrote, exemplifies an answer to that pressing question. We are of use when, and only when, we assume Christ's posture of being for the world. As early as his doctoral dissertation, *Sanctorum Communio*, which Barth read when it appeared in book form and proclaimed a "theological miracle," Bonhoeffer insisted that the vicarious representative atonement of Jesus Christ patterns the "structural principle" of the Christ community. "God's vicarious action in Jesus is a testament to the love of God; and as the love of God in action it restores the community between God and human beings," and creates a new sociality.[7]

The church is the church when it embraces its calling to be a community for the world's healing. So, again, the exemplars of the excellences of Jesus Christ, the ones who suffer for a just cause and are thereby beatified, bear witness to an experience in "which the power of Jesus Christ [becomes] manifest in fields of life where it had previously remained unknown."[8]

And then, as ever, discipleship—that most key category for Bonhoeffer. Discipleship, from the German *Nachfolge*, meaning "to follow after." The disciples of Jesus Christ are the ones who follow him into those manifold fields and ask the Spirit to let them there exemplify him.

*   *   *

People Get Ready directs our attention to twelve people who did just that—followed the example of Jesus into spaces marked by oppression and the tyranny of death, and there made manifest God's love of all that God made. White race traitors, a musician who sang the dignity of workers, and a woman who uncommonly loved the sea; a visionary architect of sanctuary; a Korean immigrant to America who at the age of ninety wrote a searing memoir of racism and survival. Each of the men and women hymned in this book shows the truth of Bonhoeffer's recognition "that God wants us to love him eternally with our whole hearts—not in such a way as to injure or weaken our earthly love," but exactly entangled with "earthly affection."

The book takes its title from Chicagoan Curtis Mayfield's gospel-inflected hit song with its message of the Lord's grace and the promise of reaching the destination of freedom and salvation. The song was also a call to action. When Martin Luther King Jr. took the SCLC (Southern Christian Leadership Conference) to Chicago in 1966, "People Get Ready" became an anthem of that campaign. "That was taken from my church or from the upbringing of messages from the church," Mayfield said. "Like there's no hiding place and get on board."[9] It is a journey bound for justice, Mayfield added, a journey that "welcomes everyone," a journey train "to the promised land, really."[10]

The essays herein are concerned less with the accomplishments of twelve remarkable people (though the accomplishments of many are profound—legislation passed, social reforms achieved, policies enacted) than with the ways their witness serves as a call to get on board—enduringly nourishing faith and activism in the present. Of her own preoccupation with Rachel Carson, a woman who didn't plan to become a climate prophet *avant la lettre* but was "propelled into public witness" by her cares and concerns, Mallory McDuff writes, "When I worry about my students' future—and that of my daughters—I yearn for a solid story to share. I don't need a vapid inspirational tale but a strategic model of inspired persistence." Or as Jemar Tisby writes in his essay on Tom Skinner, "I never had the opportunity to meet . . . Skinner, but if I could, I would tell him that his words and example helped another Black Christian who has spent a lot of time with white evangelicals to boldly proclaim, 'The Liberator has come!'" And, just as Tisby interrogates Skinner's life, so too he realizes that others may examine our lives. "Did we stay consistent? Did we betray our convictions for wealth or comfort? Did our zeal wane with age? Did we compromise with racism or courageously confront it?" These questions cannot "be answered in a single action or a short season. The most important questions about our character can only be answered by the witness of our entire lives."

"When I first started in theology, my idea of it was quite different—rather more academic," Bonhoeffer wrote in a 1935 letter to his brother Karl-Friedrich. Members of the Bonhoeffer family, it seemed, had begun to worry about the excesses of Dietrich's devotion to Jesus. "Now it has turned into something else altogether. . . . I think I am right in saying that I would only achieve true inner clarity and honesty by really starting to take the Sermon on the Mount seriously. Here alone lies the force that can blow all this hocus-pocus sky-high—like fireworks, leaving only a few burnt-out shells behind."[11] The twelve men and women considered here took the Sermon on the Mount seriously, too; their lives are the fireworks of which Bonhoeffer wrote, though I'd rather say that if they wholly spent themselves (a few, like Patty Boyle, truly burning themselves out in the work, as activists so often do), they nonetheless left behind not empty shells but kindling for our own work.

In her essay on Carson, McDuff describes Carson "doggedly claw[ing] at her writing and advocacy through illness, devoting her life (and her death) to the health of people and places." *Doggedly clawing at witness*—an estimable example for us all to follow.

*   *   *

In his late writings, Bonhoeffer pondered the idea of a new nobility: the future of the Christian movement depends on nothing less than a "new elite of people," with moral sensibilities shaped by "a higher satisfaction"— an aristocracy of responsibility, we might say, a nobility of the righteous and the prayerful. This nobility would be marked by its fierce love of this world and spirited into speech and action for the sake of the coming generation. "It is only when one loves life and the earth so much that without them everything seems to be over that one may believe in the resurrection and a new world."[12]

Some of this nobility's exemplars would come from the global, ecumenical church; others would number among the ranks of the good people, of whom Bonhoeffer had written in *Ethics*, in a positively stunning revision of the Lutheran trope of the eviscerated self—or of what Krister Stendahl once called the "introspective consciousness of the West": "Other times could preach that a man must first become a sinner, like the publican and the harlot, before he could know and find Christ, but we in our time must say rather that before a man can know and find Christ he must first become righteous like those who strive and who suffer for the sake of justice, truth and humanity."[13]

Despite the heartfelt efforts of postliberal theologians to cast Bonhoeffer as a church theologian in the tradition of Karl Barth and Stanley Hauerwas, Bonhoeffer's persistent ambivalence about the church (which long predated the war) and his dissatisfaction with most doctrinal explications render such efforts incomplete. Bonhoeffer's nobility did not require the church's nourishment, nor her blessing. For Bonhoeffer, discipleship is best read as a theological rhetoric of dissent—and sometimes what was dissented from was the church, its local expressions and its hierarchies. (*Life Together*, let us recall, was written not as a manual or a guidebook on Christian community; it was composed as a meditation on an experiment in evangelical monasticism now vanished.) Not all his new nobles would have in common churchgoing, or baptism, but all would be marked by the dispositions of compassion, honesty, forthrightness, and civil courage, and in turn—and in one of my favorite passages in Bonhoeffer's vast oeuvre—they would illuminate the path "from the newspaper and the radio to the book, from feverish activity to unhurried leisure, from dispersion to concentration, from sensationalism to reflection."[14] Likewise, the twelve characters in this book relate variously to the church—some loved church in the old familiar ways; some loved church while facing wholly, or immersed fully in, the world; and some were largely detached from the church's offices. What the twelve saints (and, yes, I do claim them thus) have in common with one another, what ranks them among Bonhoeffer's nobles, is not that they sit Sunday by Sunday in a pew, but that they stand unapologetically on the side of the stranger, the outcast, the dissident, the individual of conscience, *and the book*, against the present profanations.

"I hope to take up later this subject of 'example' and its place in the New Testament," Bonhoeffer wrote to Eberhard in his "Outline for a Book."[15] We regret the absence of a theological essay on exemplification. It is our hope that *People Get Ready* contributes toward this unfinished project.

Charles Marsh

ACKNOWLEDGMENTS

By the time we completed work on *Can I Get a Witness? Thirteen Peacemakers, Community Builders, and Agitators for Faith and Justice* in 2019, we already had in mind a second volume, not only because the need for peacemakers and misfits is ongoing and ever-urgent, but because there are so many stories worth telling. Countless peculiar people have made what the American saint John Lewis called "good trouble" in pursuit of a better, more righteous world, and we wanted to commit a few more of their stories to print. We're so grateful for all who shared this vision and helped bring this second volume into being.

Both *Witness* and *People Get Ready* are the products of collaborations hosted by the Project on Lived Theology at the University of Virginia. We are grateful to project director Charles Marsh for his vision and stewarding, as well as to Jessica Seibert and Kim Curtis, whose able and steadfast support keeps all the wheels turning.

The team at Eerdmans—past and present—has been unfailing even amid editorial transitions. Thank you to David Bratt, James Ernest, Andrew Knapp, Jenny Hoffman, and Tom Raabe, sharp and thoughtful editors all, who have made this book better. Our thanks as well to Amy Kent for keeping us in line and attending to the important details required to usher a book into the world.

The Project on Lived Theology exists by the grace of the Lilly Endowment's generosity and vision. Thank you, as always, to Jessicah Duckworth and Chris Coble for shepherding such misfits, malcontents, and dreamers.

FLORENCE JORDAN

(1912–1987)

Florence and Clarence Jordan; photo courtesy of Hargrett Rare Book and Manuscript Library / University of Georgia Libraries

STAYING PUT IN THE GOD MOVEMENT

The Life and Faith of Florence Jordan

Ansley L. Quiros

She senses the light first, savoring the shift in consciousness that heralds a new day. Moving slowly, she opens her blue eyes and extends her arms. Even after all these years, it is strange to have the extra space, to wake up alone, without him. The sorrow sometimes still surprises her.

Yet, another day, she thinks, as the chirping birds and rustling tree limbs outside remind. It's as though they've begun to sing. She joins in: "Great is Thy faithfulness! Great is Thy faithfulness! Morning by morning new mercies I see. All I have needed Thy hand hath provided. Great is Thy faithfulness, Lord, unto me."[1]

Rising, she prays, for grace, for courage, for strength to love. In the words of Saint Benedict: "Always we begin again." As she straightens the bed, she prays for her children far away—Eleanor and Jim, Jan and Lenny—as well as for her grandchildren. As she puts on a cream knit dress, she prays too for the farm, her home for these many decades, offering up to God its myriad details and relationships and travails. Neighbors and friends come to mind as she slides on her shoes; she asks God to ease their aches and pains, to be near them in suffering. "Thy kingdom come, Thy will be done." She swats at a fly, then emphatically resumes, "Deliver us from evil." *She loathes flies. Exhaling, she lifts her palms.* "For thine is the kingdom and the power and the glory, forever. Amen."[2]

It can be hard to imagine the kingdom and the power and the glory when your knees ache and the flies buzz and it's just another Monday morning.[3] Florence Jordan has learned this over her seventy-three years, most of them spent here in this plot of land called Koinonia Farm. Our mundane lives can feel inconsequential, the smallness of our attempts at goodness mocked by the scale of injustice. What match is a faithful life for war and arrogance and distraction? What spiritual transformation could possibly be wrought by a woman in rural Georgia? And yet, somehow, ordinary people, living ordinary lives, doing ordinary things, can be incarnational, can reveal Light in darkness. After all, "Who can really be faithful in great things," Dietrich Bonhoeffer asks, "if he has not learned to be faithful in the things of daily life?"[4] Somehow, small, quotidian actions of love can bring about radical transformation. Her husband, Clarence, used to talk about this sort of radical transformation, this kingdom of God, as the God Movement. She always loved that idea—that God's spirit of love was on the move, ushering in reconciliation and justice and peace.

But so much of the God Movement, for her, has simply looked like staying put. Despite the rush of redemption, the life of faith and faithfulness often feels hidden, small, what Eugene Peterson calls a "long obedience in the same direction."[5] But that is how the kingdom comes: one moment, one resurrection breath, after another.

One day at a time.

Before heading downstairs, Florence looks at her reflection. Her silvering hair and lined face reveal her age. But as she applies lipstick and turns her head, she sees for a moment the girl she once was.

On a cold day in November 1912, two days before Thanksgiving, Florence Louise Kroeger was born in Louisville, Kentucky. Her father, Fred Kroeger, had immigrated to the United States from Germany around the turn of the century, making his way to Louisville, where he worked as a builder. In 1908, he married Ida Weilage, who was also of German descent, but a Louisville native. The couple settled in the city, where they were surrounded by a tight-knit German American community. Following Florence, Fred and Ida welcomed another daughter, Lillian, and then a son they called F. C. Despite the hardships Americans confronted in those years—war, depression, war again—the Kroegers still enjoyed tulips in the spring garden, *zimtsterne* baking at Christmastime, and the organ strains at the Baptist church. Decidedly middle class, they enjoyed both a warm family life and an active social calendar. When she was ten, Florence, along with her sister, Lillian, attended an Easter party at the home of one of her friends that warranted coverage by the *Louisville Courier-Journal*. In the following years, the Kroeger girls took weekly ballroom dancing classes, participated in theater productions in Latin, and attended showers and numerous other parties.[6]

Despite this upbringing, Florence never felt particularly well suited for society life in Kentucky. For one thing, she was tall and broad. When the Kentucky Classical Association announced roles for their production of *The Marriage of Tulia*, for example, Florence discovered she had been cast as "parent" of the bride.[7] But more than having to play less dainty roles on occasion, Florence had a heft to her, a seriousness. As her friend Peyton Thurman put it later: "she always carried her head just a little higher and had just a little more substance than other girls."[8] Though reserved by nature, she had strong ideas, energy, and an uncommonly deep faith. But what could a woman in the early twentieth century do with that?

After graduating from high school, Florence, perhaps trying to make sense of it, enrolled at the University of Louisville for a course in psychology. When she confided in her friends and her sister a desire to contribute to the world, to make her life count, and to really follow Christ, they often would tilt their heads and smile, politely but blankly. But it was this desire that drew her to the job at the seminary—and to him.

Florence Kroeger lifted her ice-blue eyes at the sound of the creaking door. It was him again. As the lanky southerner strode into the Southern Seminary Library evening after evening that fall of 1933, she knew there was something odd about him. His accent, certainly, but also his jaunty walk that betrayed a hint of mischief. Sometimes she would spot him huddled over theology textbooks, mouth moving almost imperceptibly, intensely focused.

For his part, Clarence took notice of the pretty young library assistant as well but hesitated to speak to her, at least initially. He felt overwhelmed by his new course load and out of place socially. Since arriving in Louisville, he had often mistaken his fellow seminarians for professors, which made him newly self-conscious about his own clothes and appearance.[9] He was a long way from his hometown of Talbotton, in middle Georgia, a long way from what he had known or expected. He had studied agriculture at the University of Georgia and planned on becoming a farmer, but then felt a stirring of the Spirit and a call to the ministry. Which is how he found himself surrounded by dusty texts rather than pecan trees, energized but lonely. One day, though, a hearty laugh broke through the stuffy stillness of the library. Clarence followed the sound. It was her.

They began dating. But after a few love-struck months, the normally jovial Clarence turned serious. "Florence, you know I am not going to be a regular preacher. Not at First Baptist and all that and maybe not at any church."[10] For a moment his eyes darted to the floor, but then they met hers evenly, expectantly.

"I know," she said, smiling. She never aspired to marry a preacher, had never thought of herself as a preacher's wife, despite the years around Southern Seminary. She just wanted him. And she wanted what she knew now would be her life with him, unconventional maybe, but full of truth and love. And she wanted to be a part of it, a partner. Somehow in this strange boy from Georgia with an easy demeanor and a radical faith, she sensed a match. As she put it, years later, "Clarence and I are very much alike."[11] And they were. Seeing the pair around the seminary campus, onlookers often mistook them for brother and sister.[12] And, of course, in some sense, they were that too.

After knowing Florence for almost three years, Clarence asked Fred Kroeger for her hand in marriage. Her mother joked it probably wouldn't matter to the couple whether they consented or not, strong-willed as her daughter was, but added that she too approved.[13] When Clarence's father heard of his son's engagement, he wrote with congratulations and advice. "No man or woman who does not know and love God can truly love one another. Since you both love him I know you will love each other and be supremely happy." Clarence and Florence agreed. They had already vowed "not to be first with each other," agreeing that "the Lord had to be first."[14] "I want to tell you," Mr. Jordan's letter concluded, "that a good woman is one of God's greatest gifts to man, to the world, and to mankind."[15] He couldn't have known how prophetic those words would be.

Their engagement announcement appeared in the newspaper at the end of May 1936, and the couple married two months later on a warm July afternoon. It was a simple affair at the Kroeger home, attended by family and close friends. Thomas A. Johnson, the seminary librarian, officiated the ceremony, having witnessed much of the romance unfold. Florence beamed over her bouquet of pink roses and blue delphiniums as she locked eyes with Clarence. Walking toward him in her pink lace dress, blonde hair swept back, she had no idea what their life and marriage would hold. But as she vowed before God "for better or worse, richer or poorer," Florence smiled broadly. Clarence grinned right back.[16]

The bell rings, not loudly, but she can hear its bright call across the farm property. Every morning they gather for a chapel service. In the

*still room, often they just sit in meditative silence. Or pray. Some-
times someone shares a testimony or devotion from the Scripture.
This daily office, the daily practice of faith, is their collective habit.
This morning in the chapel, just a simple room without ornamenta-
tion, the rhythmic swish of her straw fan the only sound besides the
shifting saints around her, she envisions the other spaces in which
she has worshiped over the years—the stately brick Clifton Road
Baptist Church she'd attended as a girl in Louisville, the Southern
Seminary chapel, and Rehoboth Baptist, here in south Georgia, just
down the road from the farm. She thinks back to all she learned in
those places—and all she'd had to unlearn.*

"What in the Sam Hill is this I hear, Florence?" Mr. Bullard, the
business manager and her boss, leered above her desk. His face
reddened splotchily, the veins above his starched collar protruding
visibly. "Do you really think that this Seminary should let those
n——s eat in the dormitory alongside white men?" She met his eyes
but said nothing. "Do you?" he pushed, voice rising with fury.

Finally, she spoke, quiet but firm. "Yes, I do. They are the
invited guests of the Seminary prayer meeting committee and
should be treated with respect like any other visitors." Bullard
exploded, a stream of racist expletives filling the modest office.
Florence closed her eyes briefly and rested a hand protectively on
her stomach. She was almost seven months along at that point,
the baby girl kicking hard in response to the loud diatribe.[17]

After their wedding, Clarence had opted to remain at the seminary to pursue a PhD in Greek New Testament, with Florence's
support.[18] As newlyweds, they spent many nights reading together
on the couch in an easy quiet. "In his study of the Greek, he did
much research into the roots, derivation, and nuances of words.
He also studied the papyri for the common usages of phrases and
meanings," she later wrote. "A single passage could take hours
of study and meditation."[19] And yet, Florence could plainly see
Clarence delighted in it. As his biographer Dallas Lee put it, "he

began to discover theological foundations for the human impulses in him."[20] He also began to find human foundations for his theological impulses, especially among Black brothers and sisters. Clarence had begun teaching New Testament at Simmons University, a Black seminary in town, where he wrestled with the gospel's implications for American race relations. In these years Florence could sense a joyous cohesion forming in him: the Logos. The Word. The Word made flesh. Incarnation. But this understanding of the biblical ethic of racial unity was not universally shared. In fact, it was what had enraged Bullard earlier that day.

Florence was cooking supper when Clarence walked into their apartment. Seeing her, he knew something was wrong. When he asked, "Sweet, what happened?" she told him about Bullard. Some folks would rather worship the status quo than Jesus, he lamented, shaking his head. But he insisted nonetheless that the seminarians be welcomed as brothers in the Lord, and that they all break bread together in fellowship. Florence nodded. They fell silent for a minute, her eyes traveling around the small apartment. "Let's host them here," Florence said, resolutely, as she resumed stirring.

Later that week, with Florence's permission, Clarence made an appointment to speak with the seminary's president, John Sampey. As he entered the opulent office and took a seat, Clarence found himself staring into the eyes of Robert E. Lee, whose portrait loomed over the president's desk. He recalled an address that Sampey, a native of Lowndes County, Alabama, had given a few years back in which he called Lee "the greatest Christian since Paul." He knew the kind. With Lee looking on, Clarence exhaled and explained the couple's plan. They would elude the Southern Baptist seminary's segregation policy by hosting the welcome meal for the Simmons seminarians in their apartment. "And this is okay with your wife?" Sampey asked, incredulous.

Clarence chuckled. "She suggested it."[21]

Following this incident, the Jordans' commitment to racial justice deepened. In January 1939, Clarence accepted a job directing the Sunshine Center, later renamed the Baptist Fellowship Center, a home missions effort in Louisville's predominantly Black West End. There, he worked with Black pastors and churches to address a myriad of social injustices, to train and educate Black ministers and laypeople, and to collaborate with local white Baptists. While the center had previously focused on Sunday school, vacation Bible school, and other religious instruction, Clarence insisted that "people can't listen to a message if they're hungry," expanding the social services the center offered.[22] Even in addressing material needs, Clarence resisted paternalism, urging white volunteers not to assume leadership positions or presume that they could "help you dear folks run things."[23] He restructured the mission's leadership, bringing Baptist leaders together for fellowship, Bible study, worship, and deacons' planning meetings, and subverted segregationist strictures. Some white members of the Long Run Baptist Association, which had called him initially to the position, resented Jordan's "offensive and obnoxious"[24] methods as well as his increasingly outspoken articles on the need for Christians to embody the "great fact that in Jesus Christ the 'great middle wall of partition' was abolished."[25] Mistrust only increased when the Jordans started attending Virginia Avenue Baptist, a Black church. This they did, though, primarily for their own benefit. "The Negro has a great contribution to make," Clarence said, "an interpretation of Christ that the rest of the world needs."[26] Though Florence had never previously interacted much with Black people, had not, in her childhood, frequented the west side of Louisville, she felt a deep Christian kinship, a fullness of the Spirit, in that church.

The work burdened her husband, that much was clear from his heavy eyes and sloping shoulders coming through the frame of their Louisville apartment with the cold air. But she could also see the wheels turning in his mind. So many of the Black folks in Louisville, suffering on the West End from poor housing, poor health, unemployment, despair, segregation, and racism, he told her one evening, were from farms in the South. She waited for him to go on. Florence knew, of course, how important farming was to him. Many of the Black folks in Louisville had been farmers or sharecroppers, he continued, forced to leave ancestral homes and extended families by economic desperation and racial terror. But what if they could have stayed? Purchased a small plot of land and worked it? What would the harvest have been? What ecological wisdom and more, what support and joy might have been shared by generations staying put? And what if they could have continued to worship God in the clapboard churches built during Reconstruction, those churches that testified from the ends of the earth? What of that heritage of faith? What if there was a new way, a new kingdom, in a new South, where Black and white Christians could share land and faith and life together? Now, Clarence seemed almost wistful, for the past or the future, she couldn't quite tell. Slowly, as the conversations continued, she began to imagine for herself a home she had never seen among a people she had never known. It brought to mind the words of Ruth: "For where you go I will go, and where you lodge I will lodge. Your people shall be my people, and your God my God."[27]

A few years later, in the fall of 1941, Clarence attended a meeting of the Fellowship of Reconciliation in Louisville and met J. Martin England, a quiet man, but one who, from their previous correspondence, he sensed shared his fierce Christian convictions. Martin explained that he and his wife, Mabel, had been on prolonged furlough from mission work in Burma, denied returning to Asia by the outbreak of war, and longed to see a Christian community in which people of all races and classes might come together to work as equals in the United States.[28] In turn, Clarence described the discussion group that he and Florence had begun hosting. When he described the purpose of their group, which they called *koinōnia*, the Greek word for fellowship in the book of Acts, Martin seemed genuinely intrigued. The two men, along with Florence and Mabel, began meeting regularly. Over the course of several weeks, they excitedly discussed their shared commitments: to Christian community, to racial justice and integration, to resisting materialism and militarism. Clarence proposed that the rural, agricultural South could be fertile ground for their hopes. "If I ever leave Louisville," he had written a couple years earlier, "it will be for the red hills of Georgia or the valleys of Mississippi."[29] Desirous to learn some farming skills for an eventual return to Burma, Martin expressed openness, while Mabel was not only amenable but downright cheerful about a *koinōnia* in the South, saying it sounded "like a real adventure!"[30] Though they would spend only a few years in close proximity, Florence would always remember Mabel's example of open enthusiasm and willingness to venture out in obedience to God. Florence, too, was willing to give up what she could not keep to gain what she could not lose.[31] She had known since those early library conversations that they would likely never have much. "Clarence had told me that he would never make money," she recalled, but "I had faith in him. Clarence was not just idealistic; he was also sound. No matter how little we had I never worried.... He worried about not taking different job opportunities, about whether he was being fair to me and [their daughter] Eleanor, but I told him if he did what the Lord wanted, I knew we would be alright."[32] One night, late, as the four of them sat around the Englands' living room in Wakefield, Kentucky, as by this time they often did, Clarence blurted out, "Well, what are we waiting for?"[33] Florence laughed before meeting the others' eyes, all of them shining.

Outside the chapel, the morning sun shines brightly on the neat rows of pecan trees, the blueberry bushes, the garden plot. She can hear the whir of machinery gearing up, the school bus accelerating in the distance. It is time to get to work. Entering the Koinonia office, Florence lowers herself down before her trusty typewriter and looks through the recent letters and budgets. She tallies the donations coming into the Fund for Humanity, fills out expense reports, notes the fruitcake orders needing to be shipped. Straightening a stack of mail, she spies a photograph perched on the desk. It shows

around twenty people, Black and white, huddled together, children
perched on shoulders, squinting into the sun. She is holding her in-
fant daughter, Jan, wearing her favorite blue shirtdress, and staring
directly back at herself.

The early days of Koinonia were a stressful, delightful blur.
After deciding to found the farm, their "demonstration plot" for
the kingdom, and securing seed money from Arthur Steilberg,
Clarence and Martin began to search for a suitable place to root
their experiment.[34] It should be in the Black Belt, they agreed,
and by the summer of 1942, they had nearly settled on Alabama.[35]
That September, they sent out an initial newsletter announcing
the establishment of Koinonia Farm, "an agricultural missionary
enterprise," following months of "preparation and decisions."
"We have tried to lay the foundation carefully and to move only
after thorough study, consultation, and prayer," they said, and now
had adopted a "practical plan for implementing [their] convictions
about some of the vital teachings of Jesus." "Counting the cost"
of doing God's will, it continued, "all four of us [Florence and
Clarence Jordan, Mabel and Martin England] definitely and unre-
servedly gave ourselves to the execution of this plan, and agreed to
move to our chosen location, the Lord willing, before Jan. 1, 1943."
This initial mailing concluded: "We'll try to keep you informed as
to the activities, anxieties, failures, successes, joys and sorrows
of four agricultural missionaries and their families. . . . Perhaps
next time you hear from us, we shall be located on the farm in
Alabama."[36] But then Frank called. Clarence's brother told them
about a place just across the state line in southwest Georgia's
Sumter County. He thought they should see it. When Clarence
Jordan laid eyes on the dusty 440 acres just outside of Americus,
Georgia, he could see something beyond the tottering fence, the
eroded soil, the dilapidated farmhouse. He knew, "this is it."

When Florence heard the news, she looked down at their son,
James, born just a few weeks earlier, and cooed, "You'll be a Georgia

boy, after all." As she prepared for their move, people seemed surprised. Why, she did not know. Was it the new baby? Was it the South? Or had they just thought, in the end, she would stay in Louisville by her family? "Florence, I think it's just wonderful how sweet and willing you are to leave Louisville and all your dear loved ones and follow that husband of yours to Georgia and cast your lot with us," her father-in-law wrote: "I've now decided you really love us." She laughed reading that. Of course she really loved them. And she had cast her lot with Clarence Jordan—and with God—long before. The words of the Sixteenth Psalm came to mind:

> The LORD is my chosen portion and my cup;
>   you hold my lot.[37]

Clarence and Martin went down first, in November of 1942. For several weeks, Florence relied on frequent letters. Clarence described his long journey down to Georgia: running out of gas, hitchhiking with a couple of drunks, finding a forgotten gas ration ticket but also finding all the filling stations closed, and finally sleeping in the truck, only to wake feeling "like [he'd] never recuperate."[38] He wrote to her of his first days on the farm, of finding the old tenant still there, of unloading by himself, of the primitive conditions. "You no doubt remember the last bath and shave I had," he admitted, adding, "I cannot say that I particularly relish the idea of taking a bath in a zinc tub in a room with half the window lights out and the wind (it's cold here too) coming through at a rapid clip." Nor would she. Yet there were some promising developments. Within a day, two neighbors came by, and Martin would be there soon. "What would you think of drawing up plans for the kind of houses we want," he wrote, adding that whatever they came up with "could easily be made fly proof," which he knew was her main request.

Over the coming weeks, Florence anticipated each update. She read about escaped mules and her resigned husband hitched to the plow, laughing as he claimed, "I believe I'll make a better farmer than a mule. But we got it planted."[39] She gasped envisioning the sow charging at them, and again when they "decided if she was that mean now," they would have to "pass the sentence of death." "For once," Clarence added, "I'm almost sick on pork chops."[40] She nodded her head at his report that he "joined Rehoboth Church today. The people were all exceptionally nice."[41] Florence also responded to his urgent requests: "Call King Auto and ask about the license receipts"; "Keep me posted on how money comes in"; as well as his household queries: "where's the license receipt for the car?" and "where's the coffee pot?"[42] She mailed laundry and wired money. Of course, she wrote him updates too, as often as she could manage, and tried to offer encouragement. Some evenings, after Eleanor and James were finally sleeping, she would read again and again his tenderest notes: "I surely miss you. . . . It isn't going to be home until you come, cause I love you so much" and "I miss you all as much as I love you and you know how much that is." She never doubted his affection, but these words assured her they were in it together, even if separated for a little while. "I am grateful for a wife with your faith and courage," Clarence wrote to her that December. "Like you said, the Lord has always supplied our needs, but you are among the few people who will go along and give Him a chance to do so."[43] Truthfully, she couldn't wait for the chance.

Finally, in April 1943, after several months with Clarence's family in Talbotton, fifty miles north of the farm, Florence and the children moved to Koinonia. Their house was a "gray rundown tenant place sitting in a tangle of grass and weeds . . . like a worn and forgotten old woman." Well, Florence joked upon seeing it, it was "at least campable."[44] But she could also see the "promise of a new life": the apartment and shop Clarence and Martin were building; the gorgeous chicken house (nicer than hers, Florence would chide); the neat crops: "turnips, cabbage, onions, lettuce, spinach, kale, rutabaga, peas, beets, carrots, mustard . . . other fruit and berries, grapes, scuppernongs, muscadines, strawberries, raspberries, improved blackberries, youngberries, and boysenberries"; and the trees: "apple, pecan, peach, walnut, pear, plum, fig, apricot, nectarine, Chinese chestnut, Japanese persimmon," as well as the regal cedars, post oak, and seedling pecan.[45] Indeed, Florence could feel not only signs of her new life but of *the* new life, the resurrection life, breaking in. She could sense it when she gazed out the kitchen window at Bo Johnson, a Black neighbor, on the tractor alongside Clarence; when she listened to Mabel recite Scripture in their shared fellowship; when she balanced their common ledger. Though Florence had never been on a farm in her life, she knew she was home.

Over the next year, Clarence and Martin refined their agricultural techniques. They developed a mobile peanut harvester, innovated in fertilization and land use, and sought, above all, the care of creation. This attracted the attention and interest of their neighbors, both Black and white. So too did their sharing of excess crops and their offer of help at harvest time, as well as the seed cooperative, the egg business, and the so-called cow library.[46] Florence got used to cooking over a wood stove, washing in an iron pot, and doing without running water, at least initially—all while wrangling a six-year-old and a baby.[47] "We were young," she recalled, "and it was an adventure with the Lord!"[48] Not that she became a farm girl overnight. She still wore her favored printed dresses and took care to braid her hair. "Even working in the garden," her son Jim recalled, "she would have a touch of lipstick."[49] Her favorite hours were spent there actually. Weeding, meditating, watering, praying, waiting, witnessing. "For as the earth brings forth its sprouts, and as a garden causes the things sown in it to spring up, so the Lord God will cause righteousness and praise to spring up before all the nations"— could Koinonia be such a shoot, she wondered, her hands in the loamy soil?[50]

Seeds were scattered as word got out about the radical experiment. People sent donations, "love offerings," or letters, while others decided to come and see for themselves. Many of these were young people who had heard Clarence speak, as he did regularly at colleges and camps across the South, proclaiming his message of Christian pacifism, racial justice, and *koinōnia*. Henry Dunn, Howard Johnson, and Willie Pugh arrived for visits in the first months, as did Harry Atkinson, who stayed during his breaks from school. The help was needed, particularly since, in 1944, the American Baptist Mission Board contacted the Englands with news that they could return to Burma. Florence was sad to see them go. And for a while, it was quiet at the farm. But then the war ended and people arrived. One of them was Jan Elizabeth Jordan, another daughter, born in December 1946. By 1950, Koinonia had fourteen adults living at the farm, many of whom had formally joined Koinonia as full members. "We desire to make known our total, unconditional commitment to seek, express and expand the Kingdom of God as revealed in Jesus the Christ," they pledged. "Being convinced that the community of believers who make a like commitment is the continuing body of Christ on earth, I joyfully enter into a love union with the Koinonia and gladly submit myself to it, looking to it to guide me, in the knowledge of God's will and strengthen me in pursuit of it."[51]

The farm grew. The Browne and Wittkamper families both came, to Florence's delight, with children close in age to hers, while young people arrived with energy and enthusiasm. They were "a large extended family of religious dissidents and misfits,"[52] "ordinary people who by the Providence of God . . . were witnessing to the power of Christianity."[53] Their days included Bible study and worship, breakfast, work on the farm, a midday meal attended by neighbors and friends, afternoon activities, dinner, and evenings of socializing or community meetings. They ate popcorn while Clarence told stories, played volleyball, fought over a comb left in the bathroom, drove out to the Sunset Drive-In movie theater, let watermelon juice run down their faces. These were full, joyful, yet sometimes hard years spent in life together.

Florence continued to handle much of the administrative duties for Koinonia, including doling out the meager funds available for groceries and individual needs. "Brilliant in dealing with practical matters," Florence handled the farm's finances, including fund-raising and budgeting, correspondence, and general administration. "Frankly, without her," Jim later admitted, "Koinonia may not have survived financially."[54] But as the community grew, Florence's financial decisions became more complex—and more contentious. At one point, for instance, they had a lengthy discussion over whether or not the single men should be given an allowance and mileage limit for dates. Laying down linoleum occasioned a weeks-long debate. Other financial decisions were even weightier: purchasing farm equipment, covering a family's medical bills, the theological implications of purchasing insurance. Long conversations ensued over decisions regarding the children's education, the independence of families within the community, religious and theological interpretations of Scripture. It was "meetings, meetings, meetings," often late into the night.[55]

Sometimes these decisions, and the inevitable differences in personality, caused deeper resentments. "There are some rather strong tensions between you and most of the group," Koinonia member Claud Nelson told Florence in 1954, referencing a then-infamous "discussion of the upstairs linoleum." He went on to list a series of grievances: that Florence seldom attended the late-night business meetings, a sense that she felt it was "now someone else's turn to make the sacrifices," that she was "trying to protect [her] children, Eleanor in particular," and, perhaps most hurtfully, that she was spiritually and emotionally distant, on a "vacation from the inner life of the Koinonia." "Talking to you is like talking to a brick wall," his letter continued, harshly. "If you really love us, Florence, you must begin what you began in that little worship session. You must make it possible for us to love you. You must be willing to open up."[56] The words stung. Yes, she felt torn between protecting her family's autonomy and the unity in the community, but she wasn't trying to distance herself at all. The accusation of coldness was a familiar one. She had always been reserved emotionally—she was German, after all. And this temperament had benefited her in some of those tense talks. It was "rare for her to lose her temper," Jim later recalled. "No matter how much she might disagree with someone, while outspoken and often unwilling to concede, her language was generally controlled and proper."[57] Still, it hurt to hear that she was "unable to respond, unable to open up."[58] She did love, deeply, she explained tearfully to a grieved Clarence that evening in their second-story residence. "I know, Sweet," he'd said. This was just all part of it—the life of repentance and forgiveness, the "intimate life of love and work where an earnest attempt is made to practice the Way of Jesus in all relationships."[59]

Thinking about those days, Florence wanders over to the large meeting room, already lively with activity for lunch preparation. She is relieved not to have had to cook today—not that she doesn't occasionally like an adventure in the kitchen—but preparing the communal meals can be burdensome. That said, it had gotten somewhat easier to live in community over the past couple of decades, though there were always interpersonal clashes and ideological differences. Mostly, though, the fellowship was sustaining, especially now that her children were grown and Clarence was gone. After chopping vegetables in the kitchen and chatting amicably, Florence takes her regular seat at the long oak table, by the west side window, facing into the room.[60] She likes this vantage point, from which she can observe the hour's bustle and see clearly the faces of new visitors and old friends gathered. Before eating, they clasp hands and give thanks for the day, for their gifts, for those who prepared the meal, and for the communion of saints around the table. "Amen," Florence murmurs. She understands why Jesus chose a meal as the occasion for his own to remember him. She does indeed

sense Christ's presence in the shared meal. She senses the body—the
church. She chews, remembering a less unified church body.

Clarence's jaw clenched as he read the letter. "Because of
our differences in opinion on the race question, devotion to our
government, and proper relationship to the church," Ira Faglier,
the pastor of Rehoboth Baptist had written, "it seems to be the
consensus of opinion that the Members of the Koinia [*sic*] Farms
cannot be retained in the fellowship of Rehoboth Church." "Action would probably be taken on Sunday August 13," he continued, "possibly, fellowship would be withdrawn from the group,
and names stricken from the church rolls." Clarence thought back
to first going to the church just down the dirt road with Martin
England. He chuckled at the memory of the pastor saying, "You're
a farmer? You look sorta like a ministerial student."[61] They had
gone there ever since. He played the trumpet, led the choir, and
sometimes even filled the pulpit. Florence regularly taught an
adult Sunday school class. But now it had come to this.

The notion that "God has no favorite children," that the gospel
abolished the partition of Jim Crow, had undergirded Koinonia
from its inception. Black and white laborers ate together at the noon
meal and shared farm techniques, families played together, parties
and social gatherings were interracial. They offered Black children
rides to church and school. Koinonia had even hosted an integrated
vacation Bible school. Being together, and especially worshiping
God together, was at the heart of Koinonia's theological witness.
So when, on one Sunday in 1950, they had brought a visitor to the
farm, an Indian agricultural student, with them to Rehoboth, it
had raised suspicions. "The man was dark, but he did not look like
an American," Florence said. "We thought the people would be
delighted to meet him. He was not a Christian, but he had become
interested and he wanted to go to church."[62] It was this incident,
and the fear that Koinonia challenged the prevailing segregationist
order, that occasioned the letter Clarence had received.

He told Florence. Since he was slated to be out of town on a speaking engagement, Florence steeled herself to address the hostile congregation on their behalf. "You can imagine my feelings . . . all by myself to face the church," Florence explained. "So that night I prayed. I didn't know what in the world I was going to say." As happened so often, the words of the Bible came to her. In the first moments of waking, she heard: "When they bring you before the judges, take no thought of what you will say."[63] Trusting then that God would give her the words, she helped the younger children get dressed.[64]

After that Sunday's regular service, Florence took a seat with Eleanor, then thirteen, in a pew near the front for the meeting. "The church was full, expecting a big 'fight,'" Jim remembered, as the stuffy room swelled with anticipation.[65] Hands folded, Florence listened as the deacon read the accusations against them: they were "engaged in advocating views and practices contrary to [the church]"; they had "brought people of other races into the services"; they "constantly visit Negro churches in the community, and have persisted in holding services where both white and colored attend together"; and, as such, they had "caused serious friction in our church" as well as prompted theological misgivings. "Therefore," the deacon concluded, "we recommend that the Rehoboth Baptist Church . . . withdraw fellowship from any who are members of Koinonia Farm and that their names be stricken from the church roll."[66]

She rose to speak. There was a moment of pause, as she waited for God to provide her with words. When they came, they surprised even her. "I move that the recommendations of the deacons be accepted as read," Florence said, looking around the sanctuary.[67] If living out the teachings of Jesus to love one's neighbor as oneself regardless of race was cause for dismissal from the church, then, she decided, they should be dismissed. The pastor called for a vote. Later, tearful friends confided their shame over voting to expel them that day. "I kept hearing the words of the old spiritual, one friend

admitted, the one 'Were you there when they crucified my Lord?'"
This confession actually cheered her, as she recalled the words from
Romans, "For if we have been united with him in a death like his, we
shall certainly be united with him in a resurrection like his."[68]

But despite this hope of union with Christ, the following years
were punishing. After the 1954 *Brown v. Board* decision, the Koinonians were recast as, in Florence's words, "traitors to our race and
our class."[69] The farm became a "lightning rod." For their racial
treachery, Koinonia "caught holy hell."[70] They lost their farm insurance. Community businesses implemented a suffocating boycott. That, and a drought, brought the farm to the brink of financial
ruin. Then, in 1956, ire increased after Clarence vouched for two
Black students seeking admittance to the University of Georgia.
This action, as well as the establishment of an interracial summer
camp, Camp Koinonia, prompted accusations of communism, visits from the Klan, and a grand jury investigation. In some ways,
Florence understood. In testifying to God's kingdom, they were
"preaching the end of the world—their world—the end of the big
plantation owners, the end of the man who'd sit on his porch and
let somebody else do his work for nothing."[71] Still, the long legal
struggle, the threat of violence, the stress of dwindling money was
awful. Adding to the pain, in the midst of this persecution, the
Jordans experienced a private tragedy: they lost a son.[72] "We are
bearing with you in your recent sorrow of losing your little baby,"
Katie Long wrote from the Forest River community, adding, in
consolation, the words of Job: "The Lord giveth and the Lord ta-
keth away, blessed be the name of the Lord."[73]

During those years of suffering, questioning, even doubting,
Florence would sometimes just sit in her garden for a moment in
the late afternoon. She wondered about the future, about Koinonia; she worried about her children; she lamented in prayer. She
sowed her tears. Someday, she trusted, green springs would come
from this hard, cold ground. In due season, she thought, decidedly, standing up and going inside the warm house.

The meal eaten—today a green salad with vegetables from the farm, warm bread and butter, iced tea—a few people rise to begin clearing the table. But Florence lingers, engaged in conversation with a young woman with long, feathered blond hair framing her eager face. She is taking some time off from college, she explains, on a journey of peace. Koinonia is a stop along the way.

Florence had met many such young people over the years: the conscientious objectors of the earliest days who would stay up late discussing obligation and honor and war, the kids exploring faith, the reporters and journalists, the students who came in the 1960s with wide jeans and Afros and white T-shirts and bold eyeglasses. She thought of those years of the civil rights struggle. How the students, Black and white, would plan and disagree and end up praying and singing. Though her kids and farm visitors sometimes joined the marches in Albany or downtown Americus, Florence was wary. "We are not going to picket, protest, or register voters," she wrote in 1964 to a group of visitors, as a warning. Clarence too resisted provocative demonstrations. When, in the early 1960s, Jan asked them for permission to go march, Clarence said he would rather she not. "Listen," he explained, "you want to go to get a Coke with a black friend at the soda counter, go. But don't go looking for trouble, don't go just to break the law." If you do, he'd warned, "we won't bail you out."[74] Florence agreed. They were there to live as Christians. If that broke the law, then it did. But she wouldn't borrow trouble. Not after all the trouble they'd already had. "I love when you said Koinonia does not have to picket to prove a point," a friend wrote, affirming their hope that their "lives are demonstrations enough."[75] Indeed, they had witnessed to the possibilities of the beloved community before Montgomery, Birmingham, Albany, and the March on Washington. And while they supported the movement, it was not entirely theirs. Clarence used to say, "I'm not trying to change the laws, or change anything other than to live the way I believe Christians should live."[76]

In his mind they were not activists, nor overtly political. They were Christians. But while their faith didn't lead them to the picket line, it led them to defy segregation and to offer support for those in the fight. Charles Sherrod would sometimes bring large groups of SNCC (Student Nonviolent Coordinating Committee) volunteers to Koinonia for organizing workshops and for rest. Revolutionaries in repose, Florence would think, seeing them sprawled out on the grass under the pecan trees. She and Clarence both loved hosting them, though they had a sense that the movement was on its way, passing through, perhaps staying on briefly, but passing them by. The Civil Rights Act passed in 1964, the Voting Rights Act in 1965, and here they still were in southwest Georgia. In more recent years, the young visitors had talked more about world affairs, about the Middle East and South Africa, and the women were more vocal and direct. Sometimes it startled her, but she appreciated it.

Florence asks this young visitor questions, about her studies, her ideas, her family back in Michigan. Across all these decades, she still loves visiting with these young people at the farm. They remind her of herself in some ways, who she was and who she still is—headstrong, committed, searching, a bit rebellious. As the woman excuses herself, Florence leans back against her hard-back chair, catching pieces of the ambient conversations around her: yes, the seedlings were coming through; no, she hadn't heard back from the doctor yet; yes, a girl born last Thursday; a trip to the Blackshear Library this week sounded nice. "Right, Florence?" she hears above the din, before the tinny bang interrupts. Just a pot hitting the kitchen floor on its way to the soapy sink. But the piercing sound, and the sick silence before conversations resume, transports her back, for just an instant, to the terror years before.

The popping sound cut through the still April air, now charged with fear.[77] Florence could feel her heart hammering in her chest as she got to her feet and lunged for the door. Her eyes took it in all at once: Clarence sprawled over Eleanor, shattered glass, bullet holes ripped through the wall next to her daughter's bed. "Oh, Jesus, thank you," she exhaled, seeing that her husband and daughter were both still breathing. "Thank you, thank you, thank you."

This was not the first time Florence had heard the diabolical crackle of gunfire pierce the dark Georgia night. In the winter, there had been shots fired at Koinonia's sign, at the gas pump near the residential cabins, and then at them on several occasions. There had been the night Harry Atkinson was almost hit by a bullet in his car. Thank God he had leaned over. The previous months had brought mutilated pecan trees, scrawled threats, and burned crosses. Despite herself and her shaking hands, Florence almost laughed remembering the insults screamed from passing cars, her lovely friend Dorothy Day being called a "goddamn northern Communist whore." And then, of course, there had been the bombings of the refrigerated meat case, of the roadside produce stand, of the Birdsey feed store downtown. It had been hostile for several years by now. But this felt different. Or maybe she did.[78]

After making sure Eleanor and the other Koinonians were safe, Florence finally lay back down. But she couldn't sleep. The maternal side of her longed to protect her children. They had already endured so much—the taunting at school, the social isolation, the constant fear. And yet, she had always done what she felt God was calling *her*, as an individual, as a woman, as a follower of Jesus, to do. All night the restless thoughts came. Was it time to leave Georgia? The Americus city officials had made it clear that they could not curb the violence and had insisted that Koinonia relocate for its own survival. Though they'd refused, the question haunted her. Was God asking for endurance and courage in persecution? Or was God leading them somewhere else? What was fear and what was faith? So it went on. The next morning, she and Clarence prayed together and talked it over. How could they leave this land they'd worked for so many years, the "bit of ground where [their] child is buried"?[79] On the other hand, how could they stay and risk burying another? The conversation soon involved the larger Koinonia community. For over a week, members sought God's guidance. After getting the kids off to school or to the nursery, they deliberated and prayed "until the school buses ran in the afternoon." After supper, once the children went to bed, they gathered again, "sometimes till 12 or 1 o'clock at night."[80] Florence would never forget those long nights, the hours they spent praying and listening. In a particularly affecting moment, Con Browne shared that he was having a recurring nightmare in which he laid his child's lifeless body on the steps of the Americus courthouse.[81] After this season of desperate discernment, they decided to stay. "We had no leaning whatsoever to leave. Absolutely none," Florence concluded. "At the same time, things were pretty bad."[82]

Devout and independent minded, Florence processed this season of violent persecution not primarily as a wife and mother but as a Christian. While fearful for her family's safety, she nevertheless was willing to die for her faith if called to. "Christians say, I'm not my own, I've been bought with a price," she explained. "And if we really believe this, then if we feel we have to stay, we have to stay whatever the cost . . . we wouldn't be the first Christians to die, wouldn't be the last. And we decided all right, we're willing. We'll stay."[83] There was a cost, of course, to staying, one borne heavily by the children of Koinonia, including hers.

Sometimes, in the recesses of her heart, she pondered if she was a good mother. She got the letters from Jim, away at a private school, and ached for him as she taped up care packages. She had to read updates from Marion Johnson on Lenny, who'd gone to live at the Forest River community, informing her that she "didn't need to worry about his clothes" despite the North Dakota chill.[84] She saw Jan's hunched shoulders heading to Americus High under court order, the toll of lunches eaten alone day after day. Clarence, eyes glassy, told her frankly that while the court could have them admitted, there wasn't "a court in the land that can make these folks like you."[85] Eleanor had been shot at while home from college. Yes, the children had paid a high price, but, she told herself, circumspect, "we have chosen this way of living and our children have to take the consequences of it."[86] As much as she wanted to protect her kids, she had to be obedient to God. She could not shield them from taunts, or even bullets, but she could shield them from the mockery of a lukewarm faith, from the stench of Christian hypocrisy. Once, Lenny had asked her about it, about the decision to stay at Koinonia, to put them in harm's way or send them off. She had told him the truth. Following Jesus required a "full and total commitment . . . putting God first even before one another. Our love for one another will come if we love Him above all."[87]

She sets down the book she has been reading since lunch and stands, smoothing her skirt. Wandering outside, Florence breathes in the golden sweetness of the evening hour and savors this crepuscular moment alone. Well, almost alone. She can hear the cicadas' tilting whine, feel the cooling breeze, hear muffled conversations in the distance. The fields are gilded by the setting sun. Her eyes roam across the expanse of land before coming to rest on Clarence's old shack.

After the violence of the late 1950s died down, or, rather, was redirected, Koinonia, with dwindling money and only three families remaining, faced new crises and new questions. They had survived the persecution, just barely, staying solvent through donations and a mail order pecan business promising to "ship the nuts out of Georgia." Koinonia had been prophetic, a voice crying out, a witness for the possibility of integrated Christian fellowship in the Jim Crow South. The Movement had come, it had swept through and gone on, and yet they remained. "The koinonia had witnessed and could step out of the picture," Florence remembered reasoning. But, "What did the Lord want us to do now? Where did he want us to go? For over a year we asked those questions. In 1968, the answer came. Stay where you are."[88] Their God Movement was still staying put.[89]

Clarence built a shack on the property and began to write. For years, he had spoken to visitors, parishioners, and students about the radicalness of the New Testament, and he longed now to apply it "not only in his own tongue but in his own time," to "rescue the New Testament drama from the sanctuary and classroom" and place it "under God's skies where people are toiling and crying and wondering."[90] He set to work on an idiomatic version of the Bible, one he called his *Cottonpatch Translation*. Florence, always a willing reader, delighted in her husband's description of John the Baptist in blue jeans, of the Christ child in an apple crate, of the good Samaritan as Black. As he read drafts, it reminded her of their early married days in Louisville when Clarence would interrupt her reading with an epiphany about something in the Greek.

By the summer of 1969, he had completed his *Cottonpatch* version of Paul's Epistles, set to be published, and was now at work on the Gospels. Thinking of their dissemination, Florence thought of a passage from Matthew's account: "As for what was sown on good soil, this is the one who hears the word and understands it. He indeed bears fruit and yields, in one case a hundredfold, in another sixty, and in another thirty."[91]

And then, suddenly, he was gone. She was a widow at fifty-six.

The days following Clarence's heart attack were a blur. But after the shock and the stress of the burial, a deep grief settled in. For months, she received questions from journalists and friends, her voice thickening as she answered, yes, "we were very, very much in love always. To the very last day."[92] They had been. Florence thought back, gratefully, of the trip they had taken the previous spring—to Hawaii and then a tour of Africa, which included a stop for Jim's wedding.

There were so many condolence cards. From former Koinonians like the Brownes, from countless visitors, extended family.

She especially treasured the one from Coretta Scott King, who knew all too well what she felt, having just lost her husband the year before. Her tribute to Clarence moved her: "Unlike many other men who said the races could not live together in harmony, Clarence Jordan had the courage to prove men and women of different races could not only work together, but live together in peace and harmony and give the world an example of brotherhood at work. Though reviled, maligned, persecuted and physically assaulted for his belief in the beloved community, he remained undaunted in his commitment to justice and brotherhood."[93] She wondered now how Coretta was, and realized they were in much the same position: carrying the legacies of their husbands, and carrying on the work.

There was a lot of work to be done. After the community made the decision to stay in south Georgia in 1968, God surprised them all by bringing new movements to them. One of these came in the form of a letter from Millard Fuller, an astute businessman and fund-raiser, who asked Clarence, "what do you have up your sleeve?" After numerous conversations, they decided to transition Koinonia Farm into a new organization they called Koinonia Partners. This new effort would, through gospel sharing and donations to the so-called Fund for Humanity, help rural Georgians gain access to land and capital and housing. The start was promising: Clarence was energized speaking about the project for economic justice; two houses had been built using a Black construction company, with plans for two more; money was pouring in. When Bo and Emma Johnson, their friends for all of these decades, moved into their new home, Florence felt overwhelming joy. Her joy turned to incredulity in the following year. Millard and Linda left Koinonia for three years in Zaire before returning to expand on the Partners' housing vision. This project—which they called Habitat for Humanity—expanded over several years and ultimately gained national attention. In fact, Jimmy and Rosalynn Carter had volunteered at a build a month or so earlier. She knew Clarence would have wanted her to carry on with Koinonia Partners. At the funeral, Millard had read one of Clarence's translations: "In order that you all, too, might be our partners, we're plainly telling you about something that's real, something that we ourselves have heard, that we have seen with our own eyes. The darkness is lifting and the light is dawning."[94]

It had been difficult, but Florence was grateful for God's faithfulness to her in those months, and also proud of her own resilience. So often people spoke of the farm as Clarence's, and of course it had been his animating idea, his charisma, his gift for teaching the Scriptures that had really made Koinonia what it was. But it was hers too. Too often over the years, reporters would talk to her husband, never even directing questions to her. His name would appear prominently in magazine articles and newspaper clips while she would be lucky to be mentioned at all as his wife. She remembered years back, when Jan had written about walking out of her all-white graduation from Americus High for *Faith at Work*, how the editor's biography described her as "the daughter of Koinonia's director Clarence Jordan."[95] As though she did not also have a mother! Florence shook her head and snapped back to the present; it didn't matter. She was proud of Clarence, awed by him too, even after all these years. She knew he knew that they were partners, with each other and with God, and that was enough for her. But she knew too that she had toiled, she had prayed, she had welcomed, she had balanced books and responded to countless letters and washed dishes, she had repented, she had stayed. Koinonia was hers too. She knew that now.

As she stared at the green paint peeling on the wooden shack, the words of Ruth she had repeated so often in Louisville came back to her: "Where you will die I will die, and there will I be buried."[96] Her children had tried to get her to move in with them after Clarence's heart attack, but she had refused.[97] Koinonia was home.

Clarence was still her home too, and, though she wouldn't dwell on it, at least not today, she would be buried out there beside him soon enough.

It had been over forty-one years since she had first set foot at Koinonia. Then a young mother and intrepid adventurer; now a seasoned saint. Her children were living in Indiana and North Carolina, now married, some with children of their own. Her granddaughter Suzy had come to visit, delighted by the farm and its newest resident: her dog, Rusty. These days, Florence stayed busy, still managing the farm's finances as well as the mail-order pecan and candy business. Walking to the office, woven fan in hand, Florence would inhale the spicy, sweet scent of pecandy and fruitcake, often stopping in to chat with the other women, Black and white, sometimes sidestepping an unannounced visitor sleeping off the previous night. She kept up writing letters—to old friends from Louisville, to the farm's visitors, to family members. She even had a calendar to remember to send cards on birthdays and anniversaries.[98] She continued to read—mostly biographies and poetry—and to tend the garden.[99] She also told the Koinonia story, to Dallas Lee initially, and then to others, giving interviews, teaching seminars, and speaking in churches.

In some ways, so much had changed. Koinonia Partners had evolved into Habitat for Humanity. Their experiment in nonviolent Christian interracialism, once so despised, was now praised. The Koinonia story had been documented in several books and even a Broadway play. She thought of something Clarence had once said: "Have we been a big success? I don't know what success would look like for Koinonia. There's only one question I'll ever have to answer, and that is: have I been faithful?"[100] That was the only question she felt compelled to answer now too. She had been planted at Koinonia her whole life, had witnessed its seasons. She hoped it might simply be said of her:

They are planted in the house of the LORD;
   they flourish in the courts of our God.
They still bear fruit in old age;
   they are ever full of sap and green.[101]

After supper, a cup of tea, and a few hours talking, Florence heads to bed. She climbs the stairs slowly. She is still a large woman, but a bit weaker in recent years, especially after the discovery of a lump, benign thankfully, a couple of months back.[102] As she washes her face and undresses, tidying, she hums. It's an old favorite, "Day Is Dying in the West": "While the deepening shadows fall, / Heart of love, enfolding all, / Through the glory and the grace / Of the stars that veil Thy face, / Our hearts ascend."[103] She settles into bed, the stars her veil, and places her wedding band on the table before turning off the lamp. In the falling darkness, she offers her nightly prayers. She thanks God for his faithfulness and for the waning day.

Florence Jordan had lived thousands of days like this one. Ordinary days, struggling to embody love in community and faithfulness. As Annie Dillard reminds, "How we spend our days is how we spend our lives."[104] Florence spent her days, her life, as a partner in radical obedience. She left convention and comfort, defied Jim Crow in Georgia, imagined a just distribution of wealth, accepted bullets and derision and ostracization for herself and her children, and watched the nation shift before her eyes. She remembered that August day in 1963 when Rev. King had described his prophetic hope that "one day on the red hills of Georgia, the sons of former slaves and the sons of former slave-owners will be able to sit down together at the table of brotherhood." And she had actually seen it. She had seen it at Koinonia Farm—and, for that matter, so had he.[105]

Every tumultuous time finds its saints waiting. And then when the hour comes, their lives can bear witness to the kingdom of

God, to the invisible logic of resurrection. "There is no divide between 'radical' and 'ordinary' believers," Tish Harrison Warren writes. "We are all called to be willing to follow Christ in radical ways, to answer the call of the one who told us to deny ourselves and take up our cross."[106] The radical life of faith happens each day in ordinary faithfulness; "you can't get to the revolution without learning to do the dishes."[107] Florence Jordan had seen the revolution standing at the kitchen sink, hands full of suds. In 1959, she wrote a letter to a young Christian. "It is so easy to flit from place to place hunting for the spirit, when the need is to stop and wait for the spirit. Our own restlessness and impatience makes us want to 'do something' and do it quickly. I know from experience," she concluded, "that the Lord moves slowly. It has always been hard for me to remember that the Lord has eternity. 'For a thousand years in thy sight are but as yesterday when it is past, and as a watch in the night.'"[108] She helped usher in the kingdom, the God Movement, by staying put, rooting herself in God's Word and planting her days among the beloved community.

Bruce Klunder

(1937–1964)

Bruce Klunder; photo courtesy of Joanne Klunder Hardy

Remembering Bruce Klunder

An Inconvenient Martyr for Racial Justice

Carolyn Renée Dupont

America has largely forgotten Bruce Klunder. The twenty-seven-year-old minister who died during a school desegregation effort in 1964 gets little notice in our civil rights stories, popular or scholarly. Though the National Civil Rights Memorial in Montgomery, Alabama, honors him along with forty-one other "martyrs," very few Americans—indeed, even few historians of the civil rights movement—know his story.[1]

This forgetting is no accident. As with most aspects of our past, Americans prefer a certain kind of civil rights narrative—an easy, triumphal tale featuring southern racists and resolving in neat victories. Movies, memorials, memes, and MLK Day celebrations follow this arc. But Klunder's story defies these tropes and thus finds no place in the civil rights canon.

Specific myths—persistent, dogged, but useful falsehoods—in our national civil rights narrative leave no room for Bruce Klunder. His life and extraordinary death cannot pass through the filters that calibrate our vision. These lenses seek civil rights stories only in the South, while imagining the North, where he died, as a land of racial innocence. The same mechanisms register racism only as pathological hatred from white thugs, but Klunder's story features instead a horde of white parents and a throng of white churchgoers. And an insistence on triumphal progress screens out Klunder's death, since frustration and failure—not victory—flowed from his ultimate sacrifice.

Remembering Bruce Klunder challenges these cherished myths. Even more, this remembering demands a reorienting of our national civil rights vision, clarifying our understanding of the past and equipping us to chart a better future. Let us tell his story, unpack the falsehoods that have erased him, and relinquish our cherished tropes.

Let us remember Bruce Klunder.

*   *   *

Ironies billow from his story. The man who once metaphorically described America as a "majority society bulldozing over oppressed people, often without even a glance to see that a human soul was in the way," died under the weight of an actual bulldozer, driven by a worker who literally did not see him. Klunder believed that only his body could stop the construction of yet another segregated school, yet even his body proved insufficient against Cleveland's segregationist juggernaut. Recalling the death and resurrection of Jesus as an example of love that would "suffer with and for those who are oppressed . . . [and] be willing to bear personally some of the cost of that pain's removal," Klunder practiced what he preached in ways he did not fully anticipate.[2]

He struck many as remarkable. An advisor from his college days recalled "leadership qualities beyond his years." Careful consideration and thoughtfulness marked his efforts. Friends and coworkers described the tall, lanky, and bespectacled Klunder as "quiet," not "any kind of extremist," and one who "seemed to feel things deeply." One civil rights colaborer noted that "he worked hard researching the situations which were being protested, to insure that the protest was meaningful and intelligent, and he has led those around him to think through carefully the tactics they will use and their motivations for using them." A mentor praised him as "a person of real substance and character . . . a rational thinker, thoughtful, and analytical." Another recalled, "His life was in balance. He laughed a lot."[3]

Raised in Baker, Oregon, Klunder rarely interacted with African Americans in his youth. As civil rights initiatives gained increased national visibility during his college days at Oregon State in Corvallis, Klunder's consciousness grew as well. He raised money to help activists during the Montgomery Bus Boycott and traveled with an interracial delegation to a national student Christian conference on race relations. After graduating from Oregon State and then from Yale Divinity School in 1961, Klunder moved his young family to Cleveland, where he took a position as associate secretary of the Student Christian Union, working on the campus of Western Reserve University.[4]

Klunder's experiences in Cleveland deepened his understanding of America's racial hierarchy and his commitment to dismantling it. His work on an inner-city campus plopped him down in the midst of Cleveland's expanding urban ghetto, where he witnessed residential confinement and school segregation up close. This deepening understanding compelled him to reject as "too bland" the "interracial coffee klatsches . . . the 'Get-to-Know-a-Negro-Family' home visitation programs" then fashionable among "white liberals." Rather, Klunder and his wife, Joanne, embraced direct action and demanded immediate change. In May 1962, the couple became founding members of Cleveland's Congress of Racial Equality (CORE) chapter, with Bruce as vice president. With CORE, Klunder joined a fair housing sit-in at the governor's office, picketed the homes of slum landlords, demonstrated against discrimination at St. Luke's hospital, and spoke at the Cleveland Conference on Religion and Race. He also served as secretary for the Emergency Committee of Clergy for Civil Rights, a group of ministers in the metropolitan area who supported civil rights initiatives. Joanne picketed too, and even on occasion brought their two young children out to join these demonstrations.[5]

The couple's commitments put them at the heart of the civil

rights struggle in one of the nation's most segregated cities. Together they focused primarily on halting the school segregation
that underpinned and perpetuated every other aspect of Cleveland's racial hierarchy. Thus they planted their feet firmly on a
path to tragedy.

*   *   *

*We forget Bruce Klunder because he died working for civil rights in
Cleveland, Ohio, not Jackson, Mississippi, or Birmingham, Alabama.*
Trained to see racial injustice only in the backward South of our
historical imaginations, our civil rights vision fails to register his
activist life and sacrificial death.

In American mythology, northern egalitarianism contrasts
sharply with benighted southern racism. The North represents racial
innocence, the repository of America's true vision of equality, peren-
nially at odds with its less noble southern counterpart. In our minds,
abolitionists, crusading Union soldiers, and racial egalitarians populated the North. No Jim Crow demons required slaying in the land
where Blacks voted, attended integrated schools, and patronized the
same movie theaters, hotels, and restaurants as whites.

But history tells a far more complicated story, and remembering Bruce Klunder highlights a countervailing set of truths. In
Cleveland, Klunder witnessed and described the "iron ring"—a
constellation of deeply interlocked forces that consigned Black
Clevelanders to inferior status. The trio of economic marginalization, residential confinement, and educational segregation
worked in Cleveland and throughout the urban North without the
aid of Jim Crow statutes on the books.[6]

Rigid residential segregation, maintained through a repertoire
of shifting strategies, confined Cleveland's African Americans to
an urban ghetto. Low incomes kept many residential areas out of
reach. But landlords also tightened the housing market artificially
by refusing to rent to Blacks, and even those with more open policies charged rates well above the going prices in white districts.

Real estate agents notoriously steered Black home buyers away from white areas, and banks cooperated by strategically refusing loans. Whites used restrictive covenants in sales contracts, forbidding the resale of homes in white neighborhoods to Black buyers. Federal housing programs that greatly expanded homeownership for whites mostly denied their benefits to Blacks.[7] The effectiveness of such mechanisms showed up in Cleveland's racial geography: by 1960, 97 percent of Cuyahoga County's Black residents lived in the central city, while 59 percent of whites lived in suburbs. The dichotomy showed itself even more starkly in settlement patterns along an east-west axis. Ninety-six percent of Black Clevelanders lived east of the Cuyahoga River, while 80 percent of whites lived on the west side of that line.[8]

Residential confinement enabled school segregation to thrive, even without laws requiring it. The school board could easily draw district lines to create racially segregated schools. White students who fell into Black school districts could arrange "special transfers" on the pretext that their districted schools lacked certain course offerings.[9] Those few schools with racially mixed student populations practiced internal segregation, placing Black students in separate classes. Technical high schools that prepared workers for skilled trades either excluded Blacks or severely restricted their access.[10]

While inadequate funding plagued the entire district, problems of overcrowding impaired Black education most severely. The board built new schools for a declining white population but often refused to propose bond issues for constructing Black schools. Diminished resources meant that weak teachers, truncated curricula, and inferior facilities multiplied in Black schools.[11]

Compounding and feeding on these other difficulties, Cleveland's economic landscape provided few opportunities for even the best-educated Blacks. The city's steel mills and foundries relegated African Americans to jobs at the bottom of the wage ladder. Often involving difficult, dangerous, and low-skilled work, these positions offered little means of advancement or of acquiring transferable skills. In addition to low pay, workers in such jobs

41

suffered frequent bouts of unemployment, staying out of work longest during downturns. To make matters more challenging, many unions excluded Blacks or organized by trades that did not admit them. These problems intensified for Black women. Whenever employment opportunities expanded for white women, they remained closed to African Americans, and most Black women found their best option in private domestic work.

Racial tensions in Cleveland simmered most significantly around public education. In 1955, the city instituted a "relay" program, also used to ease overcrowding in other northern cities. Under this plan, the most congested schools—the largely Black schools—ran two sets of students a day, slashing the instructional day in half. Frustrated Black parents demanded a different, obvious solution to overcrowding: busing students from the congested Black schools to classrooms that sat empty in the mostly white West Side. While the board initially refused these requests, it complied at the beginning of 1962, after Black parents initiated sustained picketing at school board headquarters.[12]

The board's acquiescence first appeared to be both a victory for Black Clevelanders and an affirmation of the direct-action techniques then taking the country by storm. However, the sense of triumph evaporated when the newly bused students came home to tell about their day. Upon arrival, administrators herded them into classrooms separate from the white pupils and kept them tightly contained there the entire day. They could not use the cafeteria or physical education facilities, could not participate in assemblies or extracurricular activities, and could not see the school nurse. At one designated time each day, the Black students visited restroom facilities. Black parents soon learned that the board had promised white parents that the incoming students would remain in the receiving schools only until three new schools could be built in the Black neighborhoods.[13]

As the 1963-1964 school year opened, Cleveland's Black parents, CORE, the NAACP (National Association for the Advancement of Colored People), and a broad coalition of Black and white religious leaders united to work for a fully integrated and fair public school system. They aimed to force the school board to fully integrate the bused students into the receiving schools; to abandon its plans for constructing new, still-segregated schools; and to create a long-range plan that would address both overcrowding and segregation. In this struggle, they faced a recalcitrant board with only one African American member, white parents committed to racially exclusive schools, and a constellation of civic institutions. These included two newspapers, the city council, big business interests, and the police force—all accustomed to ignoring Black voices while taking the assumptions of whites for granted. This mix produced the city's worst racial turmoil in memory.

After brief picketing in September 1963, the school board agreed to begin immediately integrating some of the 940 bused students and then to integrate all of them starting the following semester, January 1964. However, when the second semester began, the board's "integration plan" proved nothing more than a limited "diffusion" plan whereby 20 percent of the bused pupils mixed with the other students for forty minutes each day. Nothing changed from the previous semester, other than this one token concession. Responding to organized pressure from white parents, the board had reneged on its promise.[14]

Black parents and their allies responded by picketing at the city's schools, while large and angry white crowds taunted, jeered, and pushed them. At one such demonstration, twenty-five of the city's Protestant ministers joined Black parents and community leaders in the picket line. An unruly crowd of hundreds of whites surrounded the picketers, jeering and throwing insults. A few white mothers tore signs from the hands of picketing ministers, and a man from the crowd punched a press photographer. White hecklers met them with dogs. Eventually, a fistfight broke out between a white onlooker and a picket. White police officers who roamed the site did nothing to protect the pickets.[15]

Yet these demonstrations did nothing to deter the school board from plans for the new school construction in Black areas. Activists rejected the plans on the grounds that the new schools would strengthen and preserve segregation. Even beyond the schools' placement in all-Black neighborhoods, the plans failed on other counts. Poorly and hastily designed, the construction lay near busy major thoroughfares on lots too small to include playground facilities. Furthermore, activists claimed, twelve thousand desks sat empty in mostly white schools. In spite of these objections, construction crews began working at the new sites.[16]

Believing they had exhausted all options to halt school construction intended for Black students only, activists initiated pickets and demonstrations at the construction sites. One weekend, they carried a coffin to the lots to symbolically bury Jim Crow. Some activists began trying to disrupt the construction by lying in front of machines or over areas marked for excavation. Cleveland school officials erected an eight-foot fence topped with barbed wire around the construction sites, hoping to keep demonstrators out. The city grew tense.[17]

On April 6, police pulled demonstrators at the Lakeview school site out of excavation zones and from under cement trucks. They arrested twenty demonstrators, who accused the police of beating them while inside police wagons. Local newspapers suggested that the demonstrators had behaved violently, but activists maintained otherwise.

Bruce Klunder entertained doubts about demonstrating at the Lakeview school construction site on the morning of April 7. He had been deeply involved in the school issue from the outset, and his misgivings did not arise from lack of commitment to action or fear for his physical well-being. Rather, he worried he might be arrested, and a pending trial would disrupt his plans to work in Peru that summer in a YMCA building program. He wrestled with the decision for several days, making up his mind only hours before heading out. En route, he stopped by the nursery where his wife worked, telling her, "The only way to stop that school is to put our bodies between the workmen and their work."[18]

The tragedy unfolded quickly, within a few minutes of the

demonstrators' arrival at the Lakeview school construction site. The activists broke through police lines, as they had done the day before. Two women and a man positioned themselves facedown in the mud in front of a bulldozer, while Klunder prostrated himself—also facedown—behind it. The driver apparently did not hear Klunder alert him to his presence. As he maneuvered the vehicle into reverse, other demonstrators screamed that Klunder lay behind him, but to no avail. The heavy truck instantly crushed the young minister into the mud, shattering his bones and imprinting its treads deeply into his flesh.[19]

Though widely reported and mourned at the time, Bruce Klunder's death in the North never really entered the civil rights historical canon. Almost no scholarly accounts consider it, and the wider public knows nothing of it. This forgetting flows from insistence on a southern civil rights story, one that cordons off racial injustice as a unique regional problem. Remembering Bruce Klunder's activist life and death requires a fundamental shift in the geography of the racially oppressive past, erasing the bright, clean lines that separate North from South. The racially innocent North of the American imagination has never really existed, as Klunder's death reveals.

*　　*　　*

We forget Bruce Klunder because the accident that killed him offers no archetypical racist villain. He died at the hands of an "innocent," rather than a racist, thug. John White, the bulldozer driver, seems not to have known that Klunder lay behind his vehicle, and, in fact, he backed up to avoid injuring the protestors in front of him. Deeply anguished over his part in Klunder's death, White became a killer simply by showing up for work that day.

In contrast, America's most celebrated and cherished civil rights tropes demand identifiable racist villains. Potbellied sheriffs, hooded Klansmen, and troubled ideologues offer more satisfying targets for our moral indignation. But heaping the nation's sins on the heads of a few individuals distorts past and present reality. It reduces complex, interlocking forces—Klunder's iron ring of economic marginalization, residential confinement, and educational segregation—to personal pathologies; obscures the workings of larger, more intransigent, and self-perpetuating structures; and promotes little change.

Klunder's own descriptions of Cleveland's situation explicitly rejected individual prejudicial attitudes as the main arena of racial struggle. The iron ring far more effectively marginalized Black Americans with its impersonal operations, its invisibility, and its diffusion of responsibility. Thus, the problem "involve[d] institutions [and] questions about the structure of society" far more significantly than questions "strictly of interpersonal relations—as if my responsibility ended with my attitudes toward those 5, 10, 20, or 50 Negro individuals with whom I come in contact in the process of a week," Klunder noted in an August 1963 sermon.[20]

Rather than offering a single villain we can love to hate, Klunder's story leaves us perplexed and puzzled. At once too few and too many, the culprits here seem elusive and unsatisfying to name. They include every institution and person that helped create and sustain the iron ring—landlords, realtors, bankers, the city's business elite, its police force, its school board, and its white parents.

Klunder's story expands the cast of antagonists to include institutions and people we see in that role only with great discomfort. In particular, Cleveland's ordinary white Protestant churchgoers joined these ranks. Their investment in sustaining the iron ring showed itself sporadically before Klunder's death, but it burst into ferocious display after the fateful events of April 7, 1964. Rather than spurring Cleveland's white Protestant churchgoers toward greater contrition and new resolve for justice, Klunder's death elicited an astonishing backlash against ministerial civil rights work. In reacting to Klunder's death, many white Cleveland Protestants revealed a commitment to the racial hierarchy as profound as any Klan member. Others expressed themselves with greater dignity but showed no willingness to examine Cleveland's oppressive structures.

Two days after Bruce Klunder died, twelve hundred people packed a memorial service at the Church of the Covenant; another three hundred or so spilled into the halls and filled the front steps. The congregation sang "The Kingdom of God on Earth," with its compelling lines, "Once to every man and nation, comes the moment to decide, in the strife of truth and falsehood, for the good or evil side." The United Presbyterian Church's highest-ranking official and committed activist, the Reverend Eugene Carson Blake, eulogized Klunder as a martyr who, like Jesus, "lay down his life for his friends."[21] Other civil rights notables, including James Farmer of CORE, attended the services for Klunder. Scenes such as this one memorialize a white Protestantism in solidarity with Black equality.

But tellingly, a parallel drama with an opposite impulse played out simultaneously, highlighting another mostly forgotten aspect of white Protestantism. In spite of the deep outpouring of grief and the public celebrations of Klunder's martyrdom, many of the city's white Protestants registered serious objections to his work, to clergy involvement in civil rights activity, and to the aspirations of Black Clevelanders. One woman complained that "liberal thinking people . . . would like to make a martyr of this man, but his death proves just how dedicated these demonstrators (who are being backed and pushed by communists) are."[22] Another described Klunder's actions as a "disgraceful" and "provocative display." Another simply opined, "Good riddance. Old man Klunder was a disgrace to the white race."[23] The backlash extended to Klunder's larger cohort of white ministers involved in civil rights work. One parishioner "state[d] categorically" that his minister's presence in the school construction protests "did not represent [him]." He went on to place the blame for Klunder's death squarely on the shoulders of civil rights advocates, not on those who stubbornly insisted on building an all-Black school: "everyone who has taken part in the demonstrations . . . has blood on his hands."[24] Some thought the city's religious leaders "display the complete lack of common sense."[25] Another noted: "the religious leaders of Cleveland . . . have confirmed my conclusion that it is not religion that is foolish, but instead it is religions' leaders."[26] Another woman put it simply: "How ridiculous can the clergy get?"[27]

Klunder's death uncorked an outrage that roiled Cleveland's Protestant congregations. Episcopal leaders noted how "church members reduce their pledges, leave their churches, stay away; angry letters are mailed to the clergy anonymously, people walk out of church in the middle of a sermon . . . confusion fills the parish church."[28] The sessions of three Presbyterian churches drafted letters of complaint against their activist pastors, and Presbyterian activists noted that they had lost "respectability because of action in civil rights."[29]

No congregation writhed more uncomfortably in the wake of Klunder's death than the Church of the Covenant, where the Klunder family worshiped. The pastor, the Reverend Harry Taylor, shared Klunder's commitments and participated in many of the same civil rights initiatives. Opposition to Taylor grew so intense that he regarded his pastoral position as "very much in jeopardy."[30] One parishioner scolded him for his "disgraceful exhibition," which had "subjected [the congregation] to ridicule." "Civil liberty is one thing, but social contact breeding of mongrel children do not make one wrong right," the man maintained. He claimed to once have "looked up to [Taylor] and have admired [him] from afar . . . but this has swept all that away."[31] Another church member thought Taylor could better "help this element" with whom he identified by teaching them "cleanliness, culture, decency" and ridding them of the "tribal lust [that] has long since been outlawed in our culture." "We are ashamed of the picture of you in the newspaper," she went on, "carrying a placard along with the shrieking rioters in your group; we are truly ashamed of what you have done to hurt the hearts of so many of us who knew you before these disgraceful activities." One member announced succinctly, "I am deeply humiliated to have my name associated with the Covenant Church."[32]

Other Cleveland congregations dealt even more harshly with their activist pastors. The Reverend Duane Day of Collinwood

Congregational Church resigned shortly after Klunder's death in "an attempt to retain the unity of the congregation." Both the congregation and Day struggled to put a good face on his departure, but parishioner opposition to Day's civil rights work clearly precipitated the move. One congregational leader noted that the minister's "views were not the views of some of the members of the church," and another explained, "As in most of Greater Cleveland, there are wide ranges to the opinions and feelings on the civil rights issue among those of our congregation."[33] According to one study, a dozen Cleveland-area ministers involved in racial justice initiatives lost their pulpits in the wake of Klunder's death and the school integration crisis.[34]

In fully remembering Bruce Klunder and his death, we recollect a civil rights story much less facile than the narrative featuring good civil rights workers and evil racist thugs. To remember Klunder rightly, we must drop our insistence on a white Protestantism inexorably on the side of right. Indeed, his story demands attention to deep failures in an institution and a people expected to serve as moral guides and exemplars. By attenuating the bright line that separates racist thugs from ordinary white Protestants, we demystify the workings of systemic oppression and ask more of religion—indeed, of ourselves.

*   *   *

We forget Bruce Klunder because his death resulted in no identifiable civil rights progress. Indeed, after this tragedy, Black activists in Cleveland fragmented into competing factions, and white clerical activism fizzled. Even more important, little changed in the city's racial structures. No one likes a story so lacking in moral vindication, so devoid of triumph—a narrative that peters out rather than explodes in a blaze of glorious victory.

The favored stories of the civil rights canon connect the suffering and death of activists to concrete gains. Montgomery, Alabama, Blacks walked to work for a year, but ultimately ended segregation in city buses. The lunch-counter demonstrators of 1960 endured physical and mental trauma, but their efforts opened local accommodations across the United States. The 1964 deaths of Andrew Goodman, Michael Schwerner, and James Chaney boosted support for the landmark Civil Rights Act of that year. And while thugs may have murdered Jimmie Lee Jackson and Rev. James Reeb, their deaths spurred the triumphal march from Selma to Montgomery and the even more momentous Voting Rights Act of 1965.

But events after Klunder's death followed an arc more common and sobering, one devoid of satisfying resolutions. For Cleveland's Black activists, the tragedy brought new heights of frustration. The intransigence of the school board and white parents, the continuing overuse of the police force, and long-standing disagreements about strategy and tactics among civil rights groups altered the course of Black activism in Cleveland. These factors helped encourage the growth of Black nationalist ideology within the activist community, signaling deep disillusionment with those more conservative strategies that emphasized integration and patience.[35]

Additionally, the deep parishioner backlash blunted the enthusiastic activism of Cleveland's white clergy. In 1966, the director of the Greater Cleveland Conference on Religion and Race acknowledged a declining interest in its work.[36] Two years later, the organization had folded, and its treasurer wondered what to do with the remaining $697.67 in its bank account.[37] Their ministers' pulpit preaching and civic work on racial justice seemed to have done little to change their parishioners. In 1968, a member of Fairmount Presbyterian Church bemoaned the ways the members "seem[ed] to consider Negroes as non-people, a strange brand of inferiors that do not have the same concern, interests, feelings, desires as do [whites]." The parishioner thought the congregation suffered from prejudices "so inborn that [they] fail to recognize . . . it, much less take the next step to try to change it."[38]

Most significantly, little about Cleveland's racial structures changed in the wake of Klunder's death. The school construction he sought to prevent continued apace. Named Stephen E. Howell

Elementary, the school came to symbolize for Black Clevelanders the white intransigence that thwarted their efforts for a more just and equitable city. Just two short years after the Klunder tragedy, as one of America's worst race riots engulfed the city, a large crowd gathered at the school, while law enforcement stationed about one hundred police and national guardsmen on the building's roof to prevent the mob from burning it down. Though onlookers blamed Black pathology, communism, and outside agitators for the five-day melee, an analysis revealed that failures to address long-standing Black concerns—most specifically, the iron ring of employment opportunity, housing discrimination, and school segregation—prompted the uprising. Indeed, the racial turmoil that roiled many American cities in the middle and late 1960s did not erupt "out of nowhere" in a display of innate Black pathology, as many explained at the time and as civil rights mythology often insists.[39]

Cleveland's ongoing racial struggles demonstrate the limited and unfinished nature of the civil rights revolution there. As late as 1977, a federal judge determined that segregation continued in the Cleveland school system as a result of factors unchanged from two decades before: residential segregation, the location of new school construction, and reassigning students for the purpose of segregation. The same year, the state of Ohio found that the city's public schools did not meet minimal standards of achievement.

The grand civil rights drama of sacrifice and high-visibility solidarity silences important questions about the mechanisms and nature of lasting change. Many civil rights events ended similarly to the Cleveland story, with little progress, only ephemeral change, or even outright setbacks. Remembering these frustrations and failures erases the bright line between the past and the present. With so much left undone, with such impregnable forces arrayed on the side of the racial hierarchy, Americans demanding racial justice today stand in the same stream of activism as their forebears of the mid-twentieth century.

*　　　*　　　*

51

Rightly remembering Bruce Klunder demands courage of the sort he displayed. Yet, this particular bravery doesn't require lying behind a bulldozer. It begins in telling a dramatically reframed story—one resolute in grappling with the pervasive, all-encompassing nature of the nation's racial crimes; audacious in pursuing thick, tangled webs of oppression even into sanctuaries regarded as sinless; fearless in naming as unfinished the work of racial justice. Against mythologies actively and insistently shrinking America's civil rights story to unusable proportions, telling this truer, harder story is daring indeed.

Since we live our lives on a stage set by others, only a rightly remembered past can help us negotiate our way through the props and pieces laid by our predecessors. A mythic past provides a faulty schema for that stage, leaving us groping and tripping. As high-profile protests erupted against systemic racial injustice in the summer of 2020, Americans' consternation revealed how dense a theatrical fog obscures our actual civil rights history. For those who believed in a civil rights past as a story about southern racist villains vanquished by the Civil Rights Act of 1964 and a few other pieces of legislation, these disturbances erupted out of nowhere, seemingly the work of agitators stoked by a sense of victimization.

A more appropriate and effective response could have arisen from a public prepared with the truer, broader, more complicated civil rights story that Bruce Klunder's life and death reveal. Let us contend for a civil rights history that wars against the saccharine myths of cherry-picked facts, self-congratulatory sophisms, and fantasies of exceptionalism.

Let us remember Bruce Klunder.

Tom Skinner

(1942–1994)

Tom Skinner speaking at Urbana 70, InterVarsity's student missions conference, 1970; photo courtesy of the Wheaton College Billy Graham Center Archives, Wheaton, IL

BLACK AND FREE?

Tom Skinner, White Evangelicalism, and Black Power

Jemar Tisby

They hunched over in parkas and sweaters as they hustled into the arena. The thousands of college students at the conference had come for the speeches, workshops, and friendships, not the frigid December air blasting across the plains of central Illinois.

It was 1970, the second day of the triennial Urbana student missions conference, and the program clipped along in the crisp fashion of a professionally planned event. That morning the students had heard messages entitled "What Is Evangelism?" and "Social Concern and World Evangelism," but the conference organizers had saved the most dynamic speaker for last.

After the dinner hour, twelve thousand students reassembled in the main conference venue. The session started with a time of worship under the musical direction of a band called Soul Liberation. The twelve-member group was made up entirely of Black people. They sported Afros and dashikis, played djembe drums and incorporated elements of soul, folk, gospel, and jazz into their arrangements.[1] Their style signaled to the overwhelmingly white crowd that this group was not going to merely parrot the cultural trappings of evangelicalism. It was an Afro-centric expression of faith.

Once the last notes of the singing had faded, Tom Skinner strode to the podium. Just twenty-eight years old, Skinner stood over six feet tall dressed in a dark suit with a widow's peak tracing the hairline of his black, slightly balding hair. He surveyed his audience. Even before he uttered any words, the veteran speaker commanded the stage.

"Any understanding of world evangelism and racism in our country must begin with an understanding of the history of racism," he intoned. "To understand why we are in the middle of a revolution in our time, to come to grips with what the black revolution is all about . . . I must take you back approximately 350 years, to when the early ships landed in this country, in approximately 1619."[2]

Skinner, a full-time evangelist, had spoken to tens of thousands of people, from Harlem to Barbados. He used humor, cultural critique, and emotional appeals to move his listeners. This night at Urbana, his words seemed particularly inspired.

"Proclaim liberation to the captives, preach sight to the blind, set at liberty them that are bruised, go into the world and tell men who are bound mentally, spiritually and physically, 'The liberator has come!'"[3]

The only sound louder than Skinner's ending crescendo was the shout of the students in response. They rose from their chairs in unison to give a standing ovation. Even though his audience was overwhelmingly composed of white evangelical college students, Skinner's dynamic oratory coupled with a timely dissection of the current racial climate and the role of the church energized the crowd. Everyone seemed to sense the singularity of an event when the message, the messenger, and the moment combined in perfect synchronicity.

Moments like Skinner's address at Urbana tend to have a historical adhesiveness that makes the memory stick. The speech was technically entitled "The U.S. Racial Crisis and World Evangelism," but the ending was so resonant that many people refer to it simply by the final words of the speech, "The Liberator Has Come." Several months later, in an interview, Skinner reflected,

"Urbana was the most significant missionary conference in the last decade."[4] Years later, William "Bill" Pannell, Skinner's colleague at Tom Skinner Associates, recalled, "When he finished that thing the whole audience exploded. I'd never seen a response like that anywhere. It was almost as if all of the seats had been wired and someone pressed a button and all the electricity ran through those seats and everyone jumped in the air. . . . It was astonishing."[5]

In the aftermath, however, others were not so pleased. A little more than a week after the conference ended, Warren B. Appleton, the white father of a student who attended Urbana, typed an angry letter to John Alexander, the president of InterVarsity.

Appleton decried Skinner's use of the words "revolution" and "revolutionaries." In this parent's eyes, it seemed to be an explicit endorsement of communism. "The net results are that twelve thousand of America's finest young, idealist[ic], Christian intellectuals are mis-led into giving a standing ovation to a speaker demanding overthrow of the present order he branded as Satanic, while the musicians brandished Communist clenched-fist salutes."[6]

Appleton concluded with a challenge to Alexander and the other leaders of InterVarsity to explain why they would permit such messages to be part of Urbana. Appleton may never have received a written answer, but Skinner never spoke at Urbana again.

Other white evangelicals seemed to have similar objections. A few months later, in April 1971, the Moody Bible Institute radio station, WMBI, canceled Skinner's thirty-minute weekly show. In a memo they explained, "the broadcast has been becoming increasingly political with less emphasis on God's message to all men."[7] Apparently, Skinner's insistence that the gospel includes a prophetic call to dismantle racism in the church and society was a departure from "true" biblical themes. More likely, the station's decision makers worried that Skinner's discussion of racism and injustice would alienate their largely white evangelical listeners.

To tell a people their sins seldom results in popularity. Such is the price of being a prophet.

A Christian Messenger of a Movement

Even though Skinner is most famous for the message he delivered at Urbana in 1970, the deeper story of that night is about the group of Black college students who literally sat front and center while he delivered his oration. For them, Skinner was their on-stage advocate for Black evangelicals. He was a person who understood their hopes and experiences and could powerfully articulate them to a white evangelical audience.

John Perkins, a Black evangelical and civil rights leader, said that Skinner provided a plausibility structure for young Black Christians who wondered if they had a place among their white coreligionists. He contended that before Tom Skinner came along and spoke the way he did, "Blacks didn't see evangelicalism as a place [for them]."[8]

Personally, I never describe myself using the word "evangelical," as Skinner and other Black Christians did in the mid-twentieth century. The color line within evangelicalism in the United States has been a barrier to full inclusion for anyone who is not white. At best, I am "evangelical-adjacent." Most of my Christian life has been spent "in but not of" white evangelical fellowships. I know from a firsthand perspective the difficulty of addressing racial justice in these communities and how so many Black evangelical-adjacent Christians search for others who can articulate, and possibly transcend, those hardships.

I can easily picture myself as one of those Black college students clustered in seats at the front of the auditorium as part of Skinner's "amen corner." I can even see parts of myself in him. I have stood on stages before white evangelical audiences and spoken about racism in their ranks. I have publicly spoken on the topic in articles, podcasts, and presentations, and I have felt the wounds of rejection as a result.

In 2011, I helped found a nonprofit organization called the Reformed African American Network (RAAN). At the time, I had just started seminary at Reformed Theological Seminary—a theologically and socially conservative school in Jackson, Mississippi. I had also started as an intern at an intentionally multiracial church in the city. It was part of the Presbyterian Church in America (PCA), which, I would discover, had a direct historical linkage to the Southern Presbyterians, who had broken off from their Northern counterparts in an effort to defend slavery.[9] But, in my ignorance, I was determined to get ordained in the PCA. In spite of being in a hyperminority—if memory serves, I could count on one hand the number of Black Americans at my seminary, in a city where nearly 80 percent of residents were Black, and only 1 percent of pastors ordained to preach in the PCA were Black—I was on a mission.[10]

My goal in the early 2010s was to create space and a place for Black Christians in white evangelical and Reformed circles. I wanted Black Christians like me to engage as equals at the white evangelical tables. At colleges and universities, seminaries, churches, websites, and conferences, I wanted Black Christians to be more than an afterthought in the white evangelical mind. I focused my ministry on racial reconciliation through interracial friendship, unity, and increasing the number of multiracial churches.

Over time, however, I came to see that white supremacy within white evangelical churches and institutions could not be vanquished by an interracial potluck or pulpit swap. In 2012, we started a website for RAAN and began posting articles. This was a milestone for our organization because we no longer had to rely on getting published in white evangelical outlets. We could articulate our realities on our own terms and on our own site. As soon as I started writing publicly about race and Christianity, however,

I started to experience the opposition that so many other Black Christians have endured from their white coreligionists. I learned never to read the comments section—that's where they first started calling me a communist, a Marxist, and a heretic. Those are just some of the terms white evangelicals, along with the Black people and other people of color who agree with them, use to label you as a threat to the church.

By 2016, I had withdrawn from the ordination process, due partially to the fact that I had learned that some white pastors had set their minds to sabotaging my ordination interviews with questions designed to prove I was a closet liberal whose stances on racism would mark the "theological drift" of the Presbyterian denomination. I had lost confidence in multiracial churches and the idea that people coming together in the same building for a couple of hours on Sunday morning would make a substantial difference in race relations Monday through Saturday. I had begun learning how to embrace the expansive Black Christian tradition as a source of healing and strength for the fight against racism. I was also just beginning to study history for inspiration and instruction from Black people of ages past.

In this season of my life, I encountered Tom Skinner and immediately gravitated toward him. As a Black Christian in white spaces, I thought that if I could learn more about Skinner's life, study his words, and absorb his philosophy of ministry, then perhaps I could find a way to maneuver in white evangelical circles while also offering prophetic critique for the purpose of Black liberation.

Researching Skinner's later ministry, however, I wondered whether he had changed tactics from the revolutionary rhetoric he delivered at Urbana in 1970 to a more conciliatory approach toward white evangelicals. Before his abrupt death in 1994 from leukemia at the age of fifty-two, Skinner had committed his name and voice to a new racial reconciliation project called Mission Mississippi.

Started in 1993, Mission Mississippi's slogan was "changing Mississippi one relationship at a time." These were fine-sounding words in theory, but when filtered through a white evangelical lens, in practice they became an excuse to avoid challenging racism in its systemic and institutional forms. "Real change does not come through laws and policies," the logic goes, "it comes through personal friendships that soften the heart and lead to new actions and new attitudes." Skinner himself seemed to agree with this approach to racial transformation. In a 1993 interview, he said, "What really is the problem is that we don't know each other. What Mission Mississippi is about is creating an atmosphere where we can know each other and build trust. If that happens, violence will be reduced, mistrust will be reduced, economic prosperity can increase."[11] Skinner made no mention of the laws, policies, or practices that worked to continually marginalize Black people in a place where they constituted a larger percentage of the population than any other state in the country.

The evidence against the "one relationship at a time" method of racial reform is as copious as it is ominous. It simply doesn't work. Strong interracial relationships *by themselves* do nothing to change the fact that Black people are incarcerated at disproportionately high rates, that the median white family has ten times the wealth of the median Black family, or that Black women die in maternity-related deaths at three times the rate of white women.

Skinner had to know this. He grew up in a working-class family in Harlem in the 1940s and 1950s. He lived through the civil rights and Black Power eras. He had faced the wrath of angry white evangelicals who turned on him as soon as he started identifying racism as more than merely an issue of personal piety.

What happens to Black Christians who attempt to cultivate relationships with white evangelicals while also pushing for racial equity? In his book *Open Friendship in a Closed Society*, which examines Mission Mississippi, historian Peter Slade explains, "The prophets of radical open friendship who cry in this wilderness are either marginalized or have their messages adulterated into an insipid gospel of cheap reconciliation."[12] In my own experience, Black Christians who remain in white evangelical spaces have three options. They either get pushed out, they burn out, or they sell out.

When rapper Lecrae, a Black Christian who amassed a large following of white evangelicals with his early albums, started speaking more publicly about racism, he was met with backlash on social media. People said he was playing the "race card," and some vowed never to buy another album or purchase a ticket to his concerts.[13] I have endured days of extreme exhaustion from trying to persuade, cajole, and convince white evangelicals that we need to press for racial justice and that those efforts are not a distraction from the faith but integral to it. This is not a new story. Some people close to Skinner suggested that the strain of working across racial lines for reconciliation may have contributed to his poor health and perhaps even his early death.[14] Confronting racism in its systemic and institutional forms—especially in the church—is risky work.

To find strength for this journey of racial justice, I look to men like Tom Skinner. But the more I learn of his story, the more questions I have.

Did the Tom Skinner of the relationally focused Mission Mississippi maintain the same zeal for revolution as the Tom Skinner who boldly spoke of racism, revolution, and liberation in 1970? Did he remain a man who was marginalized for his refusal to compromise with white evangelical racism? Was he a person whose message was appropriated by people who wanted to feel good about themselves through interracial friendships but hardly took any action against systemic injustice?

Is Tom Skinner really the champion for Black evangelicals that he appeared to be that night at Urbana '70?

CAPTURING THE MOOD OF THE MOMENT

Before we can make any judgments about Skinner's ministry in the 1980s and 1990s, we have to analyze his word at Urbana '70.

What exactly made it so powerful? Was it his delivery and oratorical flair? Was it the way he used history as a foundation for his contemporary critiques? Was it simply the fact that his presence there as a Black man made young white college students feel more racially progressive?

Although no single factor explains the significance of Skinner's message that night, one critical element is the extent to which his words captured the mood of the moment.

In 1966, a young Black activist with the Student Nonviolent Coordinating Committee (SNCC) named Stokely Carmichael had shouted the words "Black Power" during a march in Mississippi.[15] The phrase became the banner under which the next phase of the Black freedom struggle proceeded.

Carmichael (later Kwame Turé) and others such as Floyd McKissic; Willie Ricks, who had urged him to use the phrase that night in Mississippi; and members of the Congress of Racial Equality (CORE) argued that the exact phrase, especially its use of the word "Black," was important.[16] According to Carmichael, using the word "Black" "doesn't mean we are anti-white. We are just developing pride."[17] When Skinner spoke assertively of the need for white evangelicals to address issues of poverty, underfunded public education, and the insufficiency of white evangelical efforts to address racism, he said they referred to him as the "Stokely Carmichael of the evangelical world."[18]

Many people of African descent in the United States resonated with the forthright assertion of Black pride that Black Power represented. Weary of a struggle that had lasted in its most recent form for over a decade with significant but still incomplete gains, they were looking for a movement that stood for their frustrations as well as bolstered a sense of self-assurance and independence. They found it in Black Power.

Black Power's influence reached the church as well. In 1966, the National Committee of Negro Churchmen took out a full-page ad in the *New York Times* in support of the burgeoning Black Power movement. In the section of the letter addressed to white Christians, the committee took on the issues of power and love. "As black men who were long ago forced out of the white church to create and wield black power, we fail to understand the emotional quality of the outcry of some clergy against the use of the term today," they wrote. "All people need power, whether black or white. We regard as sheer hypocrisy or as a blind and dangerous illusion the view that opposes love to power."[19]

Black Power had such resonance because it came at a moment when people began to doubt the promise and effectiveness of the changes won by the civil rights movement. On April 4, 1968, Martin Luther King Jr., the veritable apostle of nonviolent interracial cooperation, was assassinated. Uprisings erupted in cities around the nation as Black people attempted to process the anger and the sorrow. In May of 1970, two events inflamed Black people and college students across the nation. On May 4, National Guard troops opened fire on students at Kent State who had assembled in protest of the Vietnam War. Four students were killed in the shooting. Then, less than two weeks later, on May 11, white police officers opened fire at Jackson State College, an all-Black school in Jackson, Mississippi, and killed two students. The events of the spring semester would have been fresh in the minds of college students such as those who attended Urbana '70 as they returned to classes that fall.

By December 1970, Black college students had been hearing about, debating, and defining Black Power and ongoing deadly racial conflict throughout their high school and secondary educational lives. As they sought to be faithful to Christ and pro-Black, they looked for voices who could articulate their yearnings. The most prominent of those voices in the evangelical sphere was Tom Skinner.

Recruiting Black Evangelical College Students

Skinner's appearance at Urbana in 1970 was at least three years in the making. In 1967, at the previous triennial conference, Black students began organizing for change. Of the ten thousand students who came to Urbana '67, only a handful were Black Americans.

In the middle of the conference, Paul Gibson, a Black evangelical and senior at Harvard, began spreading the word about an informal meeting of the Black students at the conference. In the midst of the Black Power movement and ongoing social upheaval, Gibson was frustrated by the lack of attention speakers had given to racial issues and by the dismal number of Black students at the conference. About twenty-three students attended the meeting, where they talked about what they could do to make their concerns a priority at the next conference.[20]

A young Black college student named Carl Ellis Jr. became instrumental in bringing Skinner to Urbana '70. Ellis, a student at Hampton College (now University), had become a Christian in 1964. With the zeal of a new convert, he shared his faith with other students on campus. In a short time he had founded the first chapter of InterVarsity on the campus of a historically Black college or university (HBCU). Leaders at InterVarsity recognized Ellis's passion and recruited him along with another Black student, Elward Ellis (no relation), to help them recruit more Black students to the campus ministry and its national missions conference.[21]

Carl Ellis first heard of Tom Skinner during a leadership training camp hosted by InterVarsity. A white evangelist named Clark Pinnock told Carl Ellis that he had to meet a man named Tom Skinner. Ellis and Skinner soon connected, and the young undergraduate found in Skinner a man who could connect his experiences as a Black person to his evangelical faith. Skinner mentored Carl and Elward, and in the years to come Carl Ellis came on staff to direct the Black campus ministry outreach of Tom Skinner Associates.

As a member of the Urbana advisory committee in the lead-up to Urbana '70, Ellis recommended Skinner as a potential speaker. The committee agreed, and the stage was set for Skinner's momentous message at the next conference.

Now Ellis had to take up the larger work of recruiting not just a Black speaker but also Black participants for the overwhelmingly white missions conference. Ellis had experienced disappointment at his first Urbana experience in 1967. The speakers emphasized evangelistic missions to foreign countries while giving relatively little attention to the Black community domestically.

"[White] evangelicalism wasn't present in the Black community so I could only conclude that God was a racist. But God couldn't be a racist. So I was beginning to have disillusionment with evangelicalism," he recalled.[22]

Instead of giving up on evangelicalism or white Christians, Ellis tried to carve out a space for Black evangelicals. He used his deflating experience at Urbana '67 as motivation to craft a message directed at Black students that centered their unique needs and priorities.

Ellis served as the principal host of a promotional film entitled *What Went Down at Urbana '67?* Organizers showed the twenty-one-minute film to groups of college students on various campuses and used it as the foundation for a discussion of Christianity, evangelism, and race.

The film unambiguously reflects a Black Power cultural ethos and aesthetic. It begins with a Black man dressed in a dashiki and pounding out rhythmic cadences on an African drum called a djembe. Images from the recent Black freedom struggle—marchers holding picket signs, the bullet-riddled door of Black Panther Fred Hampton's apartment, a fist raised in the Black Power salute—cascade across the screen. Then Carl Ellis, the guide for this journey, appears and asks the viewer, "Are you serious about solutions?"[23]

The majority of the film addresses the objections of young Black people to the idea of evangelistic missions and of Christianity itself. Student actors represent these concerns on-screen, making assertions such as "Missions ain't nothin' but Christian racism." And "Christianity's nothing but an extension of colonialism." Or "Christianity's just a tool for enslaving black people."[24]

In response, Ellis and others present a socially conscious, Afrocentric, and evangelical perspective on the racial issues of the late

1960s. "The black man's role in the great commission should be that he should go out through all the lands and preach the gospel the way it's supposed to be and not with this white man's honkified way of preaching the gospel."[25]

The "honkified" way of preaching the gospel exhibited a disregard for, even a defense of, racism. It did not address the segregation that white Christians forced on Black people. A honkified gospel remained mute or only raised its voice in support of entities like the Ku Klux Klan and the Citizens' Council that sought to enforce white dominance by any means necessary. The honkified gospel was the mid-twentieth-century version of what Frederick Douglass had described as a "slaveholding religion."

"I love the pure, peaceable, and impartial Christianity of Christ. I therefore hate the corrupt, slaveholding, women-whipping, cradle-plundering, partial and hypocritical Christianity of this land. Indeed, I can see no reason, but the most deceitful one, for calling the religion of this land Christianity."[26]

This honkified religion was described by King in his "Letter from a Birmingham Jail." He characterized it as passive in matters of racial justice. King named these Christians "white moderates." One who is "more devoted to 'order' than to justice; who prefers a negative peace which is the absence of tension to a positive peace which is the presence of justice . . . who paternalistically believes he can set the timetable for another man's freedom."[27]

Ellis's recruiting method worked. Several hundred Black Christian college students attended Urbana '70. Many of them came in anticipation of Tom Skinner and the way he articulated an Afrocentric, evangelical version of Christianity.

The honkified gospel is what Skinner spoke of that day at Urbana. He spoke of the "hyper Christian." A white Christian who was "'a Bible-believing, fundamental, orthodox, conservative, evangelical Christian,' whatever that meant." This person had "half a dozen Bible verses for every social problem that existed. But, if you asked him to get involved, he couldn't do it."[28] This kind of bold, rhetorically engaging commentary is exactly why the Black students wanted Tom Skinner to speak and exactly what they wanted the white college students at Urbana '70 to hear.

AFRO-CENTRIC EVANGELICALISM

Skinner and his colleagues had been fashioning his timely message of Black liberation and evangelical Christianity since at least 1967. That year the National Conference on Black Power took place in Newark, New Jersey. From July 20 to 23, more than one thousand delegates representing 286 organizations gathered to formulate plans to aggressively consolidate economic, political, and social power in the hands of Black people for the purposes of community restoration and self-determination.

Just days before the conference began, one of the nation's largest and deadliest uprisings took place in Newark. Once again, the old tensions between police and Black communities were the source of the conflict. John William Smith was a trumpet player, a US Army veteran of two wars, and a Black man. The latter was enough to get him pulled over on July 12 by two white police officers. Instead of simply issuing a citation, they beat him severely.[29]

Rumors flew, and local residents initially thought that the police had killed Smith. He survived, but the encounter outraged a community already strained by police brutality, poverty, and racial segregation. Five days of conflict ensued and left twenty-six people dead, most of them Black, with $10 million in property damage to the area. Along with other conflagrations in Watts and Detroit, the Newark uprising encapsulated the discontent and urgency of the Black Power movement.

The focus of the National Conference on Black Power was the workshops. Topics included: "The City and Black People,"

"Black Power in World Perspective," and "Black Power and American Religion." Out of the conference in Newark came the Black Manifesto. It decried "neo-colonialist" control of Black communities across the globe and promoted a "philosophy of blackness" to shirk off the intellectual and cultural constraints of the white racial majority.[30]

Bill Pannell thought the themes and concerns raised by the Black Manifesto ought to be incorporated into Tom Skinner's evangelistic message to Black people and his prophetic critique of white evangelicalism.

"I sent [the Manifesto] to Tom and we began to work with it. That was the genesis of some thinking about our understanding of the gospel, our understanding of how we are to address the black community," Pannell said.[31]

Three themes in particular—identity, community, and power—came to be infused into Skinner's teachings. By the time of Urbana '70, Skinner had worked and reworked his messages to incorporate these ideas but with a distinctly Christian and evangelical focus.

"The U.S. Racial Crisis and World Evangelism" stands as Skinner's most concise and passionate articulation of his attempt to apply the gospel of Jesus Christ to the issues of racial oppression and white evangelical intransigence in the Black Power era. Like others such as Martin Luther King Jr., Skinner did not reject Black Power outright either as a slogan or a movement.[32] Instead, he gave the notion of "revolution" his own spiritual spin.

"First, the definition of a revolution is to take an existing situation which has proved to be unworkable, archaic, impractical and out of date; you seek to destroy it, and overthrow it and to replace it with a system that works," he explained.[33] He then went on to describe Jesus as a revolutionary whose purpose was to overthrow an unjust world order, not a political one but a spiritual one, rife with racism, poverty, and militarism.[34]

He also denounced white evangelicals for failing to rise to the racial moment. "To a great extent, the evangelical church in America supported the status quo. It supported slavery; it supported segregation; it preached against any attempt of the black man to stand on his own two feet." Skinner recognized that white evangelicals had distanced themselves from the pressing issues that continued to curtail Black opportunity in America. They preached spiritual salvation while passively or actively supporting a racist status quo.

At the same time, Skinner did not diminish the evangelical emphasis on spiritual salvation as the key to true liberation. He subscribed neither to a gospel that promoted only material uplift nor to simple soul-saving as the "true" gospel. "If your gospel is an 'either-or' gospel, I must reject it." He went on to describe the true oppressor as Satan and the true liberator as Jesus Christ.

It was Skinner's ability to describe and validate the racial oppression that Black people faced while also expressing the need for spiritual salvation and allegiance to Christ above all that made the young Black Christians at Urbana '70 view him as their spokesperson to the white evangelical church in the United States.

Black evangelical Christians felt forced to choose between advocating for Black Power and racial advancement on one side, and loyalty to Jesus Christ and soul-saving evangelism on the other. Their concerns about racism, segregation, and poverty often found a determined silence or a polite dismissal among the white evangelical organizers of such events as the Urbana conferences and college campus ministries more broadly.

In Tom Skinner, they found a person who understood their reality as Black people in a white supremacist society as well as their faithfulness to evangelical Christianity and their desire to share the good news of Jesus Christ. He put words to their unverbalized yearnings, and did so with a force, confidence, and charisma that made white evangelicals pay attention.

EVANGELICALS LOVE A GOOD CONVERSION STORY

From his conversion in 1959 to his evangelistic rallies and crusades before Black audiences throughout the 1960s, Tom Skinner was favored by white evangelicals. In a relatively short time, word spread about his evangelistic ministry to Black people in the urban ghetto. One newspaper article about Skinner's work dubbed him "the Billy Graham of Harlem."[35] The young Black evangelist had patterned his ministry, in some ways, after Graham. The organization that became Tom Skinner Associates was originally named the Tom Skinner Crusade, and he conducted evangelist crusades in places such as Harlem and focused on big events to draw people to Christ, not unlike Billy Graham's ministry. White evangelicals frequently called on him to speak at Christian conferences and schools. In 1968, leaders at Wheaton College, a flagship educational institution for white evangelicalism, invited him to give a series of messages on campus.[36] He was an in-demand speaker and eventually had his own radio show broadcast on nine stations.[37]

Skinner could have started his own congregation or taken leadership at an established church. He could have chosen a teaching ministry at a college or seminary or through writing books. He could have been employed in any job and simply tried to live as a faithful Christian in that capacity. Instead Skinner chose to become an evangelist, and any evaluation of his life and ministry must keep that fact at the core.

Skinner's evangelistic tendencies began from the moment of his dramatic conversion. According to Skinner's own testimony, by his early teenage years he had become a violent gang leader. "By the time I left the gang I had twenty-two notches on the handle of my knife which meant that my blade had gone into twenty-two different fellows."[38]

All that changed one night when Skinner listened to a sermon on the radio. In his autobiography he wrote that he had been planning the strategy for what he contended would be the largest gang fight in the history of New York. It was to involve five gangs and an estimated three thousand people.[39]

Skinner had the radio on while he was planning, and, at nine o'clock, the station interrupted its regularly scheduled programming with a gospel presentation. An unnamed preacher preached an evangelistic message about Jesus Christ coming into your heart and changing the corrupt moral factory that manufactures evil. "That's right! His Spirit lives in that 'factory' and makes it over so you don't sin no more."[40]

Skinner began thinking about the person he had become—duplicitous, thieving, violent, and selfish. Although he had heard Black preachers, including his own father, share a similar message countless times before, this time it resonated.

"I bowed my head and prayed simply, 'God I don't understand all of this. . . . If you can forgive me of every sin that I ever committed, then I'm asking You to do it. I'm asking You to come into my life and take it over and live in me.'"[41]

From that moment on Skinner renounced his old ways and became an ambassador for Christ. He quit his gang the next day and began preaching to the people around him. Looking around at his native community of Harlem, he said, "After my conversion, these people became my 'parish.' I became deeply concerned about thousands of other fellows like Tom Skinner who needed to hear about this person Jesus Christ."[42]

Perhaps this explains Skinner's early popularity with white evangelicals. They love a good conversion story. Skinner related his encounter with Christ countless times at crusades, churches, and speaking events over the years. White evangelicals could resonate with someone who saw a personal relationship with Jesus Christ as the answer to the world's most pressing problems. What's more, Skinner was doing what white evangelicals could not or would not do—speaking to predominantly Black and urban audiences.

As long as Skinner focused on individual conversion and not cultural critique, white evangelicals could make a place for him. Such a message required no sacrifice from them. It did not mean they had to change the schools they sent their kids to or decide whether to move to a different neighborhood. Evangelistic messages did not require a shift in how they spent money or what state or federal policies they supported.

White evangelicals' love of a good conversion story also confirmed their generalizations about other Black people. If Black people did not end up converted and broadly evangelical in their convictions, then it was due to their own lack of effort, their own criminality, the shortcomings of their own culture. Such personal and social depravity could only be overcome through the "miracle motif." Sociologists Michael Emerson and Christian Smith explain: "The miracle motif is the theologically rooted idea that as more individuals become Christians, social and personal problems will be solved automatically."[43] As long as Christians preached the gospel and saw people converted to their religion, then issues of personal piety and public equity would take care of themselves.

Giving a platform to someone like Tom Skinner, a Black man who spoke their language of evangelicalism, gave white evangelicals cover for their colorblind approach to racial relations and their apathy on racial justice.[44]

MISSION MISSISSIPPI

Pat Morley was burned out. Even though he was experiencing professional success as a prosperous business owner in Florida, he didn't feel he had done enough to earn God's approval. In 1976 he attended a retreat hosted by the Young Life evangelical ministry. Its retreat center, Windy Gap, sat on 2,200 acres in the Blue Ridge Mountains of North Carolina. That year, a featured speaker at the retreat was a man named Tom Skinner.

After one of Skinner's evangelistic messages at the retreat, Morley said he "felt free." Free of the burden of proving himself to God. Free of the yoke of being perfect in order to earn his way to heaven. It just so happened that Morley ran into Skinner at the tennis courts. They both shared a love of tennis, and since Skinner's message had been so powerful, Morley invited the evangelist down to his hometown of Orlando to speak later that year. Their friendship grew and deepened over time, and they remained close until Skinner's death in 1994.[45]

At that same retreat, recalls Morley, Skinner said that "the most powerful force in the world is a relationship." Skinner's relationship with Morley, who is white, would serve as a living demonstration of the gospel's power to reconcile siblings in Christ across racial and ethnic lines. It is that philosophy that undergirded Mission Mississippi's approach to racial change.

In the mid-1980s, Morley sensed a call to full-time ministry. His work exploded onto the national evangelical scene when he published a book called *Man in the Mirror*. It was a book designed to help men overcome the works-based Christianity that Morley struggled with, and its message resonated. To date, *Man in the Mirror* has sold more than 4 million copies worldwide, and Morley started Man in the Mirror, a nonprofit whose vision was for "every church to disciple every man."[46]

The fame that came with Morley's book caught the attention of a group in Jackson, Mississippi, called the Christian Business Men's Committee (CBMC). They invited him to come speak, and it was there that he met with Jim Baird, pastor of the historic First Presbyterian Church. Morley recalls Baird explaining that "Evangelism is not our problem, our issue is that half our community is Black and half is white and nobody knows each other; our issue is racial reconciliation."[47]

The statement became a moment of clarity for Morley. "I felt the Spirit come over me. It was one of those times when a hundred things happen in a nanosecond. I realized why God had made such an investment in a relationship between me and Tom."[48]

He called up Skinner and asked if he'd be willing to go to Jackson to talk about their friendship as a demonstration of the reconciling power of the gospel. Skinner agreed, and in 1992 they spoke to a group of about eighty Black and white residents in Jackson. Morley spoke first, and when Skinner came up to speak after him, they embraced on stage.

"Several people in the audience gasped, and for years afterward that's all people talked about or remembered from that meeting," recalled Morley.

Events proceeded rapidly from there. A biracial steering committee of local Jackson men met and planned a city-wide rally for October 1993 called "Bringing Down the Walls That Divide Us: Worship and Unity Rally." The event had all the marks of a Billy Graham–style crusade, complete with a football stadium for a venue, celebrity testimonies, and a mass choir. Morley and Skinner as well as a host of others spoke, and the three-day rally drew about twenty-four thousand people. The event culminated in a group of Black and white pastors raising a large cross together as a demonstration of racial equality and unity in Christ.[49]

As poignant as that moment was, organizers quickly decided that holding such massive and expensive events annually was not a sustainable model. They pivoted to form Mission Mississippi, a nonprofit organization designed to foster cross-racial relationships.

From its start, Skinner, Morley, and others involved focused on personal relationships. Morley recalled Skinner sketching out his vision for racial reconciliation in Mississippi. "What we need is right relationships with God and right relationships with each other." This combined two of Skinner's passions—evangelism and racial reconciliation.

Skinner also explained what he believed was the source of racial strife. "The problem here is that we do not know each other."

Implicit in this framing of the problem is the solution. If the dilemma is a lack of relationships, then the answer is to build relationships. Absent from such a formulation is any acknowledgment of broader systemic and institutional forces such as voter suppression, unequal funding in public schools, or police brutality.

Yet the absence of any structural analysis of racism may have been due to the fact that Christian cross-racial efforts were still rare and novel in the late 1980s and early 1990s. The civil rights movement removed some of the legal barriers of segregation, but the subsequent decades demonstrated that people had not changed their social, professional, or economic networks. Legal desegregation did not result in racial integration.

In this context, even the mere pursuit of relationships across the color line was seen by some in Mississippi as a radical act. In a state with the highest number of recorded lynchings, one where only the bravest civil rights activists ventured, the last state in the Union that literally still flew the battle flag of the Confederacy, Black and white people coming together as relational equals was a direct confrontation with the stronghold that white supremacy held in the state.

Lee Paris, a key figure in starting Mission Mississippi and a life-long member of First Presbyterian Church, reflected on his social network in the early 1990s. "I really did not have African American friends at this time. Maybe there were folks I was friendly with, but I never had anyone over to my home socially."[50] The undeniable love and friendship that Skinner and Morley put on display was a revelation for many conservative white Christians.

But many Black people disagreed with this relational theory of change. As word of Mission Mississippi spread, Black people exhibited a mix of responses. Some hurled the "Uncle Tom" label at the Black people involved in Mission Mississippi. Others expressed skepticism by saying, "we've seen this before" or "it's just for show." Still others saw utility in befriending white people as a way to gain access to financial resources.[51]

Given the state of race relations in Mississippi, it is possible that Skinner knew that he could not begin talking about larger issues of systemic injustice until he and other Black people pierced the prejudices of many white people through relationships. Skinner's emphasis on relationships may have been a strategic entry point that he hoped would lead to broader changes in laws and policies over time.

Assimilation or Infiltration?

After Urbana, it seemed like white evangelical leaders were simply searching for a way to distance themselves from Skinner's "radical" ideas and rhetoric. Some saw Urbana '70 as the breaking point. Others used Skinner's divorce from his first wife in 1973 as an excuse to disassociate from him. In their strict views on marriage, divorce for anything except infidelity was a moral failure that disqualified one from ministry.[52]

In the 1970s and 1980s, Skinner revamped his vocation to focus on leadership training and evangelism in more secular outlets. He became the chaplain for the Washington Redskins and often preached evangelistic messages and prayed with the football team before games. He married a woman named Barbara Williams-Skinner, an accomplished political operator in DC, and together they founded the Congressional Black Caucus Prayer Breakfast. They also founded the Skinner Leadership Institute to "produce high performing morally and professionally excellent, civic-minded executive leaders."[53] Through these initiatives, Skinner cultivated friendships with many influential white Christians.

But was Skinner's method one of infiltration or assimilation? The Skinner of the late 1960s and early 1970s seemed to preach a more confrontational message of radical change. In that period he wrote three books—*Black and Free, Words of Revolution*, and *If Christ Is the Answer, What Are the Questions?*—all of which addressed both the need for conversion and the need to transform the material conditions of Black people. It is this Skinner who never spoke again at an Urbana missions conference. It is this Skinner whose radio program on WMBI got canceled. It is this Skinner that so many Black evangelicals around the nation rallied to support.

Perhaps Skinner's approach to white evangelicals in his Mission Mississippi era was to infiltrate their organizations and networks with a message that seemed broadly evangelistic on the surface but contained a subversive message upon closer examination. It is possible that Skinner mastered the technique of roundly criticizing white evangelicals while gaining their trust through humor and insight. This is not to suppose any nefarious intentions on the part of Skinner. It simply acknowledges the fact that Black people have always had to "wear the mask" in order to survive and thrive in a white supremacist society.

Or it could be that Skinner truly believed that the solution to all the problems he outlined in his books and his speech at Urbana was personal conversion. Maybe he had theologically and culturally assimilated to white evangelicalism's "one relationship at a time" approach to racial transformation. Maybe he subscribed to the "miracle motif" as the path to systemic change and encouraged others to do the same.

As sobering as that conjecture is, it might explain why he didn't write any more books after the 1970s. It might explain why he chose to partner with an organization like Mission Mississippi, with its almost singular focus on personal relationships rather than systemic change. It might explain why so few Black Christians of the millennial generation and younger have even heard of Tom Skinner.

BLACK AND FREE

History does not repeat itself—there are too many particularities and contingencies for exact reproductions of the past—but it does rhyme. The year 2014 rhymed with the year 1966; in 2014 Mike

Brown was killed by a white police officer in Ferguson, Missouri, and the phrase "Black Lives Matter" roared to the forefront of the national discourse on race. Those three words—so commonplace in isolation—when strung together proved just as disruptive to contemporary debates on race as the phrase "Black Power" had four decades prior. People from pastors to pundits to politicians weighed in on the meaning of Black Lives Matter and argued about whether it caused racial division or merely highlighted the divisions already present. The phrase became the banner under which the modern movement for Black freedom marched, protested, and picketed. To many, the words had just as much ambiguity and potency as the phrase "Black Power" in the 1960s.

Black Lives Matter shook the church in the United States, too. Just as the Black Power movement did for Black and white Christians, the phrase Black Lives Matter catapulted the stark differences in racial understanding between the races. In a Pew Research poll from 2016, a period when debate on the topic of race was vigorous, 43 percent of respondents overall either "somewhat" or "strongly" supported the Black Lives Matter movement. Disaggregated by race, 65 percent of Black people supported the movement, including 41 percent who strongly supported it; 12 percent of Black people said they opposed the movement. Among white people, 40 percent expressed support, while 28 percent said they opposed Black Lives Matter.[54]

I was among the 65 percent. I supported Black Lives Matter—whether it referred to the sentiment or the organization. To me Black Lives Matter was an assertion of the *imago Dei*. It was a racially specific application of a foundational doctrine written in the very first book of the Bible. "So God created humankind in his image, in the image of God he created them; male and female he created them" (Gen. 1:27 NRSV). Black Lives Matter is a declaration that people of African descent, too, are made in God's image. The phrase also serves as a lament, a crying out to God over the spilled blood of yet more Black people whose very existence is devalued in a white supremacist society. I supported the organization—not because I agreed with every single policy stance or action—but because Black Lives Matter activists weren't arguing about whether racism was a problem like many Christians were; instead they were actually doing something about it. They were in the fight against racism—indeed, at the forefront of the battle—and we as citizens and Christians could either join the struggle or be part of the problem.

These were not popular views in the white Christian circles of which I was a part. When I said "Black Lives Matter," many white Christians retorted, "All Lives Matter." When I said we need to pay attention to the systemic and institutional aspects of racism, they said I was being "too political." At this time I transitioned from talking about "racial reconciliation" to talking about "racial justice." It wasn't just about getting different "hues in the pews," it was about dismantling the racist policies and practices that marginalized entire people groups. But it seemed to me that many white evangelicals had erected a barrier between Jesus and justice when Jesus was precisely the reason we *must* pursue justice. As Skinner said, "We must produce in the twentieth century a radical kind of Christianity which takes its orders from God, which derives its life from Jesus Christ, and which lives oblivious to public opinion."

So I looked to Skinner to demonstrate "a radical kind of Christianity" that stood up to white evangelical sluggishness and resistance in the face of pressing racial justice problems. I looked to him for guidance about how to be a confident Black man who did not need "permission" from white evangelicals to bring his full religious identity or racial identity into any situation. I went back and studied not just his famous Urbana speech but as many of his words and writings as I could find. I searched for lessons from his life to serve as guideposts for my own. He became for me a member of that "great cloud of witnesses" who inspired and informed my own journey of faith.

It seems, however, that I may be able to walk alongside Skinner only for a portion of the path. Where he continued to work for interracial cooperation with white evangelicals, I have decided to invest more of my energy directly into building up Black people and Black institutions. No longer is my approach to try to make room at the table that white evangelicals built. Black people can build our own tables. That's why in 2017, after years of doing what I call "racial apologetics"—trying to make the case that racism is a present reality that invades institutional practices and political policies—we decided to change the name of the nonprofit I helped start from the Reformed African American Network to The Witness, a Black Christian Collective. We made a self-conscious move to center Black people in our work and exhaust less of ourselves in the work of convincing white evangelicals of the racial realities we know to be true.

I have not "given up" on white people, as so many assume—there is always room for redemption and allyship for those white evangelicals who can see the racism in their own tradition and choose to repudiate it. I also do not believe that Skinner ever stopped serving Black people or that he was a pushover with white evangelicals. Perhaps he was merely working within the historical constraints of his day. In the 1980s and 1990s, Black and white Christians still had not come together to the degree that we see in the 2020s. Multiethnic megachurches and Black pastors leading majority-white congregations, while somewhat familiar today, would have been drastic innovations for most Christian fellowships thirty years ago. So it would have been significant for a Black man such as Skinner to have such a close and visible friendship with a white man like Pat Morley or to work with white evangelical organizations to help shape their words and actions around race. Were I active in ministry in that time period, I cannot definitively say that I would have done any different.

Yet I am not pursuing racial justice in the past. God allotted me this period of time and this dwelling place in which to live out my days (Acts 17:26). Effectiveness for me is not merely about access to white spaces but racial equity throughout society. The goal is not to develop polite relationships with white evangelicals but to flip the proverbial tables of white supremacy and racial injustice to become a "city on a hill" that shines the light of justice in the world. But I would not have gained this understanding without learning about and from Tom Skinner.

Skinner came along at a time in my life when I was still steeped in white evangelicalism—its modes of thought, priorities, and ways of being in the world. I might have walked in that haze of faux harmony for much longer if Skinner's words and life had not reverberated down through the decades. We occupied very similar positions at certain points—we are both Black men speaking truth to white evangelical power and facing their backlash. In this way, he helped instill the confidence I needed to keep going, keep evolving my perspective, keep moving toward integrity in my thinking and my ministry. We all need historical mentors. Skinner will forever be one of my most important tutors.

When it comes to our life and work, someone is always watching. It is possible that after years spent vigorously pursuing some cause larger than ourselves, that ages hence, others will probe our work as I have done with Skinner. It may be that they have questions about what we have done. Did we stay consistent? Did we betray our convictions for wealth or comfort? Did our zeal wane with age? Did we compromise with racism or courageously confront it?

These are not questions that can be answered in a single action or a short season. The most important questions about our character can only be answered by the witness of our entire lives. The trajectory of Skinner's life reveals a man committed to Christ and to telling others about him. I never had the opportunity to meet Tom Skinner, but if I could, I would tell him that his words and example helped another Black Christian who has spent a lot of time with white evangelicals to boldly proclaim, "The Liberator has come!"

Rachel Carson

(1907–1964)

Rachel Carson with her colleague Bob Hines conducting marine biology research in Florida, 1952; US Fish and Wildlife Service

BEYOND WORRY TO WONDER

Rachel Carson at the Dawn of the Modern Environmental Movement

Mallory McDuff

This is a story about women who worry.

During the coronavirus pandemic, a photo of Rachel Carson (1907–1964) sat on my desk in the 900-square-foot house I shared with my daughters on an empty college campus in Appalachia. Before I met with my environmental education students on Zoom, I would glance at the black-and-white image of Carson, hair coiffed, looking curious but reserved, with her back against a tree. In another photo of her in my desk drawer, she wears shorts and a gingham button-up shirt, leaning over a tide pool to study the intricate connections of life on the shore.

Carson worried: about rising seas, pesticides, corporate industry, cancer, finances, her family's health, and more. While she didn't have her own children, she was like a single mother supporting her entire extended family. Amidst grave worries and ambitious yet relentless work, she became a best-selling author who could do what few scientists can these days—ignite public curiosity about science and transform it into advocacy.

Revered as the "mother of the environmental movement,"[1] Carson is also known as the "scientist-poet of the sea," given her trilogy of nature writing about seashores and the ocean that sustains us.[2] Her three books, *Under the Sea-Wind* (1941), *The Sea around Us* (1951), and *The Edge of the Sea* (1955), established her reputation as a writer who could translate scientific concepts into poetic, accessible language. Long before TED talks or Instagram Live, Carson combined the poetry of Wendell Berry with the cultural influence of Brené Brown. She is best known for her 1962 book, *Silent Spring,* which exposed the dangers of DDT (dichlorodiphenyltrichloroethane)—when she was fighting the cancer that would kill her.

My students are fighting too, in the midst of the climate crisis and a pandemic that brought both virtual graduations and record unemployment rates. Before social distancing, one of my undergraduates named Sally Thames occupied the municipal building in Asheville, North Carolina, with other young people from the Sunrise Movement and pressured the city council to declare a climate emergency. "The adults think we are going away, but this is our future, and we are not going away," she told me. At the federal level, my former student Kelsey Juliana is the lead plaintiff in the case *Juliana v. U.S.,* which asserts young people have a constitutional right to a climate system that can sustain human life.

Youth are living in an era when past administrations and the federal courts have repeatedly tried to halt this court case, when industries like Roundup have settled for billions of dollars to appease lymphoma victims, and when climate injustice threatens their lives. As Juliana explained, "We have everything to gain from taking action and everything to lose by not."[3] Their actions remind me of the cumulative power of bearing witness over time. Rachel Carson didn't dream of becoming an activist, but her beliefs propelled her into public witness. She had everything to lose by not taking action too.

When I worry about my students' future—and that of my daughters—I yearn for a solid story to share. I don't need a vapid inspirational tale but a strategic model of inspired persistence. I want to show them a woman who could doggedly claw at her writing and advocacy through illness, devoting her life (and her death) to the health of people and places, while marveling at the interrelationships in nature.

To do that, I have to ask: How was Carson able to move beyond worry? What spiritual beliefs drove her to persist as a woman, writer, and scientist for the good of all? Most of my students only know her from excerpts they've read of *Silent Spring* in introductory environmental studies courses. But I yearn to share her voluptuous writings of the sea and her scientific observations of warming waters as early as the 1940s and 1950s. Indeed, they might have faced a different world if this poet-scientist had lived to write about the threat of rising seas, as she'd planned.[4]

When I stare at the photo of her standing knee-deep in a tide pool, I see a woman driven by her wonder in the world, especially the sea, and her faith in the connection of all living things. Could wonder harness real worries for the good of all in an uncertain but interconnected world?

*　　　*　　　*

Rachel Carson was paying attention. She first voiced her concerns about the widespread use of DDT in a pitch to *Reader's Digest* as early as 1945 when she was working at the Bureau of Fisheries.[5] The magazine rejected the idea, but more than a decade later the Citizen's Committee against Mass Poisoning began to protest aerial spraying across the Northeast and filed a lawsuit in the state of New York in 1958. At that time, Carson received a letter from her friend, journalist Olga Owens Huckins, who described the death of birds after the state sprayed DDT over her property in Massachusetts.

Huckins had written to the *Boston Herald* expressing her horror at aerial spraying on private lands: "All of these birds died horribly and in the same way," she wrote. "Their bills were gaping open, and their splayed claws were drawn up to their breasts in agony."[6]

While care for her ailing mother and grandnephew Roger made travel impossible, Carson proposed a series to the *New Yorker* and a subsequent book to Houghton Mifflin and began research on the pesticides from her home, while a friend sent reports about the court case.

Her initial title for the serialized book was *Man against the Earth*, which would take nearly four years to research and write. In her proposal, she quoted Albert Schweitzer: "Man has lost the capacity to foresee and to forestall. He will end by destroying the earth."[7] That line later became the epigraph for *Silent Spring*. Carson continued to work on the text after her mother's death in 1959. As she wrote: "Over increasingly large areas of the United States, spring now comes unheralded by the return of birds, and the early mornings are strangely silent where once they were filled with the beauty of bird song."[8] Unlike current titles of nonfiction, this was a book that needed no subtitle.[9]

By 1960, she had written one chapter on the effects of pesticides on birds and wildlife, and other chapters on soil, groundwater, insect resistance, cell biology, and cancer. Carson decided to open the book with an allegory:

> There was once a town in the heart of America where all life seemed to live in harmony with its surroundings. The town lay in the midst of a checkerboard of prosperous farms, with fields of grain and hillsides of orchards where, in spring, white clouds of bloom drifted above the green fields. . . . Then a strange blight crept over the area and everything began to change. Some evil spell had settled on the community: mysterious maladies swept the flocks of chickens; the cattle and sheep sickened and died. Everywhere was a shadow of death. . . . No witchcraft, no enemy action had silenced the rebirth of new life in this stricken world. The people had done it themselves.[10]

She was aware, perhaps more than anyone, of the backlash that would come from both industry and government about her findings that implicated a postwar confidence in the power of technology. Indeed, her confidante and the true love of her life, Dorothy, initially discouraged her from this topic, worried about the repercussions from corporations profiting from the status quo.

As she connected DDT to cancer, Carson was plagued by her own health crisis: doctors found additional tumors after previous years of treatment and recommended a radical mastectomy. She decided to keep her illness private, in part due to her fear of industry somehow using knowledge of the cancer against her. As she dealt with ulcers, surgery, radiation, and inflammation of the iris, Carson asked her research assistant to read the chapters aloud, so she could make corrections. With a touch of dark humor, she wrote to Dorothy: "Yes, there is quite a story behind *Silent Spring*, isn't there? Such a catalogue of illnesses! If one were superstitious it would be easy to believe in some malevolent influence at work, determined by some means to keep the book from being published."[11]

In the chapter "Elixirs of Death," Carson states that for the first time in history, humans are exposed to dangerous chemicals from their conception to their death.[12] "For these chemicals are now stored in the bodies of the vast majority of human beings, regardless of age. They occur in the mother's milk, and probably in the tissues of the unborn child."[13]

Her book gives repeated examples of communities with large-scale spraying programs—from fighting the gypsy moth on Long Island to battling Japanese beetles in eastern Illinois—where pesticides had depleted wildlife species and contaminated waters. She was careful not to advocate against all pest control but promoted alternatives like biological controls and predation.

When she finally submitted the text to the *New Yorker*, she wrote Dorothy about her total sense of relief, especially given the cancer growing in her own body. At the time, she was caring for her nephew: "After Roger was asleep, I took Jeffie (her cat) into the study and suddenly the tensions of the four years were broken and I got down and put my arms around Jeffie and let the tears come. . . . I think I let you see last summer what my deeper feelings are about this when I said I could never again listen happily to a thrush song if I had not done all I could."[14]

Silent Spring was serialized in the *New Yorker* in the summer of 1962 and published as a book in September. With a strong platform, Carson's advocacy would take place on the pages of newspapers, on television, and before Congress. Indeed, on August 29, a journalist asked President Kennedy whether or not his administration would research the impacts of DDT and other pesticides: "Yes, I know that they already are," he said. "I think particularly, of course, since Miss Carson's book."[15] Kennedy subsequently convened a panel of the President's Science Advisory Committee to research the issue.

Despite that positive response, Carson experienced firsthand how those with power and money could twist the truth.[16] Using veiled threats of litigation, Vesicol Chemical Corporation tried to make the publisher suppress the book. The chemical industry reportedly spent $250,000 in a disinformation campaign to smear Carson's reputation, although, to this day, the scientific accuracy of her book has not been refuted.[17] Monsanto Chemical Company called her a "hysterical woman."[18] News coverage often began with a description of her appearance or demeanor as "shy," "petite," "soft-spoken," and even referred to her as a "spinster" and "bachelor biologist."[19] In contrast, an editorial in the *New York Times* stated that Carson deserved the Nobel Prize, which had once been given to the inventor of DDT.[20] Carson weathered the praise and critiques, taking issue when attacks came from those who had not even read her book.

In 1962, she spoke to the Women's National Press Club in the presence of TV cameras against the manipulation of truth "to serve the gods of profit and production."²¹ She warned the group of women: "It is clear that we are all to receive heavy doses of tranquilizing information, designed to lull the public into the sleep from which *Silent Spring* so rudely awakened it."²²

Photos from this era show children in cafeterias being sprayed with pesticides while eating lunch and kids running after trucks raining DDT on suburban lawns. Carson's critique challenged powerful corporations, much like calls to confront our climate emergency threaten the fossil fuel industry. In this context, she and her agent agreed to an interview as part of a CBS news special entitled "The Silent Spring of Rachel Carson." Carson's health was severely compromised by cancer; she seemed to be hanging on to her own life as she fought for the health of others.

The producer of the show interviewed individuals ranging from US Surgeon General Luther Terry to Robert White-Stevens, representing the chemical industry. Wearing a tailored suit and a broach on her lapel, Carson spoke with calm confidence and poise—and then read passages from her book. In his lab, White-Stevens wore black-rimmed glasses and a white coat and talked in a loud, foreboding, and frazzled voice. "If man were to follow the teachings of Miss Carson, we would return to the Dark Ages, and the insects and diseases and vermin would once again inherit the earth."²³ With grounded composure, Carson—the only female voice in the long parade of men—concluded with her take-home message about our place amidst the interconnections of all life: "We still haven't become mature enough to think of ourselves as only a very tiny part of a vast and incredible universe. Now I truly believe that we in this generation must come to terms with nature, and I think we're challenged, as mankind has never been challenged before, to prove our maturity and our mastery, not of nature, but of ourselves."²⁴

For the interview, she wore a brown wig, as her hair had fallen out, and cancer had spread to her vertebrae. By this time, she was often confined to a wheelchair. But still, she begged Dorothy to keep her health a secret. After the show aired in April of 1963, Carson testified before Congress in September of that year.

In our age, where writers are expected to share their lives on social media, her staunch privacy might seem almost quaint. But as a woman in a world dominated by men and money, she guarded news of the deterioration of her body to protect herself from those she challenged. She would give her final lecture in California from her wheelchair. In a poignant letter written three months before her death but delivered afterward, Carson communicated to Dorothy about her own mortality:

> I have had a rich life, full of rewards, and satisfactions that come to few and if it must end now, I can feel that I have achieved most of what I wished to do. That wouldn't have been true two years ago, when I first realized my time was short, and I am so grateful to have had this extra time.... But enough of that. What I want to write is the joy and fun and gladness we have shared—for these are the things I want you to remember—I want to live in your memories of happiness. I shall write more of those things. But tonight I'm weary and must put out the light. Meanwhile, there is this word—and my love will always live.[25]

At fifty-six, Carson died from cancer and heart disease in her home in Maryland on April 14, 1964, only eighteen months after the publication of *Silent Spring*. The previous summer, she spent her final months at her cabin in Maine, including time with her beloved Dorothy. In keeping with her quest for privacy, she had called the Reverend Duncan Howlett and asked him to preside over a simple service at All Souls Unitarian Church and include readings from *The Edge of the Sea*.

Her older brother Robert, however, commandeered the situation and arranged for a state funeral at the National Cathedral in Washington before friends could intervene. Her inner circle knew of her desire for cremation and overrode his plans to bury her body next to their mother. Later, Rev. Howlett officiated a simple service with close friends, and Dorothy scattered half of her ashes on the coast of Maine that summer.[26] The other half, as per a truce with her brother, was buried beside her mother.

The outcomes of her witness and writing were many: *Silent Spring* and Carson's advocacy helped to propel passage of the Clean Air Act (1963), the Wilderness Act (1964), and the National Environmental Policy Act (1969), among other legislation, as well as the establishment of the Environmental Protection Agency (1970). Her work is cited as influential in the Clean Water Act and the Endangered Species Act (1970).[27]

It's hard to think about another book with the same environmental impact in the history of this country. But Carson's wonder and reverence for connections in nature, much like mine, began at an early age.

*   *   *

In the town of Fairhope, Alabama, on the shores of Mobile Bay, my family of six provided an army of laypeople for St. James Episcopal Church in the 1970s and '80s. My father sang bass in the choir, my three siblings and I served as acolytes and crucifer, and my mother patrolled our behavior from the front pew. We rarely missed a service, but we never went to Sunday school. My parents realized one of the well-intentioned teachers espoused a literal interpretation of the Bible, which they did not uphold. So after coffee hour, my dad would herd us into the station wagon: "We're going to Sunday school on Mobile Bay!"

At home, we'd change into bathing suits to explore the estuarine waters that emptied into the Gulf of Mexico. In our southern landscape, Mobile Bay was famous for a rare ecological phenomenon at the edge of the sea known as a jubilee, when crabs, flounder, and other aquatic life came to shore, usually on calm summer nights. Such a spectacle prompted phone calls announcing "Jubilee!" and early-morning adventures to haul seafood into nets and coolers. Biologists speculated that specific atmospheric conditions in the summertime increased the probability of this mystery, when the fish seemed to jump from water to land in search of oxygen. As a child, I didn't have to understand a jubilee to feel a spiritual connection to the beauty on the bay.

*   *   *

Rachel viewed the sea as "the great mother of life,"[28] although she couldn't swim and didn't see the ocean until her twenties. The water was where she felt both known and at home. Her work reflected a deeply held belief that the mysteries of the universe were a part of our humanity. As she explained to a gathering of one thousand female journalists in 1954: "I am not afraid of being thought a sentimentalist when I stand here tonight and tell you that I believe natural beauty has a necessary place in the spiritual development of any individual or society. I believe that whenever we destroy beauty, or whenever we substitute something man-made and artificial for a natural feature of the earth, we have retarded some part of man's spiritual growth."[29] The persistence that defined her life may have had its roots in this reverence for such natural beauty.

Born in 1907, Carson was the granddaughter and niece of Presbyterian ministers and spent her childhood exploring the sixty-four-acre farm surrounding her home in Springdale, Pennsylvania. The youngest of three children, she was influenced by her mother Marie's devotion to the nature-study movement, which emphasized direct experiences in the natural world to foster the moral and spiritual development of children.[30] While her father struggled to sustain work and their home lacked indoor plumbing, Rachel read books such as *Birds of the Bible* and wrote stories with descriptions of the nest of a cuckoo and the eggs of a bobwhite.[31]

At the age of eleven, she published a story in a national magazine for young readers, affirming her desire to become a writer.[32]

As a teacher of environmental education, I could imagine Rachel and her brother Robert coming home from school with a copy of Anna Comstock's *Handbook of Nature Study* (1911), a classic text in my field. I pictured Marie Carson, who was trained as an educator, encouraging her children to illustrate the birds of the air or organize rocks for a collection, with the aim of cultivating imagination and a sense of the holy in nature.[33] In this context, the natural world was a place to develop both humility and reverence for the Creator. As a child, Rachel would listen to the sounds of the sea by holding to her ear a conch shell, which rested on the family mantel.

Her mother sold fruits and even her own china to help cover tuition when Rachel decided to study English at Pennsylvania College for Women, which became Chatham College. While her daughter was in college, Marie visited on weekends and typed her papers, a practice she continued later in life, even reading manuscripts aloud to her. As a student, Carson attended Calvary Episcopal Church but didn't affiliate with any denomination or church as an adult.

Known by her college friends as Ray, she fell deeply in love with biology under the influence of her mentor Mary Scott Skinker.[34] After some deliberation, she changed her major and saw the ocean for the first time when she traveled to Woods Hole Biological Laboratory in Massachusetts for summer research with her professor in 1929.

That summer, an entire world along the shore opened up to her as she watched and listened to the waves of the Atlantic Ocean, which she'd only experienced through the chamber of a conch shell. Late at night, she began explorations that would continue for the rest of her life: she'd grab a flashlight and head out into the dark to comb the seashore, studying the intricate relationships in these interstitial places where water meets the land.

Given the Depression and her family's dire financial straits, she left a PhD program for better-paying work with the Bureau of Fisheries, which became the US Fish and Wildlife Service. In 1939, she was the second female hired as a professional in this natural resource agency and would later become editor in chief of the bureau's publications.[35] Yet her entire family had moved to Baltimore to live with her while she completed her master's work in zoology at Johns Hopkins.

This counterbalance of familial obligations with her vocation defined her life until her death. After her father and sister died, Carson cared for her mother and her nieces, later adopting her grandnephew Roger. The sense that all life is connected—at an ecological and household level—was an embodied, rather than abstract, concept for her. If Carson had been a male scientist with few domestic obligations, I wonder if she would have seen the dependence of living things on their ecosystems or the effect of the death of one creature on an entire habitat.

Her writing for a national audience began as a mere introduction to a Bureau of Fisheries brochure, text that was typically as dry as an instructional manual. At the time, nature writing tended to merely catalogue species without mention of relationships or connections. Upon reviewing the essay, her supervisor suggested she send the lyrical piece to the *Atlantic*, where it was published in 1937 as "Undersea." There the editor saw her ability to write about science in a way that captured the imagination: "Every living thing of the ocean, plant, and animal alike, returns to the water at the end of its own life span the materials which had been temporarily assembled to form its body. . . . Thus, individual elements are lost to view, only to reappear again and again in different incarnations in a land of material immortality."[36]

Writing in the evenings after work, Carson published her first book, *Under the Sea-Wind*, weeks after the bombing of Pearl Harbor, and initial sales were disappointing. By this time, she was taking her mother to visit the coast in North Carolina and Georgia, combing the shores and recording her observations in journals. Two surgeries to remove cysts from her breasts—and the dearth of information provided to her by doctors—created a private burden in what became a more public life.

Serialized in the *New Yorker* in 1951, her book *The Sea around Us* stayed on the best-seller list for eighty-six weeks and won the National Book Award. At a benefit luncheon for the National Symphony Orchestra, Carson shared reflections from letters she'd received from readers, including farmers, hairdressers, businesspeople, and more.

"It has come to me very clearly through these wonderful letters that people everywhere are desperately eager for whatever will lift them out of themselves and allow them to believe in the future. I am sure that such release from tension can come through the contemplation of the beauties and mysterious rhythms of the natural world."[37]

Carson had discovered a way to mine her government job for research, especially wartime oceanographic data, that supported her writing. The earnings from *The Sea around Us* provided financial stability for the first time and allowed her to purchase a small plot on the coast of Maine and build a cabin, her sanctuary to explore the interrelationships among living things.

This reverence for the natural world seemed to ground both Carson's writing and her personal life. *The Edge of the Sea* also became a best seller, which she dedicated to Dorothy and Stanley Freeman, the close friends she'd met in Maine. Indeed, Rachel found her emotional partner in the relationship with Dorothy, although the two communicated primarily by letters and telephone, as well as periodic visits. Their letters reveal Rachel's profound need for affirmation and companionship as she cared for her aging mother and family members while navigating her ambition in a male-dominated world with the public demands of publishing and conservation.[38]

The two soulmates sometimes included separate correspondence in one envelope—one copy to read to family and another private one. They referred to the "Strong box" as a euphemism for letters they wanted the receiver to destroy, perhaps for fear of public perception than trespass, as Dorothy was devoted to her husband. Their relationship appeared to reflect a platonic friendship with the awe of romantic love, a combination that might defy categorization.[39] In a 1956 letter to the Freemans, Rachel describes watching a firefly in the phosphorescence of the water with her niece and nephew:

> To get to the full wildness, we turned off our flashlights—and then the real excitement began. Of course, you can guess— the surf was full of diamonds and emeralds, and was throwing them on the wet sand by the dozen. Dorothy dear—it was the night we were there all over, but with everything intensified. A wilder accompaniment of noise and movement, and a great deal more phosphorescence. The individual sparks were so large—we'd see them glowing in the sand, or sometimes, caught in the in-and-out play of water, just riding back and forth. . . . Now here is where my story becomes different. Once, glancing up, I said to Marjie jokingly, "Look— one of them has taken to the air!" A firefly was going by, his lamp blinking.[40]

Soon they realized the firefly had mistaken the lights in the water for other fireflies, so Carson waded into the water to the rescue. As a scientist and writer, she seemed to blend her early religious influences from childhood with scientific discovery, as seen in her letter to a reader who complained that she didn't discuss God in her books: "As far as I am concerned, however, there is absolutely no conflict between a belief in evolution and a belief in God the creator. . . . And it is a method so marvelously conceived that to study it in detail is to increase—and certainly never to diminish—one's reverence and awe both for the Creator and the process."[41]

*   *   *

With the impressive sales of *The Edge of the Sea*, national magazines courted Carson for a feature article, which she declined, citing her need for privacy. In 1956, Carson's agent suggested she write an essay about her coastal explorations with Roger. She agreed and involved her nephew in choosing anecdotes for "Help Your Child to Wonder,"[42] published in *Women's Home Companion*. Rachel soon dreamed of expanding the content into a book and sent an outline of the manuscript to her agent. The essay with photographs would be published after her death as *The Sense of Wonder*. Carson urged her readers to *feel* discoveries in nature, rather than merely create a list of species. In that regard, wonder became a functional emotion leading to a curiosity about the world.[43]

I discovered a photo of the handwritten draft of her essay in the online files of the Beinecke Rare Book and Manuscript library at Yale. Carson's cursive handwriting is as legible as typewritten words, with flourishes to the *t*s and only a few minor edits to her opening sentences: "One stormy autumn night when my nephew Roger was twenty months old I wrapped him in a blanket and carried him down to the beach in the rainy darkness. Out there, just at the edge of where-we-couldn't-see, big waves were thundering in, dimly seen white shapes that boomed and shouted and threw great handfuls of froth at us. Together we laughed for pure joy—he a baby meeting for the first time the wild tumult of Oceanus, I with the salt of half a lifetime of sea love in me. But I think we felt the same spine-tingling response to the vast, roaring ocean and the wild night around us."[44]

Carson experienced a more profound value to wonder than a simple sensory exercise: "There is something infinitely healing in the repeated refrains of nature—the assurance that dawn comes after night, and spring after winter."[45] To be sure, my own students might question if communities impacted by environmental injustice could find healing from nature while faced with polluted drinking water in Flint, Michigan, or mountaintop removal in Appalachia. But Carson's lyrical prose anticipated the quantitative evidence that exposure to green spaces promotes healthier communities.[46]

"If you are a parent who feels he has little nature lore at his disposal, there is still much you can do for your child,"[47] Carson writes. She encourages families to look up at the sky, "wherever you are and whatever your resources," to observe the moving clouds, the dawn and twilight, the stars. Listen to the wind, she says, even if it's around the corners of an apartment building, or feel the rain on your face and consider the many forms the water has taken over time.

In language that speaks to our climate emergency, Carson draws on the power of wonder in her dismay at the damage wrought by humans. "Perhaps he is intoxicated with his own power, as he goes farther and farther into experiments for the destruction of himself and his world. For this unhappy trend there is no single remedy—no panacea. But I believe that the more clearly we can focus our attention on the wonders and realities of the universe about us, the less taste we shall have for destruction."[48]

*   *   *

While Carson would applaud the establishment of the EPA, I can only imagine her dismay at an agency forced to erase any mention of climate change from its website during the Trump administration and dismiss science in the face of COVID-19. Indeed, the federal government—under Republican and Democratic leadership—has known about the dangers of a changing climate for more than fifty years. In *The Sea around Us*, Carson warned about rising sea levels. In her work, she also confronted the massive power held by corporations.

As a mother and a teacher, I worry about my own piecemeal efforts to confront our climate catastrophe in an economy dependent on fossil fuels: What should I tell my students and my children about balancing the need for climate action with a real sense of loss, anxiety, and worry? And how can Rachel Carson's sense of wonder guide us?

During the spring of 2020, the coronavirus created a flipped "silent spring," where the birds staged a full-blown chorus and daffodils bloomed but the humans were quarantined inside their homes. In my campus rental in North Carolina, my two daughters and I pecked at our computers for online school, while the bluebirds flew freely outside our windows. One morning, I finally put down my laptop and stepped outside, looking up at the blue sky and moving clouds, as she'd urged us to do. Though I still worried about the end of the story, I could feel Carson's spiritual and ecological truth: We are all connected—what happens to each of us, happens to us all. Perhaps we too must look beyond the overwhelming scientific evidence of climate change and also see the story of connection in the world around us—sea, sun, water, soil, earth.[49]

In her writing, I feel Carson's humanity, frail and strong, a poet-scientist encouraging us to see ourselves as a part of something larger. To me, her personal letters reveal a woman driven by wonder, but with her own vulnerabilities and worry as well. Her awe at the mystical interconnection of the world fueled her to advocate for its protection rather than be paralyzed by fears of its demise. The same could be said for her relentless work in the face of her own illness and mortality. From my duplex on this college campus, for this moment, I believe I can do the same.

During our virtual commencement in the first spring of COVID-19, the senior speaker, Rayna Berger, stood by the Saw Kill River in New York and spoke to her classmates scattered across the world: "There is a lot of work to be done, but there is no better time than now and no better cohort than us to rewrite the rules and change the narrative."

Rachel Carson would have agreed; she also might have shared a timeless invitation from *The Sense of Wonder*: "One way to open your eyes is to ask yourself, 'What if I had never seen this before? What if I knew I would never see this again?'"[50]

ALLAN M. TIBBELS

(1955–2010)

Allan Tibbels; reprinted by permission from Baltimore Sun Media;
all rights reserved

"Keeping at It"

Allan M. Tibbels and Rebuilding a Community
in West Baltimore

Mark R. Gornik

On the day in 1980 when Baltimore's Inner Harbor opened to great fanfare, the *Washington Post* looked two miles west to a neighborhood called Sandtown-Winchester for contrast. Ella Johnson, who lived in Sandtown and led the Sandtown-Winchester Improvement Association, told the paper, Sandtown "is just an inner-city neighborhood. . . . It's buried. A good block is where there are less than five vacant houses."[1]

A few years later, in 1987, Allan Tibbels and his family moved to Sandtown. Here Allan came to be part of a people who normally live and work, sing and worship in separate areas but in time became tightly bound together in the energies of God's love and the ends of peace for the neighborhood and city.

As a young adult of twenty-three years of age, Allan began a journal and made his first entry on June 13, 1978: "Don't know exactly what lies ahead, but to know that each day spent with you will be an adventure causes me to eagerly anticipate each tomorrow. My main concern, O Lord, is that I would set aside, completely give up, myself and my abilities so totally as to have your work done in your way. . . . Father, one thing I know right now is that I long for you to be first in my life. Make me willing to give up anything and everything to serve you."

As Allan reflected on God's grace and love for him, giving his life completely to the service of God regardless of the cost seemed the only reasonable thing to do. This was his purpose.

After moving to Sandtown in 1987, Allan stayed there for the rest of his life, working tirelessly for justice and peace. Allan sought to close the gap between reality as it was in the city and the gospel. He sought with his life to do what the Lord required, to be responsible, to follow Christ, to love with actions, to live an option for the poor. And Allan did so with a spirit of faith as calling, a sense of humor, tenacity, and passion.

The ways Allan's experience in Sandtown intersected with difficult things—race, class, place, history—can be challenging to understand. The incongruities are obvious; for starters, Allan was white in an African American neighborhood. But if in the concrete action of responsibility, of seeking to follow Christ and love one's neighbors, it is inevitable that he did not get it all right, then, as Dietrich Bonhoeffer found, he was left to turn to the mercy of God.[2]

But something unique, almost indescribable took place in Allan's life, in Sandtown, in a community. A social love lived out, a different type of politics and theology. A different way of seeing the city.

Allan was born and raised in the suburbs of Baltimore. He was the middle child of three boys, and his parents, Mel and Marie, provided a stable environment. Allan and Susan met in high school, and after graduation, at the age of eighteen, they married with plans for a life of wealth and material success. Right to work they went, starting off with a franchised cleaning company, while also becoming more involved in youth ministry.

On their way to achieving their dreams of success, something changed for Allan and Susan; a calling to turn in a different direction captured their imagination. In order to work full-time with Youth for Christ, a national Christian youth ministry focused on unchurched youth, they sold their business and gave away much of what they had. Allan and Susan moved to Columbia, a planned neighborhood closer to Washington, to work full time in youth ministry.

On May 27 of 1981, a few years after Allan's first journal entry and six years before he moved to Sandtown, Allan got up, dressed for basketball, said good-bye to his wife, Susan, and headed off to the church gym for a pickup game. He loved everything about basketball—the NBA; his favorite team, the New York Knicks; the Finals— but Allan especially loved playing. Joining with friends, staff, and students from the youth ministry where he worked, running up and down the court. Leaving nothing behind, giving his all to win.

The game underway, Allan starts in on a layup. But instead of going up in the air and then landing on his feet, the shot dropping down through the net, his legs tangle up beneath him. Allan's body, headfirst, is now in full direct flight toward the wall where the backboard is braced. The wall does not move or bend.

A complete stillness overtakes his body, and Allan crumples down on the gym floor. Sunk down into a world of physical unfeeling. His neck is broken, his spinal cord irreparably severed.

Allan suffered a C6/C7 compression fracture of his vertebrae; now he was a quadriplegic, paralyzed, without feeling from his upper chest down. Spinal cord injuries vary. This level of severe spinal injury meant that, while Allan retained some motion of his arms, but not more than a curling of his fingers, he had also lost control of his legs and bladder. Breathing was now difficult because the muscles needed to expand and contract his lungs did not work properly. Moving about would require the assistance of an electric wheelchair. Allan was twenty-six years old, married with two daughters.

Throughout his life as a quadriplegic, it was Susan who made sure Allan received the continual daily care he needed, interacting with his physicians and clinical care, and managing the problems that could arise on the part of patients with complex health conditions.

Seen in light of his first journal entry in 1978, Allan viewed breaking his neck as a part of "giving up everything." But "offering his life" to God could well mean losing his life, metaphorically, certainly, but also literally, as Allan indicated, the place where his devotion to God would take him as a quadriplegic.

Allan couldn't move the small muscles of his hands, but his curled fingers could fit around a specially devised writing implement that allowed him to type, one letter at time, first on a typewriter, and later a computer. Because he also retained some range of motion in his upper arms, it allowed him to operate a special set of controls to drive a van equipped with a lift.

Becoming a quadriplegic did not deter Allan from focusing on his vocation even more sharply. In September 1982, he wrote a prayer in his journal:

> I have so many times this week wanted to be out of this chair. What a limitation! And Susan put together a photo album of our past couple of years of pictures. Do they ever cause me to desire the normalcy of the olden days, walking and laying around on the floor and swinging the kids around. But it is not to be. God has me here in this place at this time and for His own good reasons. I do believe in its totality in my head, but how hard it is to live this out into the external world. Will I always have to deal with being in the chair with such intensity? Lord please show me it is not a "limitation" because You are sovereign. At any rate, the two thoughts I love regarding this whole situation are that I will be walking with the Father and the saints for all eternity, and the chair keeps me more dependent upon Him in the meantime. And I am determined, by His grace, to carry out all of my desires of work and service regarding the kingdom.

Allan only imagined his life as a calling, a service on behalf of God, who created and called him, like the psalmist (Ps. 139) and the prophet Jeremiah (Jer. 1:5).

After he broke his neck, Allan went back to college; a class assignment was to write his autobiography. All the expected ground is covered, including his marriage to Susan, their daughters, Jennifer and Jessica, his parents, breaking his neck. But to center his essay, and to explain what was ahead, Allan wrote about Dorothy Day. Day cofounded the Catholic Worker movement, on the Lower East Side of New York City, during the Great Depression in communities of hospitality, sharing food and companionship with the poor.

It was not just that Allan now shared Day's pacifism and commitment to the poor that moved him toward her story. Instead, he saw in her life an "idealism" that he wanted to be his, a single-minded focus on something. Allan believed a life marked by a singular passion was "a gift" from God that he had to use, whatever the cost. For Allan, it was not Day's "faith-driven life," but the "drive itself."

In the providence of God, Allan, Susan, and I were friends from before his injury, a friendship that continued over a lifetime. When I was in high school, for a short period of time, Allan and Susan were my youth leaders at church. Allan and I shared a love for music and the arts, but more than that, over the next years, we found a deepening spiritual commitment to the church and city.

Allan was inspired by the prophetic words of Martin Luther King Jr. about racism, violence, and poverty, and by the hospitable ecclesial vision of John Perkins, a civil rights leader from Mississippi who urged Christians to be the body of Christ in the most vulnerable places. John, Vera Mae, and the whole Perkins family helped to begin a church and ministry called Voice of Calvary. Their work included a day-care program, cooperative farming, a legal clinic, and a church. Voice of Calvary began drawing volunteers from around the country to this distant patch of Mississippi. It was, however, the 1960s and Mississippi, and the threat of violence, even death, against African Americans and civil rights workers was always but a moment away.

With these leaders as inspirations, Allan began to reach a new clarity on his purpose and calling, and in 1985 he wrote as much in his journal: "I am ready to relocate in the city and minister to the community in which I live! I sense great calling without the actual needs or my role. The idea of being effective there in the chair is overwhelming almost to the point of despair, but I can't let this deter me if it is calling, which it strongly is." As Allan also reflected that year, "The question is no longer whether God is on the side of the poor and oppressed, but where should I locate to be involved with them?"

The signs of the times were cities: entire neighborhoods across America were being abandoned and left in ruins, histories and communities discarded and thrown away as if unimportant. Camilo José Vergara, going from city to city—New York, Newark, Detroit, Gary, and Baltimore among them—documented what was taking place: taking photographs of urban remains, their afterlives, and continued struggles.[3] Like creation, the suffering of cities and neighborhoods was a groaning, a crying out for the wholeness and justice of God.

As a response to his Christian faith and convictions, Allan, and I, considered moving to Sandtown in West Baltimore, even if Susan wasn't as sure. After learning more, talking, and praying, Allan reached out to and met with Ella Johnson. After he explained why we were praying about moving to Sandtown, Ella offered her blessing.

The crucial step was moving to Sandtown, "relocating," to use John Perkins's language. Allan could only be a neighbor by spatially living there. In one way, "relocating" was a small act, but given Baltimore's dynamics of segregation, it was a political act, an alternative and challenge to the underlying systems of exclusion.

Allan, Susan, and daughters Jenny and Jessica moved into a tiny substandard rental house on North Gilmor Street. I moved a few blocks over. Allan now slept on a cot set up in the front room, next to the table where they took their meals; to get into the house he came in through an alley filled with trash and rats. It was not an obvious move, but all Allan could say was, "[I] wish I had done it earlier."

But moving to Sandtown wasn't to be about Allan, his needs or place. Instead, he stressed, relocating was to be about the neighborhood. Allan and Susan moved to the neighborhood to be neighbors, and as God called, to work for justice. To follow and obey Christ in the way of the Beatitudes. To share in what God was doing in reconciling all things.

At one time, there had been forty thousand residents in the seventy-two blocks of Sandtown. By the 1980s, that number had dropped to no more than fifteen thousand people. There were more than one thousand vacant and abandoned houses, and the neighborhood suffered from unemployment that exceeded levels of the Great Depression. The chronic lack of health care meant people died before their time.

Allan wanted to be a neighbor in Sandtown, to share in the mundane of daily life. To enter into the suffering and pain, but also into the joy and hope of Sandtown. To recognize his own failure, to acknowledge his role in the history built by racism and injustice, his need for repentance. Allan embraced a faith in Christ that was motivating and shaping his life, a faith that does justice.

After Allan's first years in Sandtown, a small Christian community was formed called New Song. One Sunday, neighborhood youth, Ike, Shaconda, Tyra, Cory, Chuckie, the sartorial Mr. Ulysses Carter, Allan and family, and a few others met in the front room of a row house on North Mount Street.

The group began by reading aloud a poem by Langston Hughes about what happens when dreams are deferred; next the community read Isaiah 65, what the prophet proclaimed about God and the city:

> For I am about to create new heavens
> and a new earth;
> the former things shall not be remembered
> or come to mind. . . .
> No more shall there be in it
> an infant that lives but a few days,
> or an old person who does not live out a lifetime;

111

for one who dies at a hundred years will be consid-
    ered a youth,
    and one who falls short of a hundred will be con-
        sidered accursed.
They shall build houses and inhabit them;
    they shall plant vineyards and eat their fruit.
They shall not build and another inhabit;
    they shall not plant and another eat;
for like the days of a tree shall the days of my
        people be,
    and my chosen shall long enjoy the work of
        their hands.
They shall not labor in vain,
    or bear children for calamity;
for they shall be offspring blessed by the LORD—
    and their descendants as well.
Before they call I will answer,
    while they are yet speaking I will hear.
The wolf and the lamb shall feed together,
    the lion shall eat straw like the ox;
    but the serpent—its food shall be dust!
They shall not hurt or destroy
    on all my holy mountain,
says the LORD. (Isa. 65:17, 20–25 NRSV)

Recognizing the daily challenges in the neighborhood but having heard about God's city of hope, peace, and justice, they asked a simple question: How could God's vision of peace come alive on the streets and blocks of Sandtown?

With crayons passed around and newsprint spread out on the floor, the young people drew the answer, what they believed God intended for Sandtown, their experience of the neighborhood. The image unfolded with simplicity and grace.

Vacant houses are no more. Empty storefronts become a bakery, a beauty salon, a grocery store, a car dealership, a record shop. The neighborhood now has a health center, and children walk safely on the streets. Our church is in a reconfigured row house. New names claim the street signs. Everyone *was there, present alongside one another.*

In crayon put to newsprint, the Spirit's vision of a neighborhood of justice and joy, shalom, came alive. The people of a community envisioning their families, home, and neighborhood; the imagination of urbanists with crayons—prophets, really.

If the challenges facing Sandtown were interconnected—food insecurity, no access to jobs, evictions, schools that did not send young people to high school, death before its time—then each community-based institution was integral to addressing the underlying injustices of neighborhood life. They all confronted one issue: what it means to belong together through a new system of love and justice.

Housing was the most recognizable challenge, so New Song started here. In the first weeks and months living in Sandtown, Allan saw that evictions were taking place at an epidemic level. Mere days late on your rent, and the eviction process in Baltimore could get started; the city had among the highest rates of evictions in the nation. The possibility of being "put out," the neighborhood term for being evicted and having every single one of your family's possessions—your children's clothes, your only couch, family photographs, birth certificates, and kitchen chairs—piled up on the curb in front of your home, was part of life for everyone in Sandtown. When this happened, it could shatter a sense of self and place for children and parents across generations. Economically, this meant it would be hard if not impossible for families to ever get ahead.[4]

Allan could not hammer a nail, carry lumber, or walk up the steps to see or work inside a house, but he could hear God's call, organize, recruit people, pray, tell others the story, and start to gather funds. Allan could pray as he rolled around Sandtown in his wheelchair. He could commit his life to his neighbors, together establishing Sandtown Habitat, a project with a larger national group called Habitat for Humanity.

The Habitat model was simple and just right for Sandtown: Habitat for Humanity's founder, Millard Fuller, had a vision to create stable communities through affordable home ownership, which meant no interest was to be charged on the mortgage; each homeowner put in their own work (called "sweat equity"); and the approach to homeownership was community-based, centered on partnership between people. It had a vision of the upside-down kingdom of God at its center.

A vacant house in Sandtown was not just empty; it was most often collapsing, unsafe, and filled with debris. For a few thousand dollars Allan gathered together from a local bank, on behalf of Sandtown Habitat, he was able to purchase the first vacant house, and Allan and Susan's basement turned into a construction warehouse. Frank, Fitt, Gary, Jenny, Jessica, and everyone who could picked up a hammer, carried out debris, used a paintbrush, and eventually attended the dedication. People with other needed construction skills began to join in.

LaVerne Stokes, born and raised in Sandtown, soon joined Sandtown Habitat, becoming co–executive director with Allan. Gary, Orlando, Frank, Ike, and other young people from the neighborhood joined in the work. Rehabbing one house a year became two, and then three, and then twenty. People—eventually five thousand and more a year—came to lend a hand, carrying out debris, constructing new floors, putting up new drywall, building a new roof, installing new appliances and a new heating system.

When a home was completed, a celebration and liturgy were held in the streets. A Bible was presented alongside cheers and prayers; and to close, led by local pastor Elder C. W. Harris, everyone would sing "This little light of mine . . . all around the neighborhood, we're going to let it shine."

The intertwined challenges and exclusions facing Sandtown required a holistic response. Neighborhood economic life advanced as assets and jobs were created. Susan founded and organized a community school, New Song Learning Center and Academy; her creative energies and commitment enabled her work with neighborhood parents to flourish. Jane Johnson, who had grown up in the neighborhood, shared a vision for the children of Sandtown, and shared this work with Susan and teachers and parents. For a while, a primary health-care center was opened, the first such center in the neighborhood.

Rodney, who lived on North Calhoun Street, was in elementary school when he and Allan met. Allan listened to him, hung out with him, shared meals. But the corner was tough, the systems too broken. Rodney was a young man when he died of a gunshot in a basement. Allan never forgot, never recovered. Out of his pain, the pain of his neighbors, he worked harder, creating as many jobs for young men in Sandtown as he could, building church as a place of healing. Death before his time. A city that failed Rodney. A church that failed Rodney. "I failed him too," Allan lamented, and lamented.

Community development and neighborhood life have many joyful and hopeful dimensions, moments of celebration and accomplishment. But it is mostly slow work: taking up arduous tasks, pushing forward the thankless thousands of details that make things work, the mundane. It is work filled with setbacks and painful moments, constants in any project and life together. At the end of the day, everyone is exhausted from the work. And there is always being out of money, or nearly so, for payroll, for the next house, the vital new initiative. Allan carried the weight of this.

Allan believed God wanted to heal, rebuild, and restore Sandtown. Let's keep doing more and more houses, he said, stretching every dollar that could be mustered for drywall and dumpsters.

Allan was fiercely uncompromising in his commitment to the justice-centered effort that was underway and to the flourishing of Sandtown. Imagining Sandtown twenty years in the future, Allan had a strong sense of how a community-based approach—one family, one house, one block at a time—could slowly aggregate to something new.

December 13, 2008

If how a nation treats its most vulnerable citizens shows the character of that nation, the United States is in trouble; Baltimore is in trouble. The revitalization of the "severely distressed" neighborhoods is out of vogue, has been for quite a few years now, but we will continue our house by house and block by block plan through the 30 years we originally committed. In the end the people who were living here will still be living here, most of them now in homes they own or have passed on to their children, with their children attending an academically excellent school and many others having graduated from college, and they will purchase their coffee in the morning from a neighborhood resident-owned corner store and perhaps eat dinner at a neighborhood resident-owned sit-down restaurant. The residents of Sandtown are not throw-away citizens; they love their lives and their neighborhood and desire to see it rebuilt and thriving. New Song exists for this purpose, to be partners in the realization of these dreams. The process will be messy, with many setbacks along the way; the blocks will be noisy with the sound of many children playing in the streets in which they feel secure, and at times their football or basketball will inadvertently break the glass of a car or building. But the end result will be one born of dignity and moral clarity, and the joy will be authentic and the depth of character of the neighborhood real.

Allan was clear in his conviction for Sandtown—the future needed to be one of justice and flourishing, a point of moral clarity. His lament for the suffering of Sandtown grew with each day. The historic effects of racism, continued injustices, the way leaders couldn't see that Sandtown was even there, the police as an occupying force—all this presaged for Allan a crisis bubbling up beneath the surface, coming to the fore in 2015 when in Sandtown a young man named Freddie Gray was arrested and later died of injuries suffered while in police custody. Within days, the city went up in flames.

As one decade became two decades of community development and church life, Allan grew wearier. This coincided with more serious health problems related to being a quadriplegic, and frequent hospitalization. Yet this only found Allan going deeper into Scripture, prayer, and community life. Allan was inspired by the neighborhood, and by the Catholic peace leaders Daniel and Philip Berrigan. Allan used to quote Daniel Berrigan daily, saying, "Keep at it," encouraging others to do the same; this was Allan's way of concluding every email and conversation. Allan wanted to reflect God's abundant love for Sandtown. He would not let go of his vocation, of his calling, of life in Sandtown—of his love for Baltimore.

Everything for Allan comes back to daily life in the neighborhood. Fitt and Gary are there on Stricker Street. Fitt works at the school, Gary for Habitat. Allan is nursing a cup of coffee. There is banter over the Orioles, a fuss that happened the evening before, work still to be done on a house on Gilmor. The streets of Sandtown were Allan's favorite place to be. With Mr. Kelley, Nina, Sonia, Antoine, Patty, Bubby, Jane, Frank, Gary, Ike, and Fitt. Susan, Jenny, and Jessica. And a cat.

Each of our lives is short, but from the moment Allan hit the wall and became a quadriplegic, he knew that his time was limited. He did not define his life under the power of death and the reality of his broken body, but instead through his encounter with Jesus, who overcame death.

When Allan died at age fifty-five, having lived in Sandtown most of his adult life, nearly three hundred homes had been gut-rehabbed, turned into homes for Sandtown families. Fifteen blocks had been changed, rebuilt. But it was his friendship, his sense of humor, his commitment to Christ, his compassion, his suffering with, that he is most remembered for. He connected people from all backgrounds.

Because of his brokenness as a quadriplegic, because he embodied the impact of trauma and unspeakable losses, people with their own wounds trusted Allan, spoke with him, shared with him, and he shared his life and struggles with others. Wounds inside and outside. A lost parent, brother, or sister. In shared brokenness there was ever more room for others, for Christ to heal in community. Allan would listen; friendships of trust would form.

Allan was a person of hope. He believed and lived as if his broken body, and a world of broken bodies, would experience wholeness, healing, and transformation in the resurrected body of Christ. This came through the way of the cross, life in Sandtown.

In all he did, with Susan and in community, Allan sought to honor Christ with his body, trusting that God's work was already under way. Allan believed, in the words of Saint Paul written to Roman Christians, that "just as Christ was raised from the dead by the glory of the Father, so we too might walk in newness of life" (Rom. 6:4 NRSV).

Allan's life recalls the prayer of Saint Ignatius of Loyola:

> Take, Lord, and receive all my liberty,
> my memory, my understanding,
> and my entire will,
> All I have and call my own.
> You have given all to me.
> To you, Lord, I return it.
> Everything is yours; do with it what you will.
> Give me only your love and your grace,
> that is enough for me.

A life moved by grace and committed to the purpose of love; Allan gave all he had to fifteen blocks in the city of Baltimore. Keeping at it until the end.

MARY PAIK LEE

(1900–1995)

Mary Paik Lee, with her son Tony, circa 1940; photo courtesy of Irvin Paik

A Bittersweet Life of Faith

Mary Paik Lee and Anti-Asian Racism

Jane Hong

Mary still remembers how it all began. It was just another day when three Japanese soldiers marched up to the door of her grandmother's home in the Korean countryside.

"Who lives here?" the soldiers shouted, their feet firmly planted on the land as if it already belonged to them.

Five-year-old Mary froze. She had heard the adults talking about what Japanese soldiers were doing to Korea, but it was hard for her to understand what it all meant. The men "attired in strange-looking clothes" gave them a choice.[1] The family could either leave immediately or live with the soldiers in their house— not really a possibility due to its small size. Either way, the family's days of living peacefully in the farmhouse that had been passed down for generations ended in that moment.

The next morning, at dawn's first light, little Mary and a dozen of her family members packed up and left their generational home with only basic bedding, clothes, and food. Of the journey, Mary remembers only being carried on her father's back. After walking "a day and night," they arrived at Incheon, the nearest port city. "Only God could have guided us in the right direction down dark and unclear roads," Mary's mother declared with gratitude.

In Incheon, the family learned of an opportunity. A man could work one year on Hawaii's sugar plantations in exchange for his

121

family's passage fare. Once on the Islands, he would also earn fifty cents a day for working from sunup to sundown. After one year, he could leave the plantation and go where he chose. Fearing the worst as Japanese forces steadily tightened control over Korea, Lee's grandparents made a drastic decision. They resolved to send Mary's father to the United States; with him went Mary's mother, eight-year-old Meung Sun, and five-year-old Mary. The plan was that they would earn money and do what they could to carry on the family name in a place outside Japanese control. Even though she was only a child, Mary sensed a deep sadness as her parents embraced their loved ones for what most expected would be the last time this side of heaven. God would provide for their family, her elders declared, even if an ocean divided them.

*   *   *

One of the earliest Korean immigrants in America and arguably among the first "Korean Americans," Lee is a singular figure for people like me, Asian Americans who rarely see ourselves in US history. As a scholar, I first learned about Mary Paik Lee in an Asian American history course in college. Among the people I know who've even heard of her, a class that assigned her book is usually where they were introduced. The first autobiography written by a Korean American woman in English, Lee's book *Quiet Odyssey* (1990) is a rare source—a text written by an Asian immigrant to America before the massive waves of migration that started in the 1960s.

Born Kuang Sun Paik in what is now Pyongyang, North Korea, Mary immigrated to the United States in 1905 and died at age ninety-five. During her ninety years in America, she lived through the Great Depression, World War II, and the Black civil rights movements. Lee's memoir looks at twentieth-century America through the eyes of a young Korean immigrant girl and registers the monumental social and racial progress of the twentieth century. The text records the slow dismantling of structural and legal barriers that opened new career paths and economic opportunities for her American-born children and grandchildren. Simultaneously, her book provides a historical account of anti-Asian racism, a reality that remained a through line of her long life. As such, Lee's life story reveals what has not changed: the enduring persistence of white—and often, white Christian—racism in both its vulgar and polite forms, and the myriad ways Asian immigrants and their children have sought to make sense of their racialization as outsiders and of the underlying sense of rejection that characterizes the experience of being Asian in America.

Mary Paik Lee's story is diasporic as well as American. It is also rare. Few Koreans were able to immigrate to the United States before Congress dismantled Asian exclusion laws in the 1960s. Unlike most immigrants from Asia at the time—individual men who came to work and send money back home—Lee came as part of a nuclear family that planned to make a permanent home in the United States. Legally, because of long-standing racial restrictions barring persons of Asian descent from US citizenship, Lee didn't take on an American identity until she was nearly sixty years old. But naturalization papers aside, in the day to day, she lived as an American. That said, becoming American did not mean forgetting Korea. Even as she daily battled for inclusion and acceptance in the United States, she prayed for Korea's liberation from the yoke of Japanese colonialism. The fight for Korea's independence defined the first half of her life and forged a lifelong connection to her Korean heritage.

*   *   *

On May 8, 1905, the Lees arrived in Hawaii aboard the SS *Siberia*, one of the last boats to carry Koreans to the Islands. They were among the seven thousand people who left the Korean peninsula between 1903 and 1905 for the sugar plantations of Hawaii, where labor unrest by Chinese and Japanese workers had prompted planters to look for new sources of inexpensive Asian labor. The window was short due to Japanese colonialism, which soon cut Korea off from the rest of the world. The Japanese colonial government not only actively discouraged emigration; Japan's 1910 annexation of the peninsula made Koreans subject to US exclusions on Asian immigration for the first time, limiting the possibility of migration on both sides.

The boat ride leaving Korea was long and unpleasant. A seasick Mary spent much of it in her berth, along with her equally green mother. She was so nauseous she could barely eat. Decades later, she could still recall the "wonderful-tasting" bowl of hot noodles she ate in the ship galley once she regained her appetite. The ship's Chinese cook had made them especially for her. The journey was long, but her father's friends broke the monotony by carrying her onto deck, with stern warnings about how the waves would sweep her away if she were not careful.

Once in Hawaii, the family forged a connection to a small but active Korean community. The conditions were rough, the labor hard. Being around other Koreans helped. The family joined a small immigrant church and continued worshiping on Sundays. That is how they survived the contractual year. Once the year ended, Mary's father was eager to make a better way, and at a friend's urging, he decided to move the family to Riverside, California. There he hoped to find a higher-paying job and more opportunities for young Mary and her brother.

Unfortunately, the West Coast in the early decades of the twentieth century was a hotbed of virulent anti-Asian sentiment and violence, and the Lees felt the animosity from the start. Starting in the 1870s, the California-based Workingman's Party pressured congressional lawmakers in Washington, DC, to stop the "Asiatic tide" from coming to the United States. Within a decade, political parties eager to capture California's electoral votes had adopted an anti-Chinese platform, and in 1882, Congress enacted the first federal exclusion law barring Chinese workers from immigrating to the United States. By the time Mary's family arrived in December 1906, Japanese and Korean immigrants had become the next targets of white exclusionists and nativists seeking to protect America's Anglo-Saxon civilization from a "coolie invasion." Indeed, the Japanese and Korean Exclusion League was formed precisely for that xenophobic purpose. The family had scarcely disembarked at the port in San Francisco when a group of young white men began harassing them. They spit in Mary's face, kicked up her mother's skirt, and taunted her family with names Mary had never heard before. *Jap. Chinaman.* Her first reaction was anger. "Why would we come to a place where we are not wanted?" she asked her father.[2]

His answer stuck with her for the rest of her life. She would later call this her "first lesson in living," one that she never forgot. Koreans had not treated the first white American missionaries to arrive on the peninsula much better, her father reminded her. "We were just as nasty, just as ignorant as the white people, so we're getting just what we deserve." He explained to Mary that

> [American missionaries] came to Korea without knowing any Korean. But they took all the abuse, they bowed their heads and learned the Korean language, spoke it better than we do, then they translated the American Bible into Korean. And being medical doctors, they founded a hospital, took care of our sick. Look what wonderful people they are. They were respected . . . they could go anywhere in Korea without having to spend a cent. Everybody feeds them, welcomes them, and gives them anything they want. *We are here. No matter what the white people do to us, just determine you're going to learn and show them you are just as good as they are, and you'll be respected.*[3]

To the contemporary ear, Mary's father's appeal to respectability politics and to an early model minority logic can sound cringe-worthy. If the incarceration of Japanese Americans during World War II or anti-immigrant movements across US history have proven anything, it is that perpetrators of racist violence don't care where you went to college or how much money you make. As one activist posted on social media, "Your degree will not save you."[4] Arguably one of the most important contributions the immigrant rights movements early in the twenty-first century made was to reject the idea that immigrants should have to prove their worthiness for rights or protections. According to this revised logic, migrants deserve rights and protections not because they are valedictorians or model citizens but because they are human. For Americans accustomed to white supremacy, that is not a small mind-set change; it's a massive paradigm shift.

In 1907 California, however, this thinking was still far off, and at that time nonwhite people rarely even shared space with whites. Mary's California may not have had Jim Crow as the South did, but de facto segregation remained the law of the land. As a child, she almost never interacted with white people. Her first day of school in Claremont, California, was the first time she saw a white person "close up." It was quite a shock. The teacher, a "German woman with bright yellow hair and big blue eyes," just "scared the life out of me," Mary recalled. Adding to the trauma, kids in the playground "bunched up . . . pointed fingers" and started chanting a "ching ching chime" song where a white man chops a Chinaman's "tail" off. At the time, Mary was confused, but she soon learned what the lyrics meant. But despite the hostile reception, she still liked school because it was one of the only public places where she was allowed to use the same bathroom as white people. Whenever they traveled on a train or a bus, her father wouldn't let them eat or drink for up to half a day beforehand, to avoid having to use segregated bathrooms. Black friends had similar experiences. "If you got into a predicament somewhere, it's too bad," one told her.[5]

The opportunities that Mary's father's friend had promised in Riverside failed to materialize. In 1906, the only jobs "open to orientals were picking oranges, lemons, walnuts, farm work. We couldn't even do housework because white people were afraid of us." To them, Koreans were "dirty, smelly chinks . . . they didn't know about Korea, so we were all chinks." Her father worked in the fields, and her mother cooked meals for the local Korean bachelors in order to make ends meet. Her mother woke up at 3 a.m. to start cooking, and she woke up with her to pack the workers' lunches. The labor became too much for her mother after she became pregnant, so after two years, the family moved to Claremont, where they did hand laundry. Since "white people weren't speaking to us," Mary and her brothers had to ask their schoolteachers for laundry to do. And that's how they got by. There simply weren't other options. As Asians, they "weren't allowed in American institutions" or in white people's homes—"they didn't trust us." Hand laundry worked because they did it at home. It would be "another 15 years" before Asians could get jobs doing housework.[6]

Lee credited the family's survival to her father, a resourceful and educated man who had never even done manual labor before arriving in the United States. Upon arriving in Riverside, the only shelter they could find were "small chicken shacks" next to chicken coops built in the 1850s to house Chinese working on the Southern Pacific Railroad. The shacks were so old the "lumber had shrunk," and the wood so rough "you could get splinters from touching it." The design was barebones: "no windows, no shelves, no nothing—just one big room," with no furniture. Mary's "ingenious" father had the kids "go around to the junkyard and pick up scraps of tin boards." From these he built a lean-to for the kitchen and fashioned a crude stove and oven. He constructed beds for the children with pieces of lumber, straw, and paper they had scrounged at the local dump. Mary remembered how her dad used to joke that he had originated the "bunk bed" idea.

These were very hard years for Mary's family. They had no money to buy necessities, and neither of her parents could speak English. But Lee's father could write Chinese characters that he had learned in his Korean schooling. Using this skill, he obtained credit from a local Chinese storekeeper and purchased pots and pans for cooking.[7] Since food was scarce, he commissioned Mary and her brother to pick plants to eat—usually dandelions or other "wild vegetables"— and beg for entrails at the local slaughter-house. At the time, white Americans didn't think kidneys, tripe, and heart were fit for human consumption, so butchers regularly discarded the inner organs of cows and the other animals they killed. When Mary and her brother showed up, the workers would make comments about "dirty chinks eating things not fit for hu-mans." They didn't even hand the leftovers to them because they "didn't regard us as human beings," Mary recalled. Still, she was grateful they weren't violent. Years before, people would "shoot [Chinese] like jackrabbits." Without these butcher scraps, the fam-ily "would've starved to death," Mary concluded, so any embar-rassment or harassment was worth it.[8]

Even with the creative sourcing, there were still lean times. After several years of eking out a living in Southern California, Mary's father moved the family north to Willows in search of better opportunities. As "orientals" in Southern California, they had been tolerated even if not welcomed. But farther north, they faced open hostility and blatant racial discrimination. Local white residents refused to patronize the family's hand-laundry service because they were "oriental." Less business meant less money— and less food. In Willows, a meal consisted of a biscuit and a tin cup of water, eaten three times a day. This lasted one year, but to Mary, it "felt like 10 years."[9]

The constant hunger tested Lee's faith in God. Her stomach became distended from constant hunger and made such "queer noises" while she was at school that other students would tease her. The worst was listening to her younger siblings cry for food. It was a wonder no one got sick, she marveled. Even as babies, they never had fresh milk, and the canned milk they drank was like milk-colored water, thin with barely any taste. Why did her father faithfully thank God before each meal, whose meager portions could barely fill a person's stomach?

One night, Mary was so famished she could not fall asleep. She got out of bed and went to fill her stomach with water, which helped ease the hunger pangs. As she passed the kitchen, Mary saw her parents sitting at the table, holding hands and weeping. "I realized then how much agony they were suffering, and that my own feelings were as nothing compared with theirs. I had been so absorbed in myself that the thought of my parents' suffering had never entered my mind. Seeing them that way made me realize how ignorant I was . . . and awakened me to the realities of life."[10] In her own telling, Mary "grew up" that day. By entering into the suffering of other people, she found greater strength to endure her own.[11]

*   *   *

Mary's father may have accepted the harassment the family experienced when they first arrived in San Francisco Harbor, but that did not stop Mary from fighting back as she got older. Even as a teenage girl, Mary had a strong sense of right and wrong, and an equally strong desire to crush intolerance. When her high school history teacher called Korea a "savage country" that Japan had to "civilize," she pushed back. "How the hell do you know that? Don't you know that China is one of the oldest civilizations and Korea is second oldest . . . in fact, Korea civilized Japan." Similarly, when a pastor at the first white American church Mary ever visited blocked her from entering the sanctuary, she challenged him.

"I don't want any dirty Japs in my church," he stated flatly while holding his arm outright to cover the door.

"Does it make any difference if I tell you we're not Japanese?"

"What the hell's the difference? You all look alike."

"Well for your information we're Presbyterians and Presbyterians were the first missionaries in Korea . . . and they're respected in Korea so I thought at least a Presbyterian minister would treat us kindly."

"Go to hell," the minister retorted before stalking away.[12]

This formative experience led Mary to wonder: What does it mean to share the same religious faith as your oppressors? The faith in God that had inspired and sustained Mary's family in Korea looked different on this side of the world. Like many early Korean immigrants, Lee's family had worked closely with white American missionaries before immigrating to the United States. Dr. Samuel Moffett, a Presbyterian missionary to Korea, led her grandfather to the Christian faith and baptized Mary and her brother. White American Christians in Korea had been spiritual mentors, friends, and allies. But white Christians in the United States were often cast from a different mold, Mary found, even as they ostensibly shared the same Bible and preached the same Jesus. The few times she dared step into a white church in the United States, some white folks glared at her to make it clear she was not welcome. Others, like the pastor in Willows, actively commanded her to leave.

This duality described life as an "oriental" Christian in early twentieth-century America. In the day to day, Mary and her family took solace in God and the Bible; their faith nourished and sustained them. In the absence of a Korean church or a white church that would welcome them, every Sunday her father gathered several families in their house and preached the gospel. As one scholar described it, Christianity became an "important source of homemaking for Koreans in exile," providing a sense of comfort, hope, and direction in a land where few felt welcomed or settled.[13] Living an ocean away from their family and hometown community, Mary and her family clung to Jesus. And yet, paradoxically, some of Mary's deepest wounds and worst experiences of rejection and racism came from people who professed the same faith. How does a Christian person of color reconcile such a painful reality?

As before, Mary's father offered wisdom and insight. In his words, "There are good people and bad people," and they should be grateful when "lucky" enough to meet good people. This was the view Mary herself adopted. While today many rightly describe this kind of racism as largely structural or systemic, for Mary, who lived before that kind of thinking became the norm, racism and prejudice in general were an individual failing. That meant that, for as many white pastors and churchgoing folks rejected her, there were also "good" people who used their influence to advocate for her and others like her. "Every time when I'm at a crisis I meet a good American stranger who helps me," she reflected with gratitude.

The incident at the church in Willows, where the pastor barred entrance to Mary, is a good case in point. There the good white stranger who served as Mary's advocate was her friend Margaret's dad, Superior Judge Finch. After the pastor chased Mary and her brothers away from the church doors, Judge Finch asked to meet with her and told her he would speak with the church's leaders on her behalf. The next Sunday the minister "ran down the steps, shook [her] hand," and ushered her in. "You are welcome in this church," he told her, with the countenance of a totally changed man. Seeing the transformation, Mary concluded: "It sure pays to have friends in high places!"[14]

Other white Christian leaders were more forthcoming on their own. In Hollister, California, where Mary worked as live-in domestic help for a white family in order to attend high school, a white Presbyterian pastor used his position of leadership to welcome her to the church, despite the hostility of many lay members. He was especially supportive after finding out that her family was Christian and that she had been baptized by Dr. Moffett, whose missionary work was widely known and celebrated throughout the denomination. The minister persuaded Mary to join his church, and even convinced her to teach a Sunday school class of teenagers.

On the first day of the class, the twenty students gawked at her as if she were "something from Mars." For most of the teens, it was their first time seeing an Asian up close. One especially brazen student asked if she were really a human being. Her response was gracious but direct.

> I have two eyes, a nose, a mouth, two ears, two arms, two legs—just like all of you. The only difference is the color of my skin and hair. I have black hair and dark skin. Do you know that there are more colored people in this world than there are white people? Some are black, brown, yellow, or red. They are all human beings. They speak their own languages, of course, but they love, fight, and hate—just like you. When you grow older and are able to travel to other countries, you will see that America is not the only country in the world.[15]

In this way, Mary tried to use her own cultural and racial differences to open the eyes of white Americans to the diversity of the wider world to which they all belonged. Her efforts were not always successful, but that never stopped her from trying.

*   *   *

As one of the first families to form an emerging "Korean colony" in California, the Lees joined a diasporic community of Korean nationalists devoted to doing whatever they could to liberate their homeland from Japan. As one scholar described their commitment: "Plantation and other laborers barely able to make ends meet sacrificed their time and monies to support efforts within their communities and overseas."[16] Within a few years of annexing the peninsula, Japanese officials banned the Korean language, rewrote Korean history texts, and renamed Korean historic sites to reflect a new Japanese colonial identity. Within the small Korean American community, elders strove to retain a distinct Korean identity, as if to flout from afar Tokyo's systematic efforts to erase Korean identity and absorb the peninsula into its empire.

For someone who spent ninety of her ninety-five years in the United States, it speaks volumes that Mary begins and ends her autobiography by talking about her homeland, Korea. Like thousands of ethnic Koreans scattered across a global diaspora, she understood her Korean identity as inextricably tied up with fighting for her homeland's independence from Japanese oppression. In 1919, Mary and her family were among those who cheered at news of the March First Movement, when millions of Koreans gathered in defiance of Japanese colonial authorities and risked their lives to support the cause of Korean independence. The centrality of Korea's independence movement is clear from the fact that she closes the book with a remembrance of the "thirty-three brave Korean patriots" who signed the 1919 Korean Declaration of Independence "knowing full well they would be killed by Japanese soldiers." That she wrote these words more than seventy years later is testament to how formative the Korean independence struggle was in shaping pride in her Korean identity from a young age.[17]

Other Koreans echoed the meaning that their homeland's independence struggle gave their lives in the United States, which many saw more in terms of exile than choice. In 1919, two hundred Korean community leaders gathered in Philadelphia for what they called the First Korean Congress. The goal of the meeting was to mobilize and inspire fellow Koreans in the United States and win support from influential white Americans for the Korean independence cause. After marching in the streets of downtown Philadelphia, the delegation of Korean immigrant patriots stood in Independence Hall for a public reading of the Korean Declaration of Independence. There they affirmed Korea as an independent state and Koreans as a self-governing people.

Like most of the working-class Koreans who made up the community in America, Mary was not able to be present at the First Korean Congress. But she later hosted at her home Syngman

Rhee, one of the delegation's keynote speakers, during one of his trips to Los Angeles. Rhee had been elected the first president of the Korean provisional government in exile founded in 1919. He would later become the first president of South Korea after the peninsula's post–World War II division and independence. Rhee was a controversial figure, to be sure, but Mary found deep satisfaction and pride in supporting his education and years of lobbying in Washington, DC, on Korea's behalf.

*   *   *

On December 7, 1941, Japanese planes bombed Hawaii's Pearl Harbor, and Mary felt the renewed brunt of anti-Asian racism once again. The next day, President Franklin Roosevelt declared the United States at war with the Empire of Japan, and the country formally entered World War II. The surprise attack set off alarm bells in Washington, DC, but anti-Japanese feelings flared nationwide from cities to small farming towns and communities like the one in California where Mary, now married and a mother to three sons, lived. Within months, the US government detained and incarcerated more than 120,000 Japanese Americans, roughly two-thirds of whom were native-born US citizens. For the next four years, the government deprived them of rights and freedoms in the name of national security. Mary and her family watched as members of their community got rounded up and taken away.

While some older Koreans remained wary of Japanese Americans as extensions of their colonizers in Asia, Mary and her husband, H. M., were part of a younger generation who had grown up with *nisei*, or second-generation Japanese Americans, and who saw them as neighbors and friends to support. At the request of a one *nisei* friend, Mary and her family moved to their farm after they were incarcerated, and worked the land until the war ended. Mary remembers white people who came in trucks to "take away all kinds of belongings" but left when they saw Mary and her husband watching.[18]

As ethnic Koreans, Mary and her family were not incarcerated, but they faced constant danger from white Americans who mistook them for Japanese. Given how centrally Koreans' fight for independence from Japan had shaped her own life and her family's lives, their targeting as Japanese can only be described as ironic.

On the evening of the December 7 attack, Mary stopped by her usual grocery store in town. Having gone into the fields early that day, she had not yet heard the news and was surprised to see a room full of angry white faces staring at her with hate-filled eyes. The store belonged to the Nixon family, and future president Richard Nixon's mother was tending the counter when another customer noticed Mary and declared loudly, "There's one of them damned Japs now. What's she doing here?" Mrs. Hannah Nixon swiftly came to her defense. In Mary's words, Mrs. Nixon proved to be the "angel" her son often described her to be. A devout Quaker, she was widely known for her piety and religious commitment to justice and peace. Mrs. Nixon declared to the crowd: "Shame on you, all of you. You've known Mrs. Lee for years. You know she's not Japanese, and even if she were, she is not to blame for what happened at Pearl Harbor! This is the time to remember your religion and practice it."[19]

Eager to avoid trouble, Mary exited the store without buying anything. Anticipating a quick transaction, she had left her one-year-old son in the car. She hurried back to find him surrounded by teenagers with raised fists threatening violence. Her motherly instincts kicked into gear. "Does it take three of you to beat up a one-year-old baby?" she shouted.[20] They scattered, but Mary never forgot the terror she felt. In the months that followed, white customers at the family's roadside stand cursed at and even slapped her young boys.

Still, Mary's family largely escaped serious harm. Others were not so lucky. Chinese and Korean Americans reported verbal abuse and even physical violence at the hands of white Americans who conflated them with the Japanese enemy. As she recalled, "Even after all the Japanese were taken away to concentration camps, other Orientals were subjected to all kinds of violence. They were afraid to go out at night; many were beaten even during the day. Their cars were wrecked. The tires were slashed, the radios and batteries removed. Some friends driving on highways were stopped and their cars were overturned. It was a bad time for all of us."[21] Many Korean Americans she knew didn't go out at night at all for fear of being stopped and beaten up. People had their tires slashed and car radios and batteries stolen. In one especially vicious episode, local vigilantes stopped some of Mary's friends on the highway and flipped their car as retribution for the brutality of Japanese soldiers in the Pacific.

The United States won the war, but anti-Asian sentiment did not disappear with the Japanese defeat in August 1945. Five years later, Mary tried to rent a house for her family in the same community but was rejected over and over. Each time she visited a new place, she said, "every person took one look at me and shut the door without a word." More than a decade after the war, she recalled signs along the highway declaring "Japs are not wanted here."[22]

Years of experience with anti-Asian racism nurtured in Mary a strong sense of solidarity with other oppressed groups. "Due to our mutual problems, all minorities felt a sympathetic bond with one another," she observed, and often they went out of their way to help one another. Stories of discrimination against other groups stayed with Mary even decades later, and evoked her compassion. Writing in the 1980s, she called out the injustice of the 1982 murder of Vincent Chin, a Chinese American auto worker beaten to death by two white men who thought he was Japanese. She also recalled how anti-Semitism had prevented a Jewish friend's son from attending his dream college. In particular, she expressed a special kinship with her Black friends. Like Asians, they "spoke English, but that did not help them in their struggle for a better life," she once said. Well into her seventies and eighties, Mary attended a Black church because it was where she felt "most comfortable."[23] The racism and rejection she experienced as a young person stayed with her for the rest of her life, and she leveraged its sting to become an ally and advocate for all those with similar experiences.

*　　*　　*

By the 1960s, civil rights reforms and immigration liberalization had opened greater professional opportunities for Mary's children and newer immigrants coming from Korea and other parts of Asia. In describing her grandchildren's prospects, Mary noted that this "third generation of Orientals" was "fortunate to be born into a different world, where everything is possible if they work hard enough." Meeting younger Koreans led her to reflect on her own immigration experience. As she told one anxious family just off the plane, "You have arrived in Heaven compared with the place we came to in 1906."[24]

Read through the lens of today's racial politics, it can be tempting to read Lee's autobiography as an early model minority narrative, that is, an immigrant tale of hard work and perseverance that ultimately pays off in middle-class success. But the way Mary writes about her own three sons suggests that she sees her own life as more complicated than a prototypical or prescriptive tale of immigrant upward mobility. Her son Henry earned a doctorate and went on to become one of the first Asian Americans to work for the Federal Reserve Bank, representing the United States in countries across Latin America and Asia, and later worked in the US State and Treasury Departments. In Lee's words, Henry's career was a "miracle from Heaven," proof of an "attitude change we had been hoping for since 1906, a change that took nearly one hundred years to bring about."[25] But a tragic plane crash cut his life short, leaving behind his wife and three children. To Mary, Henry's death was yet another reminder that America might have changed and her children might have greater opportunities available to them, but professional success was no ward against suffering.

The way Mary describes her youngest son, Tony, speaks perhaps most clearly to how she valued the hardships as much as the successes. As gratified as she was by the professional and educational accomplishments of her two older sons, she expressed singular pride in Tony's comparatively modest achievements, and in the endurance and the strong character his personal trials had produced in him. Born without muscles in his eyelids, Tony had to undergo multiple painful surgeries and physical therapy from a young age; a bout with polio led to another two years of surgeries and interventions focused on his spine. Lee described her son's ordeal through "agonizing" and "intense pain" that reduced him to "skin and bones." After high school, Tony worked as a janitor at a Macy's store. Mary ascribed deep value to her son's suffering and perseverance. He "never had the opportunities other people have had," Lee wrote, but his "strong, patient spirit; his ability to endure misfortune without blaming anyone; and the way he tries to be optimistic about life" were praiseworthy.[26]

*   *   *

Lee's life exemplifies how, when you are Asian in the United States, racialized assumptions about your Asian roots shape your daily life in a hundred different ways. It is telling that Mary originally titled her autobiography *Life Is Bittersweet*, an appellation that reflects her theological belief that suffering was the main through line of her life. To her, it was never a suffering in vain but one that she believed God inscribed with meaning and promised to redeem. As controversial and contested as a theology of redemptive suffering understandably is today among faith communities of color, there is no denying that for Mary Paik Lee, that theology functioned as a means of survival.[27] Time and again, Mary's belief in redemptive suffering helped her endure and make sense of difficult encounters with racism while growing up as an "oriental" in early twentieth-century America.

It is nothing short of a travesty that as I write this chapter, we again find ourselves in a place where Asian Americans face widespread harassment and violence. We continue to be treated as easy scapegoats for circumstances beyond our control. In Mary's youth, to be Asian meant to be dirty, unwelcome, a threat to the white Christian nation. In the era of COVID-19 and its aftermath, to be Asian means to be a vector of contagion, the carrier of a "Chinese virus." It means the murder of six Asian American women by a white Christian man on March 19, 2021. These are challenging times, when US power and supremacy are being tested in myriad ways. And now, as in Mary Paik Lee's time, Asian Americans too often pay the price.

Flannery O'Connor

(1925–1964)

Flannery O'Connor, 1950s; photo courtesy of the Flannery O'Connor Collection, Ina Dillard Russell Library, Georgia College and State University

Race, Grace, and God's Typewriter

Loving the Canceled Flannery O'Connor

Jacqueline A. Bussie

On Tuesday, February 25, 1964, the thirty-nine-year-old renowned southern Catholic author Flannery O'Connor was admitted to the hospital for surgery to remove a tumor. The doctors in the Georgia hospital expressed concern that the procedure could reactivate her lupus, a severe autoimmune disorder that she had had since age twenty-five and that had killed her father. Unfortunately, the doctor's fears came true. Postsurgery, Flannery suffered from a kidney infection. The doctors administered so many antibiotics—five different rounds—that Flannery's eyes swelled shut; subsequent cortisone shots reopened her eyes but gave her a swollen "moon-like face."[1]

Sitting upright in the white-sheeted hospital bed, Flannery, moon-faced, nauseated from the antibiotics, and in severe pain, gripped her ink pen and notebook. Even on the brink of death, she wrote. Every. Single. Day. She hid the papers under her pillow, for fear that her caregivers might take them away. The patient was like a woman obsessed. The nurses were in awe at the writer's peculiar persistence, and when they passed in the hallways to change shifts or bedpans, they whispered their incredulity in hushed but hearable tones. Even Flannery's own mother, Regina, her primary caregiver with whom she lived on the family farm, tried to no avail to get her stubborn daughter to put down the pen.

In Flannery's opinion, what no one understood, what no one ever understood, was that the story she was revising, "Revelation," wouldn't let her be. It begged to be written; it came to her faster than any other story she'd ever written; faster, she hoped, even than death. "God, please don't let me die without getting this sent to my publisher," she silently prayed, as she dragged her pen across the page.

At last the author was discharged from the hospital. In order to accommodate Flannery's inability to walk any considerable distance, her mother moved her writing desk with its new electric Smith Corona typewriter just two feet to the left of her bed.

Flannery felt weak and was able to write only a couple of hours per day, but, thank God, she managed to finish revising "Revelation." In the tale, a racist, classist, self-righteous, and obscenely smug white woman named Ruby Turpin thanks Jesus every day that she is not "white-trash" or a "n***er." But Ruby gets her comeuppance when a young girl named Mary Grace calls her an old warthog from hell and smacks her upside the head with a Human Development textbook. This violent act of grace complicates, then reverses, Ruby's vision of the world. Later that day while washing down the hogs on her farm, Ruby growls at God, "What do you send me a message like that for? . . . How am I a hog and me both? How am I saved and from hell too?"[2] God answers by granting Ruby a life-altering divine vision in which the (allegedly) last are first, and the (supposedly) first are last: "A vast horde of souls were rumbling toward heaven. There were companies of white trash . . . and bands of black n***ers in white robes, and battalions of freaks and lunatics. . . . And bringing up the end of the procession was . . . herself and Claud. . . . Yet she could see by their shocked and altered faces that even their virtues were being burned away."[3] After she typed these final lines, Flannery sent the story off to her editor.

Lauded by critics to this day as one of O'Connor's finest anti-racist parables, "Revelation" was the author's last fictional gift to her readers. A few short months later, on August 3, 1964, she died of lupus.

*   *   *

Have you ever fallen in love with someone, gotten to know them better, fallen out of love with them, and then, to your surprise, fallen back in love with them but for completely different reasons? Well, that sums up my rickety relationship with Flannery O'Connor, and the tumultuous path my heart traveled while writing this chapter.

Like Flannery O'Connor, I grew up in small-town Georgia. I first encountered O'Connor's work in a college English class, and promptly fell in love. "Revelation" was my favorite of her stories. It liberated me from the all-too-familiar Bible Belt racism that I had imbibed, by revealing it as grotesque, absurd, and opposed to the Divine's dream. Marvelously, O'Connor taught me that "love is efficacious in the looooong run," and that God's grace, contrary to pious platitudes, greets us more like a gut punch than a warm fuzzy.[4] Her stories challenged me, a young white Christian of privilege, to broaden love's bandwidth and to see the sin within my smugness. I read every word, and was changed. Inspired, I became not only an author but also a public theologian-activist with a PhD in religion and literature. My love affair with O'Connor continued for decades, disrupted only during the writing of this essay.

In July 2019, to begin my research for this chapter, I made my first pilgrimage to Andalusia.[5] I strolled among the peacocks, listened to the cicadas' screech, and stood reverently in O'Connor's bedroom before her shiny Smith Corona typewriter and its now-silent silver keys. I returned from the trip eager to plumb Flannery O'Connor's progressive imagination and socially conscious life for some much-needed prophetic wisdom.

Never before having published anything on O'Connor, I had a lot of homework to do. I first read Brad Gooch's newly released definitive biography, and then set about reading every published letter that Flannery ever wrote, most of which I'd never read. O'Connor, as stated in her will, intended for her letters to be published after her death. However, they have been released to the public only in dribs and drabs, with the first (heavily edited) compilation published in 1979 by O'Connor's best friend Sally Fitzgerald (*The Habit of Being*), a previously uncollected set published in 2019 (*Good Things out of Nazareth*), and some new fragments released during the writing of this essay (2020).

To my shock, as I began to read all six hundred pages of *The Habit of Being*, almost immediately disenchantment and disappointment slapped me across the face. Every other page stung with what felt like an adulterous betrayal. The real-life Flannery of the letters bore little resemblance to the Flannery of the fiction. And to my despair, I strongly disliked the former. I was disappointed by the way, as a wealthy woman of privilege, she spiritualized poverty, writing to a friend, "Everybody, as far as I am concerned, is the Poor."[6] I was appalled that she participated in the Red Scare by making an unsubstantiated and unfounded report that her colleague Elizabeth Ames, the director of Yaddo—the artist community of which O'Connor was a member—"colluded" with a communist.[7]

I was annoyed that Flannery obsequiously requested permission from male priests to read books on the *Index Librorum Prohibitorum*, Catholicism's list of banned books (written largely by Protestants).[8] I couldn't comprehend why such a forward-thinking author declined an invitation in 1957 to visit nearby Koinonia Farm, the interracial, ecumenical community farm founded by Florence and Clarence Jordan.[9] I winced as I stumbled upon her wounding anti-LGBTQ comments, "as for lesbianism I regard that as any other form of uncleanness"; and "Mr. Truman Capote makes me plumb sick, as does Mr. Tennessee Williams."[10] I was bewildered when I unearthed O'Connor's critiques of Dorothy Day and the Catholic Worker movement, "What I can't understand about them is the pacifism," and disillusioned when I learned that she refused to ever speak again to the man she once loved—Erik Langkjaer—after he wrote a "naïve" pro-nuclear-disarmament piece for the Catholic Worker journal.[11]

Worst of all, I couldn't stave off the sickening, sinking suspicion that Flannery O'Connor was . . . well, racist. As the editor of the 2019 volume of O'Connor's previously unpublished letters observed, "O'Connor witnessed campaigns for racial integration but would not meet with activists such as John Howard Griffin, James Baldwin, or Martin Luther King."[12] I was dismayed to discover that when her friend Maryat Lee offered to introduce her to fellow author James Baldwin, O'Connor refused to meet him, in spite of the fact that at Andalusia she entertained "a constant stream of visitors" that included many strangers.[13]

I was baffled that Flannery, a mere four years older than Martin Luther King Jr. and *a native of the very same state*, rarely commented about his work or the civil rights movement, though she frequently made jokes about the KKK and the kinds of crosses they burned on lawns: "It ain't much but I'm able to take nourishment and participate in a few Klan rallies."[14] I was horrified to find that she once remarked to award-winning novelist James B. Hall's wife, "Mama and me got a n***er that drives us around."[15] I was repulsed by the way she repeatedly used the N-word in her private correspondence and once in all seriousness took a *Catholic Bulletin* journalist to task for "think[ing] that nothing is so important as stories about Racial Justice."[16] I was heartbroken by this anti-integration sentence she wrote to friend Janet McKane in September 1963: "What do you think of that business of hauling children out of their neighborhood so that they can attend a 'racially balanced' school? I should think it would be hard on all concerned, children and teachers, and do nothing to help the race situation."[17]

But then my conscience nagged me with the inevitable question: Isn't it unfair to judge a mid-twentieth-century author by 2020 standards? Am I, and are we, guilty of moral anachronism if we expect more of O'Connor? Was she merely, as her contemporary ardent defenders argue, a product of her time? Quite possibly, yes. But aren't the people whom we admire most those who reject the status quo and who are *more* than a product of their time? Aren't moral exemplars precisely the ones who reverse the cliché—those who don't merely *reflect* their cultural moment, but instead *refashion* it into a product of their liberating vision? True followers of the gospel don't merely *portray* their era, but instead in a very real sense *produce* it.

Case in point: Flannery O'Connor's contemporaries, who include Maya Angelou, Gabriel García Márquez, Dorothy Day, and Martin Luther King Jr. These author-activists did more than simply *display* the theological wisdom of their day; instead, they *defined* it. Their Christian faith fueled not only their progressive writing but also their lived lives as pioneer activists. If we make excuses for O'Connor's woeful lack of "wokeness" and social activism, then don't we in the same breath discredit the actual race consciousness and life-risking activism of so many of her forward-thinking contemporaries?

Moreover, if we *fail* to critique Flannery's letters and life for lacking the very same prophetic vision we celebrate in her fiction, don't we become hypocrites, even by her standards? After all, in 1961 Flannery herself penned, "When the herd is wrong, the one who leaves it is not doing evil but the right thing."[18] She also once famously claimed, "You have to push as hard as the age that pushes against you."[19] These bold assertions should compel us to ask: Fiction aside, how hard did the southern author really push against the racism of her age?

At the very same time I asked myself these tough questions, I came across important evidence that debunked the charge of moral anachronism. Flannery's very same letters indicate that many race-conscious white folks in the 1950's, unlike herself, did indeed deem the N-word degrading, offensive, and objectionable. For example, the poet John Crowe Ransom, founder and editor of the *Kenyon Review*, desired to publish *The Artificial N***er* but worried about its racist title. "I hate to insult the black folks' sensibilities," he wrote Flannery. She spat back, "The story as a whole is much more damaging to white folks' sensibilities than to black," and unequivocally refused to change the title for publication.[20] Similarly, when Ransom chose to read that same story aloud to the class at the Iowa Writers' Workshop, he refused to say the N-word and instead substituted the word "Negro." Complained O'Connor, "It did spoil the story."[21]

Many of Flannery's female white classmates at the Georgia State College for Women engaged in powerful antiracist social activism: for example, traveling as a group to Atlanta University where they stayed in the dorm and ate in the cafeteria with Black women students. However, O'Connor's former college classmate Helen Matthews Lewis recalled that Flannery refused to participate: "We kept trying to get her [Flannery] to come to these things . . . but she was apolitical or non-political."[22] A less charitable but equally plausible explanation: such antiracist activities didn't align with Flannery's own politics and privately held point of view.

These historical facts led me to conclude that, no, I was not being unfair to Flannery or anachronistic when, as a follower of Jesus, I longed for more congruence between her privileged conservative life and her radically progressive literature. Nor was I alone. Many of those closest to the author also struggled with the incongruity. Robert Giroux, her editor, once remarked, "Flannery was a paradoxical person and a paradoxical writer. It's what fascinates us. It's a natural human reaction when a person is so contradictory."[23] Similarly, Maryat Lee confessed of her dear friend, "The writing is one thing and the thinking and speeches are another . . . Jekyll and Hyde if you will. Perhaps."[24]

Sally Fitzgerald, the editor and publisher of *The Habit of Being*, also arguably detected a disconnect between the Flannery of the letters and the Flannery of the literature but chose to hide that dissonance from the public. As stated above, from its publication in 1979 until a few short years ago, *The Habit of Being* was the only published text of O'Connor's letters. But the letters compiled in *The Habit of Being* are heavily—and at times frustratingly—redacted. Reading the book from cover to cover for this chapter, I noticed repeatedly that just when O'Connor's letters would start to get interesting and touch on the socio-political issues of her day, Fitzgerald irritatingly and inexplicably interrupted the letter itself and inserted the dreaded editorial ellipses, ellipses that she acknowledges in the introduction "indicate editor's deletions."

I first encountered, and read small sections of, *The Habit of Being* in college. At the time, it did occur to me to ask why Fitzgerald repeatedly made deletions; however, it did *not* occur to me that the reason was perhaps that she desired to hide from the world her best friend's shameful racism. Obviously, I should have paid closer attention to Fitzgerald's cryptic thou-dost-protest-too-much claim from the collection's preface: "Her [Flannery's] tongue could take on a quite unsaintly edge. There was an area of sensibility in her that seems to have remained imperfectly developed, as her letters suggest. . . . I have found myself thinking that her own being would have been likewise raised and perfected, completed, by a greater personal empathy with the blacks . . . with whose redemption she was so truly and deeply concerned. Her will was never in danger on the score of racism."[25]

Returning to Fitzgerald's words now that I have read some of the newly released sections of letters she chose to excise, I am forced to conclude that Fitzgerald deleted the parts she did precisely because she worried about her best friend's legacy. Unable to reconcile the racist Flannery of the letters with the long-standing critical interpretation of Flannery's literature as antiracist, Fitzgerald chose to bury the side she couldn't stomach. And she succeeded . . . until 2020.

And with this discovery, I, who once upon a time adored Flannery O'Connor, fell *out* of love with her just as strongly as I had once fallen *in* love with her. The literary crush of my youth shipwrecked hard on the rough-cut rocks of her racism.

*   *   *

In November 2019 I reported to my fellow *People Get Ready* authors that I feared I might have to change my chapter's subject or withdraw. They urged me not to abandon the project but instead to be honest about what I was uncovering and experiencing.[26] Taking their advice to heart, I decided to stick with it, but put my writing on hold until the spring/summer of 2020.

And then, the pandemic hit. On May 25, 2020, the police murdered George Floyd in broad daylight on a downtown Minneapolis street. In the ensuing collective protest for racial justice, *Flannery O'Connor, in stark contrast to all the other moral exemplars featured in this volume, got canceled.*[27]

In July 2020, Loyola University Maryland, a Catholic institution, made headlines when it removed Flannery O'Connor's name from a residence hall and renamed the building after Sister Thea Bowman, the first African American member of the Franciscan Sisters of Spiritual Adoration.

The reason for the name change? On June 2, 2020, scholar Angela Alaimo O'Donnell released *Radical Ambivalence: Race in Flannery O'Connor*, a book that published for the first time several of O'Connor's most controversial letters—letters that contained blatantly racist and derogatory comments about Black people. When students of color at Loyola learned of this correspondence, they successfully circulated an online petition with over one thousand signatures arguing for the name change.

What did Flannery O'Connor pen that caused such a stir?

*   *   *

Homebound after her surgery, Flannery completed her story "Revelation," and then turned her attention to her second-favorite pastime: letter writing. On May 3, 1964, Richard Russell, a Democrat in Georgia, led a filibuster in the Senate to block the Civil Rights Act. Seemingly in response, Flannery sat down at her bedside desk a few days later. She inserted a clean, crisp sheet of white paper into her electric typewriter and typed this candid missive to her progressive friend Maryat Lee, the civil rights activist who had invited her to meet James Baldwin: "You know I'm an integrationist by principle and segregationist by taste anyway. I don't like negroes. They all give me a pain and the more of them I see, the less and less I like them."[28]

Two weeks later, O'Connor continued this disturbing conversation in a second letter to Maryat:

About the Negroes, the kind I don't like is the philosophizing prophesying pontificating kind, the James Baldwin kind. Very ignorant but never silent. Baldwin can tell us what it feels like to be a Negro in Harlem but he tries to tell us everything else too. M. L. King I don't think is the age's greatest saint but he's at least doing what he can do & has to do. Don't know anything about Ossie David except that you like him but you probably like them all. My question is usually would this person be endurable if white. If Baldwin were white nobody could stand him a minute. I prefer Cassius Clay. "If a tiger move into the room with you," says Cassius, "and you leave, that don't mean you hate the tiger. Just means you know you and him can't make out. Too much talk about hate." Cassius is too good for the Moslems.[29]

Ten short weeks after writing this letter, Flannery O'Connor died at age thirty-nine. The red wolf of lupus that had hunted her for fourteen years finally caught and consumed her physical body, leaving behind only her body of written work.

* * *

Flash forward fifty-six years. After Loyola University removed Flannery's name from the dormitory, a massive social media war ensued, with reputable scholars—of all races—taking sides. Some such as Alice Walker, Richard Rodriguez, and Angela O'Donnell herself argued against the canceling, while others such as Paul Elie embraced it as a necessary form of essential truth telling in the quest for racial justice. Still others, such as Benjamin Alexander, editor of O'Connor's previously uncollected letters published in 2019, contend that Flannery O'Connor should be considered for sainthood alongside Dorothy Day.[30]

On July 31, 2020, two hundred scholarly defenders of O'Connor, including Alice Walker, issued a public letter protesting Loyola's cancellation of O'Connor. The letter argues that Flannery's racist remarks are the words of a person "struggling against the racist legacy she inherited. O'Connor 'grew,' as Alice Walker observes . . . and she grew in remarkable ways. . . . O'Connor may—and does—make some racially insensitive statements in her private correspondence. There is no excusing this. But in her stories her better angel rules. . . . She lays claim to America's original sin of racism, seeks atonement, and she atones. . . . Few, if any, of the great writers of the past can survive the purity test they are currently being subject to."[31]

The "Letter in Protest of Cancelling Flannery O'Connor," which notably fails to quote or even mention a single one of the disturbing passages cited in this essay, raises important questions. First, as scholar Paul Elie suggests, is it fair to say that a white person "grew" with regard to her own racial prejudice when throughout her entire life she used the N-word, and ten short weeks before her death wrote scathing and derogatory statements about Black folks, including esteemed civil rights leaders? Second, how are these the words of a person who is wrestling against the racist legacy of the South, rather than succumbing to it? Third, how and when and through what means precisely do the letter's authors understand Flannery to have atoned for her wounding words? Fourth, why pretend that Flannery's statements are merely "racially insensitive" when they should more honestly be called what they really are, which is flat-out racist? Fifth and finally, is the letter accurate in identifying the source of the disturbing discrepancy between Flannery's letters and her fiction as her better angel winning out? Or is it, as I prefer to argue, God's grace that makes her fiction transcend her own racism? I dare say I think the grace-obsessed author would assert the latter, if given the choice, as I will now explain.

So there I was, suddenly out of love with one of my favorite authors, and desperately longing for a divorce . . . that is, until I picked up O'Connor's *A Prayer Journal.* This poignant journal tracks Flannery's innermost spiritual journey during her first year in the Iowa Writers' Workshop (January 10, 1946–September 1947). The young grad student never could have imagined that, sixty-seven years later, her heartfelt handwritten prayers would be published, raw and unedited.

She also never could have imagined that the prayer journal's private insights would lead this reader (and hopefully many more) to fall in love with her anew after she had been canceled in a 2020 collective uprising for racial justice.

As a twenty-first-century scholar-activist, I longed to cherish and seek racial equity and to cherish and respect Flannery O'Connor . . . was it possible to do both? The answer was yes, and the most unexpected and splendid part was: Flannery herself left behind the breadcrumbs that led me to the reconciliation I craved.

Like a sleuth seeking clues, I unearthed within O'Connor's prayer journal's pages a neglected interpretive key that reconciled the incongruity between her radically liberating fiction and her racist letters and actions. The key was O'Connor's deeply theological understanding of the act of writing, and of herself as a writer-mystic-prophet-freak. The answer had to do with four main concepts O'Connor mentions in the journal and remained obsessed with for the rest of her writing life: vocation, mystery, vision, and grace.

*   *   *

In June 1945, just as World War II was drawing to a close, twenty-year-old Mary Flannery O'Connor graduated from college and entered a master's degree program in journalism at the University of Iowa. A devout Catholic and a lifelong southerner, Mary Flannery uprooted her life in her hometown of Milledgeville, Georgia, and moved that summer to Iowa City, Iowa. Almost immediately, she struck up a robust correspondence with her mother, Regina, back in Milledgeville.

In one of her first letters, the eager student asked her strong-minded mother if she would mind if, in tandem with her transition, she changed her name. Regina, who disagreed with her daughter on most matters, surprisingly gave her blessing. As if to symbolize the transformation in her identity from young student to professional writer, Mary Flannery henceforth shortened her name to Flannery, the name she would be called for the rest of her life.

After one unhappy semester in Iowa, Flannery paid a visit to Professor Paul Engle. Engle, the director of the university's prestigious creative writing program, commonly known as the Iowa Writers' Workshop, was a formidable presence on campus. One Monday morning in December, lacking both an appointment and a coat suitable for a Midwest winter, an eager Flannery entered Engle's office and sat down. Several seconds of awkward silence passed in which she kept her shy gaze fixed on the Iowa River outside his window. And then, she mustered up the courage to speak. Her southern accent—jokingly nicknamed "magnolia mouth" by her Midwestern classmates—was so thick that Engle at first believed Flannery spoke a secret or foreign language.[32]

A few moments of embarrassing incomprehension passed . . . until Engle improvised. He slid a fat white notepad and thin black pen across his desk to O'Connor. "I'm sorry, I don't follow," he said. "Why don't you write it down?" Flannery grabbed the pen and scribbled on the notepad's topmost fresh white page: "My name is Flannery O'Connor. I am not a journalist. Can I come to the Writers' Workshop?" The next day, Engle read the young woman's portfolio of one-of-a-kind stories and, awestruck, admitted her to the program. She was one of only three women to receive such a coveted place.

On January 19, 1946, at the start of the second term, Flannery O'Connor, the aspiring writer with a new name to show for it, sat down in her dorm room at her desk. It was a new semester, and a new day. Outside her window, fresh white snow carpeted the university lawn. Pencil in right hand, Flannery used the other to reach into her desk and fish out her newly purchased Sterling composition notebook No. 110 with its signature mottled black and white cover. On the blank line next to "Property of," she wrote in her finest flowery cursive: Flannery O'Connor. She vigorously crossed through "School," and on the empty line next to it wrote the day's date instead. She took a deep breath, opened the book's cover, and began to write.

What poured forth were raw and intimate missives aimed straight at God's own heart. Pleas such as: "Oh Lord, at present I am saying, I am a cheese, make me a mystic, immediately," and "Help me get to what is more than natural in my work . . . God must be in all my work . . . will I ever know anything?"[33]

Over the next nineteen months, the little composition notebook became the young woman's own private prayer journal, the trustworthy space where she confided to a God who listened. As the often-homesick young woman struggled to find her place among the most talented writers of her day, she returned to the journal's pages whenever she longed to talk directly to God. She discovered there a safe container for all her insecurities, longings, disappointments, and dreams. "I am stupid, quite as stupid as the people I ridicule. Please help me to stop this selfishness because I love you, dear God. I don't want to be all excuses though. I am not much."[34]

On November 6, 1946, Flannery, black-rimmed glasses perched on her nose, sat quietly in front of her prayer journal after a long hard day of peer workshopping. Ashamed of her gluttony, she stared at the already empty box of her favorite Scotch oatmeal cookies in front of her on her desk. Ashamed of her mediocrity, she cringed as she recalled her male colleague's critiques of her writing. She longed to be—and to do—better.

As she shared this secret with God, her pen began to flow with a completely new understanding of the writing process, and a revelation of Who would be ultimately responsible should she ever succeed. Suddenly she found herself writing these unexpected words:

> I want to be a fine writer. If I ever do get to be a fine writer, it will not be because I am a fine writer but because God has given me credit for a few of the things He kindly wrote for me. . . . I'll continue to try—that is the point. And at every dry point, I will be reminded Who is doing the work when it is done & Who is not doing it at that moment. Right now I wonder if God will ever do any more writing for me. He has promised His grace.[35]

In another undated journal entry, O'Connor rejoiced that her prayer had been answered:

> Dear God, tonight it is not disappointing because you have given me a story. Don't ever let me think, dear God, that I was anything but the instrument for Your story—just like the typewriter was mine. . . . I didn't know exactly what I was trying to do or what it was going to mean. . . . Dear God,

I wish you would take care of making it a sound story because
I don't know how, just like I didn't know how to write it but
it came.[36]

Another afternoon, the aspiring mystic confessed to the page,
"All my requests seem to melt down to one for Grace—that supernatural grace that does whatever it does. My mind is in a little box,
dear God, down inside other boxes inside other boxes and on and
on. There is very little air in my box. Dear God, please give me as
much air as it is not presumptuous to ask for."[37]

*   *   *

God answered the devout MFA (master of fine arts) student's
prayers. Flannery O'Connor became one of the greatest writers of
her time. But according to her own private mystical interpretation
of the writing process, God was the real author of the fiction, not
herself. O'Connor's name might be on the book cover, but God
was the ghostwriter. God's grace, in her view, gets the byline.

O'Connor here begs us to understand that any good that
emerged from her hand was *in spite of herself*, for on its own her
narrow mind contained a set of airless boxes nestled inside one
another like Russian dolls. In O'Connor's understanding, she was
called to be God's mouthpiece, a mere conduit, a divine instrument. She served, as her journal so beautifully suggests, as God's
typewriter.

What if we took this theological claim seriously: that O'Connor didn't *create* her fiction, but instead *received* it, in the same
manner that a prophet speaks but God provides the words? In our
wrestling with O'Connor's racism, have we paid sufficient attention to this claim? What if we actually believed her that her mind
sits inside airless boxes, and we understood those airless boxes
to be her racism, her homophobia, her white privilege, and her
parochialism?

Asking myself these questions, I realized with a start that if we had taken O'Connor's prayer journal at its word, not one of us should ever have been shocked to discover the massive incongruity between her personhood and her fiction. We wouldn't even have been surprised that the beloved author eventually got canceled. After all, *she warned us*. Repeatedly. I mean, the person Mary Flannery literally renamed herself with an author name as if to say with the biblical Jacob/Israel: *I am a different person when God gets hold of me*.

Mary Flannery never hid from her friends and family who she was apart from God's grace: a broken, egocentric, hypocritical sinner. She openly declared, "Grace . . . can and does use as its medium the imperfect, purely human, and hypocritical."[38] She admitted to a friend the frightening limits of her self-knowledge: "I doubt if anyone ever touches the limits at either end of his personality. We are not our own light."[39]

Flannery the writer never took responsibility for her stories' content, only for having been faithful enough to show up to write them. She described her own writing as "self-abandonment."[40] She believed "the Holy Ghost . . . work[s] through the given talent. You see this in biblical inspiration, so why would you think it would be different in a lesser kind of inspiration?"[41] She confided to a fellow writer, "Most of us only have talent and this is simply something that has to be assisted all the time by physical and mental habits or it dries up and blows away. . . . I write only about two hours every day because that's all the energy I have, but I don't let anything interfere with those two hours. . . . The fact is if you don't sit there every day, the day it would come well, you won't be sitting there."[42] All of us who are writers know showing up for the empty page day after day can feel terrifying and lonely. For that reason, I see O'Connor's faithfulness and discipline in this regard as awesome . . . and loveworthy.

Suddenly, as I reflected upon this insight, so many unusual things Flannery repeated to friends and audiences clicked. For example, the way she consistently compared novelists to prophets: "The Lord doesn't speak to the novelist as he did to his servant, Moses, mouth-to-mouth. He speaks to him as he did to those two complainers, Aaron and Aaron's sister, Mary: through dreams and visions . . . and by . . . the imagination."[43] The way she understood prophets to be recipients of a "vision": "[My] vision . . . I have had it given me whole by faith because I couldn't possibly have arrived at it by my own powers."[44] The way for her, writing was a mysterious (read: divinely inspired) process: "It is the business of fiction to embody mystery," and "There is no excuse for anyone to write fiction for public consumption unless he has been called to do so by the presence of a gift. . . . It is a mystery in itself, something gratuitous and wholly undeserved, something whose real uses will probably always be hidden from us."[45]

And the list of things that clicked doesn't stop there. I saw with new eyes Flannery's repeated understanding of writing as a vocation, a God-given calling: "A vocation is a limiting factor which extends even to the kind of material that the writer is able to apprehend imaginatively. The writer can choose what he writes about but he cannot choose what he is able to make alive. . . . The Christian writer particularly will feel that whatever his initial gift is, it comes from God."[46] Her comprehension of her fiction as finding its source in God: "To be true to the particularity of his own vocation . . . [the writer] will have to descend far enough into himself to reach those underground springs that give life to his work." Her comparison of the artist to the blind man in the Gospels whom Jesus grants sight: "[The] storyteller . . . is like the blind man whom Christ touched, who looked then and saw men as if they were trees, but walking. This is the beginning of vision, and it is an invitation to deeper and stranger visions that we shall have to learn to accept if we want to realize a truly Christian literature."[47]

Rereading *Mystery and Manners*, the definitive collection of O'Connor's talks and essays, I experienced the deceased author's words like a sledgehammer. How could I have missed something so obvious? Her own words offer us a liberating third path—a middle way that avoids the false binaries of cancellation or sainthood, of exclusion or excuses. And yet almost no contemporary literary scholar concerned with O'Connor's racism seemed to have taken O'Connor's artistic philosophy seriously, most likely because it is 0 percent literary and 100 percent theological and mystical, grounded in her Christian faith. Nothing makes literary theory blush more than theology. Likewise, nothing makes theology blush more than ugly biographical details.

O'Connor laid down breadcrumbs to lead us out of bafflement, but we chose not to follow them. We (myself included) desired her vision to mirror—not contradict—her moral life. We wanted to excise all the ugly, delete all her uses of the N-word, whitewash her racism. If Sally Fitzgerald had just told the truth from the very beginning and published all of O'Connor's letters unedited, would things have been different? Would contemporary progressives ever have felt the need to cancel her? Or could we have honestly wrestled with her racism and sinfulness and parochialism from the very beginning? Would doing so have helped us to glorify more the miraculous gift of God's grace that transformed O'Connor's personal prejudice into a literary form of *agapē* so expansive it bordered on scandalous? I dare answer yes.

Instead of heeding Flannery's own mystical philosophy of artistic grace, however, many of us strove to make her a progressive saint. Even while alive, the thought horrified her. When friend Robert Lowell allegedly once referred to her as a saint, she responded, "Let me right now correct, stash, and obliterate this revolting story about Lowell introducing me as a saint. . . . Impress on him the impropriety of repeating this kind of slop."[48]

O'Connor unequivocally abhorred hagiography—writing the lives of saints—so we must avoid writing one about her. When asked to write one to honor a thirteen-year-old orphan who died of cancer, O'Connor refused, explaining that hagiography was not only dishonest but in many ways grotesque. In lieu of a hagiography, she wrote a beautiful introduction to the young girl's "memoir" that included this fascinating commentary: "Most of us have learned to be dispassionate about evil, to look it in the face and find, as often as not, our own grinning reflections with which we do not argue, but good is another matter. Few have stared at that long enough to accept the fact that its face too is grotesque, that in us the good is something under construction."[49] In this passage, as in many others in the prayer journal, if we listen closely, Flannery admits to her own evil. The good in her, she claimed, was something under construction. God's grace was the bulldozer. Why can't we believe her?

O'Connor throughout her life implicitly claimed to be a prophet, while she explicitly claimed to *not* be a saint. In the Scripture, God's prophets are not somehow worthy, superior, pure, or perfect. On the contrary, they're as maimed and imperfect as the rest of us—if not more so. The prophets aren't saints; what they are is *chosen*, and most often chosen *in spite* of who they are and not *because* of it. "You have to be chosen. And in between times of being chosen, you have to keep on writing."[50] Flannery understood this in the deepest way possible, as she once acknowledged to her friend Betty Hester: "The prophetic vision is dependent on the *imagination* of the prophet, not his moral life."[51]

O'Connor often repeated to her readers, "It is the free act, the acceptance of grace particularly, that I always have my eye on as the thing which will make the story work."[52] What if we took this seriously with regard to the author herself? Where is the moment in her own life in which she freely accepts grace? I would argue: every moment she sat down at her typewriter.

What if the most astonishing greatness about Flannery O'Connor is not some moral life she lived but the grace her own writing brought into her own airless, privileged box of whiteness? The way grace liberated much of her writing from her own bias, prejudice, and racism? What if by making excuses for her, whitewashing her racism, and rewriting her biography as hagiography the very thing we wrote out of her life was GRACE—the very thing she was obsessed with in all of her characters and would have most wanted us to see working within her own character? (Remember Ruby Turpin in "Revelation," who is saved from false righteousness and her own racism by a girl named Mary Grace, who violently smacks her in the face?) The grace that transforms, upends, reverses, revolutionizes? Honestly, I think Flannery would be pissed off at us for our cowardly redactions. She wouldn't want us to edit, delete, revise, pretend, make excuses, call her a product of her time. Her writing was bigger and better than the confines of her own mind and culture and white privilege, and *that* is the miracle. To God be the glory.

Flannery O'Connor was great as a writer for the same reason every prophet was great. She was willing to step aside and allow herself to become God's mouthpiece.

Of course, we must acknowledge the theological danger and contestability inherent in the assertion that any finite human speaks for God. After all, many people have publicly claimed to be God's mouthpiece, but history ultimately revealed that they sought none other than the selfish reinforcement of their own privilege and power. What makes Flannery such a fascinating—and distinct—case is that the passage of time has revealed the exact opposite. As God's mouthpiece, her words revealed her own selfishness and racism, and unspun the coil of her own privilege and power. As such, her story reveals a potential litmus test for anyone who claims to speak for or with God.

The epiphany? We can't erase the grotesqueness of Flannery O'Connor herself, of her life, any more than we can erase the grotesqueness of her fiction. She wouldn't want us to, because to do so erases grace, deletes God—the one constant Flannery always pointed us toward—right out of her biography. When we redact the author's letters, make excuses for her bigoted and biased claims, or shrink from directly identifying her racist words and actions as racist, what we expunge in the end is Godself. Were she alive today, she would no doubt protest this.

Flannery O'Connor got canceled, yes. But ironically, when we attempt to overturn her cancellation, we cancel the action of God's grace within and behind the fiction. A grace that permeates Flannery's writing and allows it to transcend its author's personal limitations. We end up denying the Holy Spirit's "underground springs." Concealing the ugly truth about Flannery's personal grotesqueness leads us to efface an ancillary truth, which is this: God called Flannery to the vocation of the Divine's own Smith Corona. Faithfully, she answered.

Flannery O'Connor wasn't a faithful Christian because she was antiracist. She was a faithful Christian because as an author she showed up for the page, and got out of the way so grace could perform its mystery. The writer Flannery is a miracle, created by God's grace and her own willingness to show up for the page . . . no matter what wildness emerged. For this faithfulness, she should be praised and recognized. Just as for her own sin and racism, she should be critiqued.

What if from this moment on, all of us lovers of O'Connor just stopped all these frenetic efforts to angelize, hagiographize, revise, besaint, ensky, beatify, and canonize her? What if at long last we put an end to all the defensiveness? the excuses? the textual gloss? the cultural justifications? The endless redaction with its vigilant eye hell-bent on deleting all the nasty bits from Flannery's life? *What if we just accepted her for the sinner she was?* What if we just accepted her own bald-faced categorization of herself as selfish, narrow-minded, desperately in need of grace, and as a writer whom God mysteriously uses to critique the very sins she herself participated in?

I think we would find ourselves led, splendidly, to the offensive miraculousness of God's extraordinary grace.

I propose we do something radically new and use O'Connor's unusual understanding of grace to interpret not only her fiction, as has been done for decades, but also the author's own life. Writing on the use of the grotesque in her fiction, O'Connor famously once observed, "Our age not only does not have a very sharp eye for the almost imperceptible intrusions of grace, it no longer has a feeling for the nature of the violences which preceded and followed them. The Devil's greatest wile, Baudelaire has said, is to convince us that he does not exist."[53] When we read Flannery O'Connor and ignore her personal racism, aren't we falling into this very trap?

In my view, racism is the grotesque violence that, tragically, precedes and follows the grace of O'Connor's fiction.[54] Yet most critics and readers deny its very existence. The irony!

O'Connor also wrote, "Violence is strangely capable of returning my characters to reality and preparing them to accept their moments of grace. Their heads are so hard that almost nothing else will do the work." And so I ask: Where is the moment of grace in the hardheaded author's own life and legacy? If Flannery O'Connor could hear us now, would she see our antiracist critiques and her own cancellation as an act of grace, an act of grace as violent as any that happened to her self-righteous protagonists like the grandma and Ruby Turpin? I think she would, and I want to believe if she read that odd sentence on this page, she might even chuckle.

O'Connor, after all, repeatedly compared herself not only to Ruby Turpin[55] but also to the self-righteous grandmother in her story "A Good Man Is Hard to Find." The grandma only recognizes her shared humanity with those she perceives as beneath her at the moment when she stares down the barrel of a serial killer's gun. After murdering her, the serial killer in the story concludes, "She would of been a good woman . . . if it had been somebody there to shoot her every day of her life."[56]

Is it possible to conceive of cancel culture as a violent act of grace, a blow to the head that can reverse our vision like Ruby Turpin's? Would Flannery O'Connor have been a better antiracist if people of color and their white allies had been empowered to cancel her, or at least call her out, every day of her life? I dare say she might've been. I want to believe that she was open to grace, even the violent kind of grace that hurts to receive. I could be wrong, but I crave to believe she would've changed and repented.

From the day she first set pen to paper, Flannery O'Connor longed for her work to glorify God. And guess what? It does. But only if we her readers unflinchingly name, claim, and confront— not hide, whitewash, or excuse—the reality of her lived racism. Seen in this light, O'Connor can remain beloved—though never besainted—in our hearts forever.

PETE SEEGER

(1919–2014)

Pete Seeger, 1969, at the University of Chicago Folk Festival; photo by Marc Pokempner, courtesy of the Hanna Holborn Gray Special Collections Research Center, University of Chicago Library

Finding the Joyful Struggle

Pete Seeger on the March from Selma to Montgomery

Peter Slade

The Reverend James Bevel was pleased to see Pete and Toshi on the road. The short Baptist preacher with a colorful kippah on his head swung down the line toward the couple. "Hello there, Brother Seeger," he said, embracing them. "We are still down here fighting Sin."[1] But Bevel didn't linger; this nonviolent general needed to get his small army on the move.

The marchers had spent a damp and muddy night under canvas and had eaten their breakfast of oatmeal and lukewarm coffee brought by the "fish and loaves committee" all the way from Selma: thirty-four miles back down Highway 80.[2] Now, just after seven in the morning on Wednesday, March 25, 1965, they formed up in a raggedy line.[3]

We're gonna march when the Spirit says march.

Pete threw back his head and added his baritone to the voices around him.

And if the Spirit say march, why then you march with the Spirit.

National guardsmen stopped the traffic, and a helicopter clattered overhead as the column crossed over the highway and turned right toward Montgomery—sixteen miles ahead. As Pete wrote that evening, they were "three hundred foot-weary but light-souled people."[4] Looking around him, the forty-five-year-old folk singer could see mostly "younger people." He judged about two-thirds were African Americans from Selma, the other third were a mix of Blacks and whites from across the country, "about 10 percent, it seemed to me, were clergy. . . . I've never been surrounded by such an ecumenical group."[5]

Pete loped along in his usual work attire. A plain sweater, collared shirt, and a notepad and pen in his pocket.[6] This tall, skinny Yankee with a Harvard accent could be mistaken for another one of the white ministers who had poured into Selma for the civil rights march, except he was not wearing a clerical collar. Toshi strode next to him, a bag slung over her shoulder and a camera in her hand.[7] After sleeping only one night in the tents, the couple was fresher than most of the marchers. They had flown down to Montgomery from their home in New York the day before, and, with a return flight that evening, they were traveling light.[8]

It was none other than Martin Luther King Jr. who had sent the Seegers a telegram requesting their presence, but he wasn't there when they joined the marchers.[9] King had been with the march when it set off from Brown Chapel in Selma on Sunday, March 21—the first day of spring. King led the column of three thousand across the Edmund Pettus Bridge and down the Jefferson Davis Highway toward the state capitol in Montgomery.[10] At the end of the first day, the crowds returned to Selma, and King camped that first cold night with the core group of 350. With feigned gravity, the urbane civil rights leader announced to the press the next morning, "I am happy to say that I have slept in a sleeping bag for the first time in my life. I feel fine."[11] That day, Monday, the marchers had crossed into Lowndes County, and, following the court's order, only three hundred had continued. With the trees and bushes still bare of leaves, King and his companions felt exposed on the two-lane highway, and the national guardsmen were on high alert. The second night was not so cold, but it was wet. On Tuesday morning King, nursing his blistered feet, left the marchers in the rain and flew to Cleveland for an SCLC (Southern Christian Leadership Conference) fundraiser.[12] Now, on the fourth day, the Seegers were participating in the final push to get to Montgomery.

After three hours of steady walking from their camp, they crossed from Lowndes into Montgomery County. The road widened to four lanes. Everyone breathed a little easier. Cars and buses started pulling over on the southern shoulder disgorging clean reinforcements who rushed across the median to join the muddy three hundred. The sun rose in a clear sky and the temperature climbed into the seventies.[13] Sweaters and coats came off, and the marching songs of the movement rang out.

"Ain't gonna let Jim Clark turn me 'round!"

The sheriff of Dallas County frequently made an appearance in the freedom songs. Like Bull Connor in Birmingham, Clark cut a cartoonish figure in Selma. Historian and eyewitness Howard Zinn described Clark strutting along his line of billy-club-wielding officers, "a six-footer with a big stomach, on his green helmet a gold medallion with an eagle, a big gold star on his shirt, the Confederate flag stamped on his helmet, an open collar, epaulets on his shoulders. Gun at his hip."[14]

"Ain't gonna let nobody turn me 'round!"

People came out on their front porches and stared. The marchers drew encouragement from the African Americans who showed their support. Whites were less friendly. One marcher recalled their looks of "utter disdain" and the "great deal of profanity . . . yelled from passing cars."[15] But it wasn't the yelling that concerned the march's organizers and the commanders of the soldiers swarming over the route. They were worried about snipers. The white Alabama guardsmen protecting the protestors were now under the direct command of the president of the United States, not Sheriff Clark or Governor Wallace. John Lewis, his wounds from Bloody Sunday inflicted on him by Alabama state troopers only two weeks before, appreciated the irony: "It was almost a contradiction . . . these unarmed few nonviolent soldiers—some of us carrying a book, an apple, an orange, or something in a bag—were being guarded by men with guns riding in jeeps."[16]

The marchers wanted equal voting rights for all, but many whites in Alabama, the region, and the country saw what Lewis called a "nonviolent crusade" as nothing less than a threat to America. On the second day out from Selma, a plane of "the Confederate Air Force" dropped leaflets courtesy of the White Citizens Action Inc. of Tuscaloosa that threatened economic retaliation: "An unemployed agitator ceases to agitate."[17]

That same day, the marchers had passed the first of a number of billboards showing a photograph taken at Highlander Folk School with the caption, "MARTIN LUTHER KING AT COMMUNIST TRAINING SCHOOL." King dismissed the accusation, telling reporters, "There are as many Communists in the civil rights movement as there are Eskimos in Florida."[18] Fortunately for him, the Census Bureau didn't have a count of Inuit in Florida for comparison, but communists were indeed involved in the civil rights movement. Pete Seeger was one, and he was no stranger to violent opposition or economic reprisals.

Pete, for reasons of professional self-preservation and the safety of his family, tried not to be outspoken about the particularities of his political beliefs.[19] When asked if he was a communist, he had a well-worn set of evasive answers. The questioner might get something like, "I'm afraid anyone who wants to find out my opinions can do so easily enough simply listening to the songs I have sung. . . . I am about as communist as my songs are. I'm about as anti-communist as my songs are."[20] Or perhaps he would say that he'd been entranced as a boy by the stories of Native Americans who, "if there was food, everyone ate. If there was hunger, everyone was hungry, even the learned chief and his children. When I was twenty I learned that anthropologists call this 'tribal communism.'"[21] But, if he could have been open about his politics that Wednesday in 1965, he would have explained, "Being a communist has helped me, I believe, to be a better singer and folklorist, and a more selfless citizen."[22]

Seeger's formal involvement with the Communist Party USA (CPUSA) dated back to his truncated student career at Harvard. His arrival at college coincided with the zenith of the Communist Party in America. Like many intellectuals and artists of the time, the energy, moral clarity, and possibilities of communism attracted the young Seeger. He devoted more time to the activities of the Young Communist League than to his classes.[23] Dropping out of school in 1938, he departed Boston for New York, where his father introduced him to the music and art scene of the Far Left.

Seeger's interests and passions overlapped with much of the prewar Communist Party's doctrinaire pronouncements and programs. As a teenager in the Depression, he had longed for an end to mass unemployment and poverty wages. "The words 'freedom' and 'justice': only Commies talked about things like that," he remembered.[24] Under the influence of Party teaching, Seeger developed what one biographer described as "[a] zeal for unions [that was] near religious."[25] And though living in an almost completely white New England world, he shared the communists' outrage at Jim Crow and white supremacy. Pete Seeger's interests extended beyond politics. He loved writing and thought he might become a journalist. He enjoyed painting and toyed with the idea of a career as an artist. He also had an extraordinary affinity for the old songs and fiddle tunes that musicologists like his father's friend John Lomax collected, transcribed, and catalogued. Always a contrarian, he eschewed formal musical instruction and chose instead to spend hours figuring out how to play the five-string banjo.

In the 1930s and '40s, the Communist Party USA saw potential in this music of "the People"—a term it now preferred to "the Workers" or "the Proletariat"—as an appropriate soundtrack for an authentically American revolutionary movement.[26] The party encouraged Seeger and the unruly group of musicians and songwriters he had assembled. The communists hoped that Pete and his friends would help lead the cultural charge against fascism in the Popular Front, its newfound cooperation with unions, socialists, and New Dealers. Naming themselves the Almanac Singers and living together in "Almanac House," the rotating musical collective—not all of whom were members of the party—performed at union fund-raisers, at bars, at clubs, on sidewalks, and in their own house parties they dubbed "Hootenannies."[27] The Almanac's "folk" music was no exercise in preserving old musical forms; they wrote new songs, and they wanted people to sing them. Pete and the Almanacs had songs against Jim Crow; in support of the Congress of Industrial Organizations (CIO); for the fight against fascists in Spain; against fighting fascists in Europe while the Soviet Union had a peace treaty with Nazi Germany; and, confusingly, in favor of fighting fascists again when Germany invaded the Soviet Union. They made a few records, but the ill-disciplined crew struggled to pay the rent and utility bills for Almanac House.

All the while, Pete honed his craft as a singer and instrumentalist and slowly developed his own voice and performance style. He learned the driving twelve-string bass lines from Huddie "Lead Belly" Ledbetter and the power of a simple melody in service of an honest song from fellow Almanac Woody Guthrie. (The Okie minstrel, seven years Pete's senior, called his musical disciple and traveling companion "my long tall banjo playing pardner.")[28] And he was building an encyclopedic repertoire. Lee Hays, who brought gospel songs from the interracial Southern Tenant Farmers' Union to the Almanacs, remembered, "When I first met [Pete], he made up a list of songs he knew—I was astonished—he knew as many as three hundred."[29]

America's entry into the Second World War put an end to the Almanacs. When Pete returned to New York from his three years in the army, he had even more songs and his energies were focused on harnessing the power of singing for "the people's struggle for a better world."[30] "Somebody asked me around January '46, 'What is your purpose in life?'" Pete later recalled. "And I said to make a singing labor movement. I was hoping to find hundreds, thousands, tens of thousands of union choruses. Just as every church has a choir, why not every union have a chorus?"[31] All these choruses would need songs. Joined by Lee Hays and many of his friends from the Almanac days, he formed People's Songs to provide them. The first newsletter of People's Songs proclaimed their motto and single purpose, "The People are on the march and must have songs to sing."[32] Alongside the folk songs and spirituals, they produced union songs setting encouraging doggerel to familiar tunes. "The Scabs crawl in, the scabs crawl out," Pete sang to a children's tune.[33] The dehumanization of "scabs," "stoolies," and "bosses" is jarring when set alongside the universal humanitarian themes of Seeger's most popular work.

After its initial burst of energy, People's Songs hit a problem: the days of a singing union movement were over. The musicians were seen as entertainers, not movement song leaders, and gigs at union halls didn't pay the talent very well. People's Songs' final failed hurrah was supporting the Progressive Party's Henry Wallace in his doomed 1948 presidential campaign. Pete declared in a letter to the supporters of People's Songs, "A trumpet blew down the Walls of Jericho. And songs—of, by, and for the people—can help you shatter the walls of reaction in 1948."[34] But they didn't. Instead, Pete found himself as Wallace's warm-up act facing angry crowds across the South who had come to throw eggs and worse at the "Commie." Wallace failed, and People's Songs went bust the next year.

Pete swore off the office work required to run an organization like People's Songs and refocused his energy on performing with his new group, the Weavers. Guitarist Fred Hellerman and classically trained singer Ronnie Gilbert joined their voices with Pete and Lee Hays to form a folk-singing quartet. But Seeger didn't leave his politics behind. "What I learned from the Communists," he explained to a journalist thirty years later, "[is] that an artist has a responsibility as a citizen. That is what Paul Robeson taught us."[35] This lesson came at a high cost. When Pete opened for Robeson, the great African American singer and actor, at an open-air concert for the Civil Rights Congress in Peekskill, New York, in 1949, he and thousands of those attending had to run a screaming white gauntlet of racist and anticommunist epithets as they tried to drive home. The mob hurled more than words. Rocks the size of baseballs crashed through the windshield and windows. In the back seat, Seeger's father-in-law tried to shield Pete's two-year-old son Danny from the shards. It was a violent prelude to the troubled and briefly spectacularly successful career of the Weavers.

The unvarnished politics and opinions of the Almanacs and then People's Songs were there for all to hear in the words of the songs. The Weavers, though, with their commercial aspirations and contract with Decca, traded explicit ideology in their songs for a wide audience. Pete hoped the range of repertoire itself could bring change. The Weavers, with their tight harmonies of three baritones and an alto, brought together American work songs, ballads, sea shanties, spirituals and hymns, along with a smattering of songs from other countries. Pete saw this "great synthesis, pulling together wonderful ideas from many different cultures" as his musical contribution to "a movement which would put an end forever to racism, would put an end forever to poverty in the midst of plenty, would put an end forever to war, sexism, ageism, all sorts of stupidities."[36]

The young people marching that Wednesday on the road into Montgomery would all have been able to sing the Weavers' hits from their childhood—"Irene, Goodnight," "Tzena, Tzena, Tzena," "Wimoweh," "On Top of Old Smokey," "If I Had a Hammer," and "This Land Is Your Land"—even though most of them had no idea that skinny middle-aged man walking with them had been the one who put them on the charts.

Pete Seeger, with his natural puritanical inclinations ("I don't smoke, I don't drink, I don't like nightclubs"), struggled with the

Weavers' commercial success and demanding touring schedule; meanwhile, outside forces were working to silence the group.[37] It was the height of the McCarthy era, and the FBI-connected anti-communist newsletter *Counterattack* dogged the Weavers, labeling them "the party-favored singing group."[38] With their names on the blacklist, the group lost TV appearances and bookings dried up. Pete and Lee both appeared before the House Un-American Activities Committee (HUAC), which was determined to pin them as members of the Communist Party. Lee, like so many other artists hauled before the inquisition, pleaded the Fifth, claiming his constitutional right not to answer their questions. Pete pleaded the First: that the committee had no right even to ask him the questions. "I resent the implication," he explained, "that because some of my opinions may be different than yours, that I am any less of an American. You have the right to your opinions, and I have a right to mine."[39] HUAC was neither convinced nor amused. The courts convicted Pete of contempt of Congress, sentencing him to a year in jail only for the sentence to be overturned on appeal.[40] Pete remembered this time as "six and a half years of overriding uncertainty."[41] Ronnie Gilbert offered a succinct summary of the impact of HUAC on the Weavers: "We lost our livelihood, We lost our careers, We lost the sense we were living in a democratic society."[42]

All through this period Pete maintained an abiding loyalty to communism, his first political love. He resisted criticism of either the Soviet Union or its iconic leader, Stalin. In a letter to Woody Guthrie in 1956, he was still holding the USSR up as a model state despite acknowledging what he called "some bad injustices [which] were done during Stalin's hard driving (and he did some mighty valuable things, too)."[43] Later that year, as he faced possible prison time, Seeger wrote a letter to his yet-unborn grandchildren, sharing with them his understanding of communism and the role it had played in his life. He wrote "Not to be opened 'til after death of both C. L. Seeger II and Peter Seeger. Or around the year 2000 A.D." on the envelope and sealed it. In the letter, he explained how he was still a communist, even though "in this year of 1956 it now appears by admission of Russians themselves, that all was, and possibly is, not as sweet as American communists hoped or believed." Now he was a communist by his own definition: "If you ask, am I in favor of slave labor camps, of stifling opinion, of violent revolution, etc. I say 'NO!' You bet I am not. On the other hand, if you ask, am I in favor of cooperative ownership and planning production and consumption, and do I believe that only under such socialism will eventually wars cease, and arts and science truly flourish, then I say: 'You bet!'" He resisted the criticisms with what we now call "whataboutism." "I'll stick with Russia and China . . . in spite of their mistakes. After all, American democracy has made undemocratic errors, too."[44]

As Pete and Toshi walked along the Alabama highway that Wednesday in 1965, they both had very recent memories and impressions of communism in the Soviet Union. Less than a year before the Selma to Montgomery march, they had been touring the USSR with their three children—Danny (seventeen), Mika (fifteen), and Tinya (eight). It was part of their ten-month world tour that Pete called "a one family musical Peace Corps."[45] Countering the stories circulating about the harsh reality of life for common people behind the Iron Curtain, his letters home to friends were full of positive comparisons between life under Soviet rule and back in the USA. "There were no shortages of necessities obvious, but there were obviously damn few luxuries for anyone," he wrote. "After seeing cities around the world where shiny limousines rolled through the streets past humans in rags, here was a land where there were no beggars or rags."[46] Far more than conducting a concert tour, the Seegers met with workers in factories and laborers on collectivized farms, and they were in Moscow's Red Square for the May Day parade.[47] As they traveled through the vast country, the ubiquitous propaganda posters and the endless statues of Lenin bothered the young Seegers, but their father explained they shouldn't find it so odd. "Every Catholic home, or school has its crucifix or madonna, and so many US schoolrooms have pictures of Washington or Lincoln or a current President."[48]

Everywhere they went on their world tour, Pete asked to hear people sing their old songs, and he in turn would sing the people's songs he had spent his adult life collecting and interpreting. And then he would invite his audience, Kenyan, Dutch, Russian, Japanese—it didn't matter—to join in on the chorus. He still believed that somehow if there was any hope for the future, it lay in a singing movement.

Raising up a cadre of song leaders had always been key to Pete Seeger's plan. Back in 1954, he dedicated his new column in *Sing Out!* "to Johnny Appleseed Jrs." The original Johnny Appleseed, Seeger reminded his readers, was "a deeply religious man . . . [who] scorned usual business methods." At the turn of the nineteenth century, Johnny Appleseed had eschewed violence, befriended Native Americans, embraced the abolitionist cause, and planted his apple seeds through the frontiers of the young United States. Seeger's modern-day Johnny Appleseed Jrs. were the teenagers of the new folk revival: "the thousands of boys and girls who today are using their guitars and their songs to plant the seeds of a better tomorrow in the homes across the land."[49]

On the Jefferson Davis Highway heading toward Montgomery, there was perhaps the greatest concentration of song leaders per capita ever assembled in the civil rights movement. Three Johnny Appleseed Jrs.—two black and one white—were getting sunburned and sweaty in the swelling column right alongside Seeger. Jimmy Collier, SCLC's young song leader, with his battered and mud-streaked guitar, had been with the march all the way from Selma.[50] Collier was delighted to have Pete, one of his musical heroes, join him in this intense experience. "You know what happens when people are really scareder than shit? They sing like they're not going to ever be able to sing again," Collier later explained. "People were really scared but they felt they had to carry on. So the music was very important to making people feel good. Many of the songs were old union songs, you know, right out of the thirties and so on, just different words. So I am sure for Peter it was just a dream come true."[51] Seeger was delighted to make the acquaintance of this "fine young guitar picker and singer from Chicago."[52]

At the head of the column, flanking the determined and one-legged Jim Letherer, came a civil rights honor guard holding high the Stars and Stripes and the blue flag of the United Nations. Alongside Jim, swinging along on his crutches, marched Len Chandler, the most conspicuous of the Johnny Appleseed Jrs. on the Selma campaign. Wearing a yellow hard hat and an impro-vised blue poncho made from a beach towel covered with white stars, classically trained Chandler trilled out "Yankee Doodle" on a child's melody flute (a fife with a whistle mouthpiece).[53] It wasn't quite the scene Chandler had hoped for. "I looked all over hell to try and find a snare drum because I wanted to recreate [the painting] 'The Spirit of '76,'" he recalled half a century later.[54] Still, it was close enough. Those around him started to sing the old Revolutionary War song:

Stuck a feather in his cap and called it Macaroni.

Chandler improvised a new verse:

Wallace said we couldn't march
We knew he was a phony
Now we're marching all the way
To make him eat baloney
Freedom fighters keep it up
Even though you're weary
Freedom fighters keep it up
We love our Freedom dearly.[55]

Chandler repeated the verse until the singers caught on to the new words, then he took up the fife again and added a shrill counterpoint. He had developed this skill—coming up with a few punchy lines with singable choruses on the fly—leading singing in mass meetings, protests, and on occasion, prison cells. Chandler called them "songs of the line."[56] All through Lowndes County, Chandler hustled up and down the column of three hundred marchers with his guitar calling out songs. One song of the line came to him as an inversion of the army drill sergeant's marching cadence "left, left, left-right, left." He didn't want anyone to get left. Left was too negative. Chandler thought, "Why don't we accent on the right foot?" And so, he just started singing:

> *Pick 'em up and lay 'em down*
> *Right. Right.*

By the time he called out the second line, the marchers were ready with their response:

> *All the way from Selma town*
> **Right. Right.**
> *Pick 'em up and lay 'em down*
> **Right. Right.**
> *Don't you know we're Freedom-bound*
> **Right. Right.**

John Lewis said, "I will never forget a little song that one of the guys would sing—'Pick 'em up, put 'em down—all the way from Selma.' [The march] was like a holy crusade, like Gandhi's march to the sea."[57] But surely Gandhi didn't have anything as cool or as funny as a Len Chandler soundtrack for his protest against the British Empire.

I've been walkin' so long
Right. Right.
I put blisters on the street.
Right. Right.
I caught the Freedom fever
Right. Right.
He done settled in my feet
Right. Right.[58]

The third of Pete's Johnny Appleseed Jrs. was Guy Carawan, who, in partnership with Pete, played a key role in bringing the movement its greatest anthem. Carawan, a tall white Californian, marched all the way from Selma to Montgomery carrying his guitar. Inspired by People's Songs and the Weavers, Carawan had studied sociology at UCLA before he moved to New York and joined the folk scene around Washington Square.[59] Since 1959, he had been the music director at Highlander Folk School in Tennessee—the "Communist Training School" of the Citizen's Councils' billboards.[60] Pete Seeger had learned the union song "We Will Overcome"—a black church hymn adapted for the picket line—on a visit to Highlander back in 1947.[61] Pete changed "will" to "shall"—the open vowel was more pleasing to sing—and added the verses "the whole wide world around" and "we'll walk hand in hand."[62] Carawan learned the song from Seeger and used it in his work at Highlander, which, following the success of the Montgomery Bus Boycott, was busy training civil rights workers for the freedom struggle.[63] In 1960, students involved in the sit-ins in Nashville invited Guy Carawan to lead singing at the gathering of student activists at Shaw University in Raleigh over the Easter weekend. Back in 1948, at the start of the People's Songs project, Lee Hays had written these prophetic words: "One dreams of a great people's song, of our marching song which will come again, but hasn't yet; of the great song which is still unsung. It will be a hymn, for it will be born in faith, and love, and united purpose.

It will be a battle hymn, for we are at war against the powers of evil. . . . And that song will be sung in many days of defeat; and it will be sung on the day we celebrate our victory."[64] That Easter at Shaw, the students of the fledgling Student Nonviolent Coordinating Committee (SNCC) took up "We Shall Overcome" and made it their battle hymn.

Just like his mentor Pete Seeger, Carawan worked hard to sow the seeds of movement singing in the unshakeable belief that the long folk tradition of people's songs was an indispensable resource for the struggle. In May 1964, he brought activists from across the South to Atlanta to meet with singers their grandparents' age to hear their blues, spirituals, and work songs. The young SNCC field workers preferred Ray Charles to the Sea Island Singers. Songs that evoked the era of slavery just didn't seem relevant. But Len Chandler spoke up for the importance of the tradition for the contemporary battle. "This music is great, and the boys on the radios and the TVs have stopped you from hearing it—but this is it, man, this is the stuff."[65]

This was the stuff that Pete Seeger had spent his life pursuing. Not the commercial music of Tin Pan Alley and the Top Ten but the song traditions of the common people that carried the "hidden heritage of militancy which comes and goes, but never completely dies."[66] And, on the road to Montgomery, the militancy and the singing were very much alive.

A group of teenage girls walked behind Toshi and Pete. For mile after mile they sang.[67] They sang church songs and school songs and freedom songs. Pete smiled. The girls hoisted up the songs like sails to catch the wind. Some filled and went on for chorus after chorus with voices up and down the line joining in. Others just flapped against the mast to be lowered after only a couple of verses. He jotted down the words, marveling at the power of their singing and the way the girls were putting new words to old songs and adding their own verses—seemingly making some of them up on the spot.

The girls started an old spiritual that had become a popular song in the movement.

> *I love everybody, I love everybody, I love everybody in my heart.*

More people joined the march. More voices took up the song. Pete sang along while scribbling down the words and snatches of notation. It was a musicologist's dream. As a boy he had traveled the backroads of North Carolina with his father asking fiddlers to play them their old tunes; as a Harvard dropout, he had spent hours transcribing recordings of old singers for John Lomax at the Library of Congress; but those were old folk tunes and old folk songs. Here on Highway 80, the marchers were birthing new songs and transforming and changing well-known songs all around him. His musicologist father had once told him that "a folk song in a book is like a photograph of a bird in flight."[68] Now, as he struggled to capture the shifting melodies with standard musical notation—why hadn't he brought his tape recorder?—that phrase echoed through his head. He wished his father could be here to witness this moment with him.[69] After this he could write, "I've read arguments about how folk songs of the past must have been created. For me there is no argument anymore. I've seen it."[70]

The swelling line of marchers crept along toward Montgomery, stopping frequently for the weary to rest their feet. A second army of volunteers in fleets of cars tended to their needs. Seminarians in a truck with four porta-johns strapped on the back stopped by the side of the road. The "Green Dragon" station wagon rolled up with its crew of doctors from the Medical Committee for Human Rights.[71] Shoes and socks came off, and the doctors put Band-Aids on blisters and had salt tablets and water for those showing signs of dehydration.[72] Pete went around the resting marchers asking them to tell him the words to the songs they had just been singing. Toshi took pictures.

At eleven o'clock there was a stir in the crowd. Martin Luther King, his wife, Coretta, and Ralph Abernathy had rejoined the march for the final push into the state's capital and the seat of Governor Wallace.[73]

Pete Seeger was not the only folklorist working the march. Bernice Johnson Reagon was there too, scribbling down the words:

> *Oh Wallace you never*
> *Can jail us all*
> *Oh Wallace*
> *Segregation's bound to fall.*[74]

Bernice first met Pete in Atlanta in the fall of 1962 in the house of Andrew Young, Martin Luther King's lieutenant.[75] Bernice was only twenty years old but already a veteran song leader from the Albany movement; her rich alto seemed to rise from the floor of mass meetings bearing the community up in song. Writing about himself in 1965, Seeger acknowledged his limitations when it came to singing "spirituals and gospel songs." He noted that his "voice tends to get tense and hard, and rarely achieves that full, relaxed, but powerful tone that most good Negro singers have naturally."[76] He could have been describing Bernice's voice. But she didn't believe she came by it naturally. After her time singing in Chief Pritchett's jail, her voice had changed. "It was bigger than I'd ever heard it before. It had this ringing in it. It filled all of the space of the church. I thought that was because I had been to jail. It was because I had stepped outside of the safety zone."[77]

Sitting there in Andrew Young's living room, Seeger had been excited to hear from Bernice that SNCC had pulled together some of its best singers to perform the new freedom songs. Drawing on his years of experience touring the country promoting unions and other good causes, he suggested to Bernice that SNCC could organize the group to raise money for SNCC and spread the word to audiences across the country. Bernice took Pete's advice. With

Toshi Seeger as their agent, the newly formed SNCC Freedom Singers, Bernice Johnson, Rutha Harris, Cordell Reagon, and Charles Neblett, made their debut with Pete Seeger at Carnegie Hall on November 11, 1962.[78] This group toured the country for the next year, sharing a stage with Bob Dylan at the Newport Folk Festival, returning to Carnegie Hall to sing with Mahalia Jackson, and singing out across the Mall from the steps of the Lincoln Memorial before Martin Luther King gave his "Dream" speech.

Pete Seeger took to singing these freedom songs in his concerts. That same summer of 1963, Columbia recorded his concert in Carnegie Hall and released the biggest-selling album of Seeger's career.[79] With handpicked musical friends on the stage to fill out the audience's singing for Columbia's microphones, Seeger beat out the urgent 12/8 tempo of "We Shall Overcome" on his twelve-string guitar.[80] Enveloped in the sound of nearly three thousand voices, Seeger unself-consciously abandoned the tune, singing bass and tenor harmonies at the top of his voice. Historian Howard Zinn witnessed the effect of Seeger singing the same song at another concert. "I have seen several hundred white people in Atlanta who came to a Negro college to hear a favorite folk singer . . . caught up in the spirit of his singing, and joining hands with Negroes and whites near them to sing 'We Shall Overcome,' the battle song of the student sit-in movement," Zinn wrote.[81]

Bernice Johnson Reagon adjusted Zinn's impression of that same night in Georgia: "It was Peter Seeger . . . chained to a struggle by the physical and musical presence of some of its most radical organizers, the SNCC 'Freedom Singers,' that created the power of the moment."[82]

Seeger had long sought out authenticity—the holy grail of folklorists and musicologists. He had also attempted to project "authenticity" in his performance style, though he learned to avoid some of the more embarrassing affectations of the earnest citybilly folk musicians (Toshi used to tease him about being the Harvard boy wearing work boots and a flannel shirt when he performed).

"While I am a singer of folk songs, I am not a folk singer," he explained.[83] He sought out real folk singers, apprenticing himself to and performing with the real deal. Huddie Ledbetter had served on chain gangs in Louisiana, and Woody Guthrie had been an Okie displaced by the dust storms. This time was different. As his young protégé Bernice explained, in working with the Freedom Singers, he was now "chained to a struggle."[84] This struggle had deep roots in the Black church, and its music was a potent force. As Andrew Young discovered in Albany and through many subsequent campaigns, the songs of the Black church that became the songs of the movement were "a bottomless reservoir of spiritual power."[85]

Bernice Johnson Reagon had grown up in the Black church, her father a preacher; now, through the intersection of song and struggle, she connected with the faith of her ancestors in a new and profound way. "In jail I met up with a few of those Bible stories. I got common with Paul and Silas," she remembered with laughter. "They sang and prayed until the jail's door opened. Well, the same thing happened to us in Albany." Scripture came alive. "Sermons [came] down out of the pulpit and [were] just walking around in the jail cells. And I said, 'Oh, okay, this is what you were talking about.' And I always thought from then on that Paul and Silas was like SNCC workers. . . . No wonder they got arrested!"[86]

Pete Seeger, unlike Bernice, had next to no church tradition in his New England childhood, and what there was, was very white: his mother was a Unitarian, and his father, as Pete explained, was "a member of the Marxist church."[87] A lifelong communist, Seeger was committed to what he jokingly referred to as his "diabolical materialism."[88] Spirituals had, however, always been a part of his repertoire. "I sang 'em for the fun of it, 'Swing Low Sweet Chariot,' or 'Didn't My Lord Deliver Daniel,' or 'Joshua Fought the Battle of Jericho.'"[89] For years, Seeger felt he had to justify his use of this religious material to his friends. Writing to a left-wing musicologist and labor historian in 1959, he said, "I do not like to arbitrarily categorize many Negro spirituals simply as religious songs because I think they are great songs from any point of view."[90] Similarly, Lee Hays explained People's Songs' promotion of hymns and spirituals: "I think this appealed to something in the left wing, some kind of sense of good old Americanism of some sort."[91] But the songs Seeger sang in the movement were not simply fun to sing, nor did they express "a good old Americanism."

The music started working a change in Seeger, one he wouldn't acknowledge until many years later when he had almost lost his own voice. "I was deeply, deeply changed by the civil rights movement," he confessed.[92] "At age 74, [I] finally decided I have made my peace with at least the word 'God.' Most of my youth, thinking religion was the opiate of the people, I disliked using the word. But I found, like many other European-Americans, that I truly loved the religious songs of African-Americans. It was as though I rediscovered my own humanity through them."[93]

Just like for Bernice, words from the Christian Scriptures gained a fresh resonance for Pete Seeger.

> *I love everybody, I love everybody, I love everybody in*
> *my heart.*

The teenage girls were still singing behind Toshi and Pete on the road. The syncopation of the song gave them a restless, dancing energy. Pete's hand twitched along to the rhythm as he committed it to memory. And then one of the new verses surprised the veteran folk singer.

> *I love Governor Wallace in my heart.*
> *I love Governor Wallace in my heart.*

Governor George Wallace of Alabama, who had famously intoned, "I say segregation now, segregation tomorrow, segregation forever."

For Pete Seeger, this joyful burst of singing brought alive a piece of Christian teaching, "If any one says, 'I love God,' and hates his brother, he is a liar; for he who does not love his brother whom he has seen, cannot love God whom he has not seen" (1 John 4:20 RSV). It played over in his mind in the succeeding weeks. In June he gave the baccalaureate address at a college. Telling the students about the march and the girls singing, he said, "I'd like to commend this spirit to you, because I believe that in the period of history we are entering, it is going to be very difficult to love a large portion of the human race living here in the USA."[94]

Seeger was anticipating the escalating conflict and political polarization around the war in Vietnam and poverty at home: divisions that over the next few years brought riots to cities and death to college campuses and mass protests to the capital. He knew as well as anyone that it could be hard to love your neighbor. "Pete Seeger! That Commie!" exclaimed one of his neighbors in his hometown. "American boys are dying in Vietnam, and he wants to sing here. He doesn't even deserve to live here. If he likes Russia so much, why doesn't he go there?"[95] Drawing from his experience of the HUAC witch hunts that nearly sent him to jail and the violence directed toward him and his family on the road from Peekskill, he delivered what must be one of the strangest lines ever given to students at their graduation. "I believe the best thing you can do is make up your mind that you will be living in an unpleasant world for much of your lives." It could be a depressing prospect. A couple of years earlier he had explained to teenagers, "More people die from discouragement than any disease. And why do people get discouraged? Because they feel that life's a joyless struggle."[96]

But on Alabama's Highway 80, Seeger encountered the spirit of unity and the joyful song of love and forgiveness.[97] Listening to the girls singing, he "realized that this March had something unique in the whole world. Anybody in America that thought that this March was full of a bunch of angry people shouting out malignant thoughts [were wrong]," he told the students. "On the contrary, it was one of the most happy—purely joyful things—you could imagine."[98]

For Pete, the Selma march meant far more to him than simply proving a theory of folk song production. It was a vindication of the hope that drove his work: he had spent his life helping to create the conditions for this very burst of joyful, creative, unifying, defiant, power-challenging, and world-changing singing. It brought to his mind another scripture. "If we are in for a struggle to keep our country from falling into bad ways don't think it need be a joyless struggle. Far from it. As Jesus urged his disciples, 'Be of Good Cheer.'"[99]

Soon after lunch, they reached the outskirts of Montgomery. Now numbering well over a thousand, the protestors filled the two westbound lanes of the highway. They marched past the airport where celebrities and dignitaries were flying in from all over the country for the next day's march to the capitol building. Black maids and janitors in the motels lining the road stopped their work and stared.[100] Press photographers swarmed around Martin Luther King and Coretta at the head of the line. Then the heavens opened—a hard rain soaking everyone to the skin.

The joyful harmony of the united voices defied both the elements and the governor. Scripture came out of the pulpit, as Bernice said, and walked the streaming steaming asphalt of Alabama: "In the world ye shall have tribulation: but be of good cheer; I have overcome the world" (John 16:33 KJV).

> *We shall overcome*
> *We shall overcome*
> *We shall overcome someday*

The song had different layers of meaning. By marching across the Edmund Pettus Bridge and following the highway all the way to the state's capitol, the marchers had overcome Sheriff Jim Clark and Governor Wallace. Those who had answered the call and traveled to Selma yearned to overcome segregation and America's systems of white supremacy. For Pete, as the rain fell, the emphasis in the song lay with the "We"— it was the collective—"the whole human race, which must stick together if we are going to solve crucial problems that face us all."[101] Here in Montgomery, as he had seen many times before and would see many times again, it was the power of singing that helped bridge what Seeger called "the oceans of misunderstanding between the peoples of this world."[102] He knew that this song he had helped shape and popularize "wasn't just a song for Alabama and Mississippi but for any member of the human race anyplace that gets a little discouraged and wonders what the future is going to bring. And this song has a kind of calm confidence that says we can, *we* can."[103]

For fifteen solid saturating minutes it rained, and for fifteen minutes they sang. Then, as suddenly as it had started, the rain stopped. The song leaders seized on the metaphor:

> *The sun breaks through the clouds*
> *The sun breaks through the clouds*
> *The sun breaks through the clouds today!*[104]

The bedraggled and triumphant column entered the gates of the City of St. Jude and headed across the muddy athletic fields toward the tents.[105] As everything sank in the mud, volunteers struggled to construct a makeshift stage from plywood and coffin crates donated by a local funeral home.[106] They were trying to get it ready for Harry Belafonte's "Stars for Freedom" concert, set to feature Nina Simone; Peter, Paul, and Mary; Mahalia Jackson; Joan Baez; Dick Gregory; Leonard Bernstein; Sammy Davis Jr.; and James Baldwin, among others.[107] But Pete and Toshi could not stay. They gathered their bags and found a ride to the airport.[108]

The couple walked into the terminal of the Montgomery Municipal Airport. Mud-streaked and damp, Pete carried his long banjo slung over his shoulder in a homemade leatherette bag.[109] He decided he would wash up before their flight. Toshi realized how conspicuous they both looked and was suddenly nervous. "Anybody looking at us knows we would have been on that march," she said quietly to her oblivious husband. "Be very careful when you go to the men's room."[110] Pete returned to his wife without incident, and the two made their way to the gate.

Once they were safely on the plane and in their seats, the indefatigable apostle of the Joyful Struggle pulled out his notebook and started writing an epistle to the folk-singing readers of *Broadside* magazine:

Montgomery, Alabama
Wednesday, March 24, 1965

Dear Broadside—Herewith I send you a few songs heard during the past day and a half, sung by a very wonderful group of people . . . [111]

Toni Morrison

(1931–2019)

Toni Morrison in 2012; Justin Knight Photography

QUIET AS IT'S KEPT

Embedded Theology in Toni Morrison's Fiction

Ann Hostetler

When the second biennial conference of the Toni Morrison Society was held in 2000 in Lorain, Ohio, Morrison's birthplace, my friend Katharine and I decided to make the pilgrimage. We were both English professors at small liberal arts colleges in Indiana, a four hours' drive from Lorain. As readers and teachers of Toni Morrison's novels, we were passionate about the value of her beautifully wrought, morally engaged art both in the classroom and for ourselves. Teaching her novels enabled us to open multiple perspectives at once for our students, prompting them to examine their own lives and assumptions. Her evocative exploration of African American characters and consciousness dignified her subjects and widened the imaginative territory of American literature. Morrison had published her first novel, *The Bluest Eye*, as a single working mother in 1970. Katharine and I were both working mothers; Katharine brought her nursing baby on our trip, and my husband stayed home to care for our four children. Morrison was a beacon of hope and possibility. By 2000, Morrison had published six novels over a span of thirty years, won both the Pulitzer Prize and the Nobel Prize, and was possibly the best-known living novelist in America. The conference would take us to her hometown, which had inspired the setting for *The Bluest Eye*. Although we knew her work well, we knew much less about Toni Morrison herself.

*   *   *

Toni Morrison was born Chloe Ardelia Wofford to working-class parents in Lorain, Ohio, a steel town on the shores of Lake Erie, on February 18, 1931. The second of four children, she came of age in an era before television broadcast its stories to a mass audience. Chloe and her older sister, Lois, remained close friends throughout their long lives. Chloe learned to read at the age of four and recalled her home being filled with music and storytelling. The families of their parents—George Carl Wofford and Ellah Ramah Wofford (née Willis)— had migrated to northern Ohio from the South (Georgia and Alabama, respectively) in search of better jobs and living conditions. Lorain provided work and an integrated working-class neighborhood in which George and Ella met and where they raised their family. "I never lived in a black neighborhood," Morrison said. "There was always a mix of races and nationalities." All the local teens attended a single high school but separated to worship in a large variety of churches on Sundays.[1] In her early years, Morrison suffered many of the physical hardships that her characters do. Although her father always worked—"he held three jobs at once for seventeen years"—the family never owned their own home while Morrison was growing up.[2] Instead, they lived in a series of rentals, moving frequently. Once, when they were unable to pay the rent, the landlord set fire to the building while they were inside.

Although Morrison's family lived frugally, her parents were devoted to family life and instilled a sense of dignity in their children. Her mother subscribed to several book clubs, a significant investment in a family that scraped together the money to pay the rent. Music was essential. Her mother made sure her children had piano lessons, although Morrison recalled that she and her sister Lois wondered after their first lessons whether something was wrong with them, since everyone else in their extended family could play so easily. Morrison's grandfather, John Solomon Willis, born into slavery, was also an accomplished violinist. He was "a musician who managed to hold onto his violin but not his land," Morrison recalls in an early essay, "A Slow Walk of Trees (as Grandmother Would Say), Hopeless (as Grandfather Would Say)."[3] Although "he lost eighty-eight acres of his mother's Indian land [allotment] to legal predators," he held onto his violin, using it as a source of income when his carpentry skills were not able to earn. His name, Solomon, along with his musical expressiveness, was immortalized in Morrison's third novel, *Song of Solomon.* In addition to music, education was important in Morrison's family. Her grandmother, Ardelia Wilkins, Solomon's wife, insisted that the family leave the Kentucky town they had moved to "because the teacher did not know long division."[4]

The Bluest Eye, Morrison's debut novel, begins with the text of the "Dick and Jane" primer used to teach over 85 million American children to read between 1930 and 1970.[5] The books, published for beginning readers by Scott Foresman, feature a white family with two children, a boy and a girl, and two pets, a cat and a dog. The primer text is repeated three times in the book before the novel proper begins, the letters growing closer and closer, until the text is completely run together, suggesting the ways in which repetition embeds propaganda into the consumer. With this frame for her novel, Morrison evokes the site of instruction, demonstrating how even an innocent-seeming text can be deeply complicit in the promulgation of white supremacy. Over fifty years later, *The Bluest Eye* still serves as a primer on white racism, revealing its damaging effects on the lives of its young, black female protagonists, and the ways in which racism is internalized, not only by individuals, but by a culture. Whereas Morrison's primary first-person narrator, a young black girl named Claudia MacTeer, resists the larger culture's mania for blue-eyed dolls and Shirley Temple movies,

Pecola Breedlove, the unwanted child from next door who comes to live at the MacTeer home, has absorbed these values—and the concomitant self-loathing—completely. She believes that if only she had blue eyes, she would be loved and healed. Antiracism is, of course, a project much larger than the individual. As the novel demonstrates in the lives of children in a midcentury Ohio town, it takes a village. Ultimately, it takes a nation.

"Quiet as it's kept." The first words of Morrison's text to follow the primer contrast with its formulaic language. Such a colloquial phrase might have been overheard by young girls as their mothers and female relatives and neighbors gossiped in the kitchen. Morrison uses it to signal the reader's entry into an intimate and particular social world. The narrator, Claudia, lived in such a world with her older sister, and Morrison draws the reader into that world through its specific phrases, sight, sounds, rhythms. It was a world akin to Morrison's own growing up. Claudia Mac-Teer's family cares for the welfare of its members and extends that care to others in the community, such as the destitute girl, Pecola Breedlove, put "outdoors" by her own family.

* * *

Morrison wasn't expected to attend the Lorain conference in person, but she was everywhere present in spirit. Morrison's sister and several of her childhood friends showed up and looked very much as though they were enjoying themselves, nudging each other and laughing frequently in the front row when mention of a salient detail from *The Bluest Eye* overlapped with their childhood memories of growing up in Lorain. It was a setting in which literature and life could freely intermingle, at least for a weekend. In addition to guest speakers and scholarly papers, the conference offered a tour of local sites that appeared in *The Bluest Eye*. We piled into a couple of school buses in search of the street where Isaly's Ice Cream Parlor once offered cold sweets to sweating children, then to the waterfront with its big houses where the character Pauline Breedlove, Pecola's mother, had worked as domestic help, escaping the drab violence of her own life in a crisp white uniform. The young Chloe Wofford had also worked in one of these big houses when she was a teenager.

There was no "Toni Morrison home" to tour because the author's family had occupied at least half a dozen rentals while she was growing up. A few doors down from one of the rentals, we saw a house that had been converted from a storefront: it bore an uncanny resemblance to the Breedlove home described in *The Bluest Eye*.

The theme of the conference was, fittingly, "The Meanings of Home in the Work of Toni Morrison." I remember one presentation in particular that focused on Morrison's novel *Paradise*. Eleanor Traylor, a contemporary of Morrison's when she taught at Howard University in the early 1960s, explored the mysterious man who appears to Dovey, the wife of one of the town's leaders, in the garden. All of a sudden, her rich voice swelled with a hymn:

> *I come to the garden alone*
> *While the dew is still on the roses*
> *And the voice I hear whispered in my ear*
> *The love of God discloses.*

The audience responded, joining the chorus:

> *And He walks with me and He talks with me*
> *And He tells me I am His own*
> *And the joy we share as we tarry there*
> *None other has ever known.*

I had never heard anyone sing in an academic session before. Tears surged to my eyes as speaker and audience sang back and forth to one another. A sense of wonder lifted my chest, trembling with fear and joy. Beneath the surface of this delivery something else was happening—something more profound than anything I'd ever experienced in the academy. More layers of Morrison's text began to open up to me through this powerful readerly response to her work. The African American scholars and attendees in the room revealed a common bond through the familiar hymn, and it resonated with the importance of hymn singing in my own Mennonite background, something I usually kept carefully hidden in professional settings. Perhaps it was I who was being opened up.

As though our collective attention to her work in her hometown had summoned her, Morrison made a surprise visit to the conference on the last afternoon. She was warm and appreciative of the society, apologizing for being unable to attend the earlier sessions, and joking about the ordeal of walking in the elegant high-heeled shoes she preferred. Society members were directed to sit surrounding Morrison in the auditorium seats and pose for a picture. I was invited into a community where I felt mysteriously at home.

*   *   *

To understand the soundtrack of Morrison's imagination, it is necessary to delve into her past and her religious formation. Morrison's mother was a staunch member of the AME (African Methodist Episcopal) church in Lorain, which Morrison attended as a child with her family, absorbing the language and rhythms of sermons, Scripture, and hymns.[6] Morrison describes her mother as "one of those people who sang all the time, and with a beautiful voice. She never took any lessons; she was just a natural singer. She sang better than anybody I ever heard."[7] In a 2017 interview with David Carrasco, a historian of religion, Morrison attributes much of her own religious formation to her mother's singing: "I learned religious language through the hymns and sermons," she says. "[My mother] sang opera, the blues, and religious music. She not only sang in the church, she sang all the time, when she was cooking, sweeping, hanging out clothes." The sound of her mother's singing voice also taught Morrison to listen for what lay beneath the words. "When she sang, I could hear if she was sad, I could hear if she was happy, and her ability to communicate that way gave me a sense of how to write that way. I know how I feel when I get something right in my writing, and now I wonder if my interior feeling is like hers when she sang in very satisfying ways, in ways that lifted her and us up in our little lower-middle-class lives."[8]

At the age of twelve, Morrison became a Catholic, inspired by a cousin who had taken her to Mass. Several other family members were Catholic as well, which likely softened the decision for her mother.[9] "I liked the aesthetics of being in the Catholic church, and so my mother agreed. I was taken by the liturgy and beauty." Morrison also found church to be a place that taught more than doctrine: "[The] church setting taught me a social closeness, and I learned black people's assumptions of the ways people should treat each other."[10] With her conversion, she took the name "Anthony" as her saint's name, using it to replace her middle name, Ardelia, her maternal grandmother's name. But it wasn't until she became a college student at Howard University in Washington, DC, that she changed her first name to Toni, because her fellow students had trouble pronouncing her given name.

Throughout her life, Morrison didn't exactly hide her Catholicism, but she kept her own practice private, often referring to herself as a lapsed Catholic in interviews, and voicing criticisms of the church. However, David Carrasco, a colleague of Morrison's at Princeton and a good friend during her last twenty years, told me that during her time at Princeton, she often attended early morning mass, and that her funeral was held at the Catholic church she attended close to her home on the Hudson River.[11]

Always an avid reader, Morrison majored in English and minored in classics at Howard, but found her most engaging literary education in the theater department. She joined the modern

dance troupe and toured with the Howard Players. After graduation, she earned an MA in English from Cornell University, writing
her thesis on alienation in the works of Virginia Woolf and William
Faulkner. Two years of teaching at Texas Southern University, a
historically Black institution, ensued before Morrison returned
to Howard as a junior faculty member. While teaching at Howard, she met her future husband, Harold Morrison. The marriage
ended in divorce in 1964, after the birth of her first son, a trip to
Europe, and her second pregnancy. But Toni Morrison held onto
her married surname, the surname of her sons.

Morrison's first attempts at fiction were prompted by the writers' group she joined at Howard University in the early 1960s when
she was on the faculty. At first, she brought short pieces to the
group that she had written as an undergraduate, but, as she told
Terry Gross on *Fresh Air*, the group served amazing lunches and
"they wouldn't let you continue to come if you were just reading
old stuff. So I had to think up something new if I was going to continue to have this really good food and really good company."[12]

After her divorce, as a young single mother of a baby and a
toddler, Morrison left her job at Howard and moved back to live
with her parents in Lorain for a short time. Determined to make
her own way, she found a job in textbook editing in Syracuse, New
York, with the understanding that the company would soon be
moving to New York City. Alone in an unfamiliar place with her
young boys, Morrison returned to the story she had begun at Howard, filling the quiet hours when they slept with writing. "It took
five years . . . to write that little book because I wasn't thinking
about publishing, I was thinking about that narrative and what I
wanted to say."[13] Once Morrison discovered her secret oasis, the
act of writing became "the place where I live. It's where I have
control. It's where nobody tells me what to do. It's where my imagination is fecund and I am really at my best," she observed at the
age of eighty-four. Meanwhile, as her editing career soon moved
to the prestigious fiction division of Random House, Morrison be-

came an arbiter of culture in her role as an advocate for new Black writers such Toni Cade Bambara, Angela Davis, Henry Dumas, Leon Forrest, and June Jordan.[14] Here she also sponsored the creation of *The Black Book*, a compendium of images and newspaper clippings pertaining to Black life over the past century. The book proved popular with Black readers who were more reluctant to invest in fiction. In this book, Morrison also discovered the story of Margaret Garner, a slave woman who killed her own child when she and her family were recaptured by slave catchers, a story that would later become the kernel of her Pulitzer Prize–winning novel, *Beloved*.

Morrison published her first two novels, *The Bluest Eye* (1970) and *Sula* (1972), while working as an editor at Random House. For her third novel, *Song of Solomon* (1977), Morrison chose a male protagonist and a quest motif. Invoking the spirit of her recently deceased father, Morrison found the courage and insight to write a novel from a male perspective that created a major sensation. When *Song of Solomon* won the National Book Critics' Circle Award, Morrison finally felt that she could claim "writer" as her occupation. She continued working for Random House in an editorial role, during which time she published one more novel, *Tar Baby* (1981), before resigning in 1983 to take an endowed professorship at SUNY Albany. *Beloved* (1987), Morrison's landmark book about slavery, was awarded the Pulitzer Prize in 1988. In 1989, Morrison became the Albert F. Goheen Professor in Humanities at Princeton University. During her tenure at Princeton, Morrison published three more novels: *Jazz* (1992), *Paradise* (1998), and *Love* (2003). She also wrote a book of literary criticism and edited several collections of essays.

Rising before dawn and fully entering the private world of her imagination to write, Morrison always viewed the publication of her fiction as an act that served the community, the African American community in particular. But the private imagination is also fed by the great storehouse of artistic manifestations in the wider world. Her inclination to draw upon the oral storytelling of her childhood, including ancestral myths, was reinforced when she discovered the novels of Gabriel García Márquez, especially *One Hundred Years of Solitude*, whose English translation was published in the United States in 1970, the same year that Morrison's first novel appeared. She recalled: "I was sitting in my office at Random House . . . just turning the pages of *One Hundred Years of Solitude*. There was something so familiar about the novel, so recognizable to me. It was a certain kind of freedom, a structural freedom, a [different] notion of a beginning, middle, and end. Culturally, I felt intimate with him because he was happy to mix the living and the dead. His characters were on intimate terms with the supernatural world, and that's the way stories were told in my house."[15] Recognizing the resonance between Márquez's cultural cosmos and that of her African American community, Morrison felt empowered to more fully articulate a mythic subtext for the novel. This is just one example among many of how Morrison continued to explore and expand her vision through her work as a reader and editor, feeding her writer's imagination.

Morrison's increasing fame as a writer required the crafting of a public persona—an image guarded and curated. She limited photographs, carefully selected interviewers, and chose to speak in venues she could support with integrity. In a 1993 interview with David Streitfeld for the *Washington Post*, Morrison said she had "mastered the art of staying behind the curtain,"[16] but after winning the Nobel, staying behind the curtain was no longer an option. Media coverage, interviews, and opinion pieces reveal the incredible generosity with which she opened herself to public conversation. Through these personal appearances, Morrison herself took on the role of cultural storyteller, revealing, bit by bit, more of her heritage, more of her values, and taking on the role of a cultural and moral arbiter. There is as yet no official biography, but certain elements recur and are even developed in her interviews over the years: her preferred time to write before dawn in the quiet of morning; the powerful influence of storytelling in her own family; her father's strong work ethic and support; the culturally diverse working-class neighborhood in which she grew up. Toni Morrison was ultimately Chloe Wofford's most powerful creation. She lived her theology, entering public discourse through editing, teaching, and, most of all, writing.

In her last decades she began to share more details from her closely guarded personal life, including the Catholic faith that guided her artistic imagination. Speaking at the Catholic Worker House in Washington, DC, in November 2012 on the occasion of Dorothy Day's 116th birthday, Morrison's friend Cornel West offered, "You know Toni Morrison is Catholic. Many people do not realize that she is one of the great Catholic writers. Like Flannery O'Connor, she has an incarnational conception of human existence. We Protestants are too individualistic. I think we need to learn from Catholics who are always centered on community."[17]

*   *   *

Artists nudge us toward epiphanies—shifts in our ways of seeing—but they rarely offer a catechism. "I am not an 'ist' novelist," Morrison told Zia Jaffrey in response to her question as to whether *Paradise* (1998) is a feminist novel. "In order to be as free as I possibly can, in my own imagination, I can't take positions that are closed. Everything I've ever done, in the writing world, has been to expand articulation, rather than to close it, to open doors, sometimes, not even closing the book—leaving the endings open for reinterpretation, revisitation, a little ambiguity."[18] Looking at Morrison's work in theological terms requires us to take the same open approach. As Shirley Stave says in the introduction to *Toni Morrison and the Bible: Contested Intertextualities*, "She requires her readers to push back the parameters of received knowledge and tread on holy ground not merely with reverence, but also with a fully engaged political and critical consciousness."[19]

Trained as a literary scholar, I had never been asked to read Toni Morrison theologically until I received the invitation to write a chapter for this book. Yet the invitation prompted me to recognize theological content everywhere in Morrison's work. Even as Morrison probes the belief systems of her characters, she embeds theological inquiry in the craft of her fiction. Her novels include biblical references and an array of preachers, both ordained and self-appointed, showing human traits and limitations. These preachers may expound or act on theological conviction, but for Morrison, the location of theological inquiry is in the relationships between characters in her fiction. "Lived theology emerges from the movements, transactions, and exchanges of the spirit of God in human experience," says theologian Charles Marsh, and this is exactly what Morrison portrays in her novels.[20]

In a chapter of this length, it is impossible to delve into all eleven of Morrison's novels, but it should be noted that each one is rooted in a particular historical and cultural matrix, even as it contextualizes profound theological questions in the form of stories: What is the meaning of human life? Why does evil exist? What is to be learned from our failure to love and care for each other? What is the process by which we should live in creation and with each other? And why do stories matter—those we've been told, those we create, those we reinterpret and live into?

Morrison's novels engage with the forgotten, the overlooked, the wounded, the despised. They invite readers to vicariously embody the thoughts, emotions, and experiences of Black women, girls, veterans; orphans and displaced survivors of trauma; slaves and pioneers; the disenfranchised and the powerful; the marginal, the wild, the holy. They strive to embody a fully developed African American culture and consciousness for Black readers, yet their invitation calls to all readers who believe that racism limits the imagination. Morrison's concern for "the least of these," her invitation to readers to enter the minds and thoughts of others with respect and regard for their humanity, echoes the voice of Jesus:

not a doctrinal call to salvation, not a sentimentalized panacea for life's brutal injustices, but a challenge to love one's neighbor as one's self, an acknowledgment of how hard that is to do, and a call to forgive the unforgivable in order to open the door to recognition and reconciliation.

"In the stories, I place the characters on a cliff. I push them as far as I can to see what they are made of," Morrison explained. "I say to them, 'You really think you're in love? Well, let me see what it's like under these circumstances. You think this is important: what about this?' I place them in that tragic mode so that I can get at what those emotions really are. What is interesting to me is that under the circumstances in which the people in my books live there is this press toward love."[21] Love is at the heart of Morrison's embedded theology. Learning to love—both self and other—is the purpose of life. The love we receive from parents and caregivers forms the basis of our own sense of worthiness. We experience love when another person witnesses and creates space for us. We need the mirror of the other in order to see the self. But love is conditioned by the fallen world in which we live. Thus "love is never any better than the lover," Morrison concludes in *The Bluest Eye*. Sometimes we can only see love when it is missing. Morrison characterized her method as "sublimely didactic in the sense that I can only warn by taking something away."[22]

*　　　*　　　*

When Morrison arrived in Princeton in 1989, her colleague Elaine Pagels, well known for her work on the gnostic gospels, invited her to lunch.[23] Pagels had first encountered Morrison's work through *Song of Solomon*, recommended to her enthusiastically by her friend, theologian James Cone. Since Pagels had been recently widowed and Morrison was divorced, Pagels thought the two women might develop a friendship. Before leaving her office to meet Morrison, Pagels slipped a copy of her book *The Gnostic*

Gospels—just issued in paperback that fall—into her purse. When she presented the book to Morrison, Morrison laughed, "You're not fast enough for me!" Clearly Morrison, already devouring and enjoying Pagels's work in feminist theology and alternative scriptures, was hungry for more. Pagels introduced Morrison to "Thunder, Perfect Mind," one of the gnostic gospels, which captivated Morrison's imagination.[24]

As an imaginative thinker and creative artist, Morrison dismantled categories, stereotypes, and clichés as she probed the human condition. She also continued to develop and widen her perspectives on theology and spiritual authority, finding resonance in multiple sources and filtering them back through her fiction. Pagels described walking into the Atelier at Princeton[25] and seeing several musicians and dancer Jacques D'Amboise performing what she described as gorgeous songs, written by Toni Morrison, inspired by "Thunder." Morrison's five poems inspired by "Thunder"—her only published poetry—were issued in a limited edition in 2002.[26] The female voice of "Thunder" makes sweeping, paradoxical claims as it embraces contradictions: "I am the first and last. / I am the honored and scorned. / I am the whore and the holy. / I am the wife and the virgin. / I am the mother and daughter. / I am the members of my mother and the barren one with many sons."[27] This voice both claims and destabilizes authority and seems to come from both spiritual and earthly sources at once. It appears to have influenced the narrators of subsequent novels *Jazz* and *Love*, who are partially identified but also disembodied.

I asked Elaine Pagels about the juxtaposition of Protestant and Catholic communities in Morrison's novel *Paradise*, and where she thought the novelist's mature sympathies lay. Pagels noted that Morrison was deeply engaged with biblical sources and admired the art of preaching displayed in Protestant churches. But Catholicism—visually rich, full of stories, and hagiography—offered more fertile ground for her imagination, especially cross-culturally. For instance, in *Paradise*, the Catholicism of the convent blends with native religious beliefs and Santeria from Brazil and ulti-mately merges with a Black Madonna figure and fragments of the Nag Hammadi.

*   *   *

In 2002, two years after the Lorain conference, Toni Morrison granted me an interview for a paper I was developing on the prob-lem of pedagogy in *Paradise*, her then most recent novel. When I was ushered into her Princeton office, she had just finished some Chinese takeout, the residue congealing in an open Styrofoam container. She was smoking a cigarette, exhaling toward a mini-air purifier on her desk. She looked up and smiled warmly, the famous dreadlocks framing her graceful face, and motioned for me to have a seat. I had sent some questions in advance, and they sat, printed out, on her desk, her flowing cursive filling the spaces between the printed text. I wanted to pick them up and read them, but of course I did not. It took me a few moments to find words. She helped out. "There was something you said about one of my novels that interested me," she began.

We talked for nearly two hours about teaching, about charac-ters in her novels, about her own practice as a teacher, me try-ing to jot down notes as she spoke, since she did not want me to tape the conversation—until the conversation got so interesting that I forgot to write anything at all.[28] When I mentioned the mo-ment at the Lorain conference when Eleanor Traylor had led a call-and-response to "He Comes to Me in the Garden," Morrison responded with a few bars of the chorus.

"Was that Jesus in Dovey's garden?" I asked, referring to the character in *Paradise* who has sporadic encounters in her garden with a handsome stranger.[29]

"She's like a lot of women I knew when I was growing up," Morrison replied. "There were many women who had a personal relationship with Jesus and would talk with him regularly during their day. My own mother, for instance." Morrison told me that when she earned her first substantial check from publishing a novel, she offered to take her family on a vacation to Aruba, but her mother was deathly afraid of flying. Morrison stayed firm in her determination to travel, and her mother eventually packed her suitcase. When they arrived on the island, Morrison said she asked her mother what had made her change her mind. Her mother reported that she had had a talk with her maker, and that she had told him that she would not think much of him if he let her down in the middle of the ocean on this special trip her daughter had planned for her.

We then delved into *Paradise*, Morrison's sixth novel, that contrasts a Black utopian community, Ruby, in Oklahoma and the convent seventeen miles down the road that takes in abandoned and lost women. In true Morrison style, it begins shockingly, highlighting both race and the novel's climax: "They shoot the white girl first." The "they" are the male posse of leaders from Ruby who view the women at the convent as a threat to the order and safety they have created in this earthly refuge. We never learn who the "white girl" is—but the mention of a white presence indicates that the convent embraces racial diversity, whereas in Ruby, the darkest skin is prized. The novel is full of religious imagery, sermons, arguments about salvation and safety. Although the book begins in violence, Morrison says: "Love of God is what the book is about. It's about spiritual love—how it gets played out and how it gets corrupted. For instance, the old nuns at the convent are literally abandoned by the church to which they have given their lives. Ruby is founded by the vigor of black Protestants who survived and prospered. But what saved them in the past could not be transferred along the generations."[30] Thus true theology is not housed in institutions, but in the relations of everyday life. The way we live our theology can undermine or subvert or redeem the institutional versions we espouse. Still disturbed by the murder of the women at the convent, characters who had won my imaginative sympathy in the novel, I asked Morrison why the women had lost the struggle for their version of love and redemption in the novel. She countered:

> To say that the women lost is to forget all that they learned. They claimed their own voices and found a ground from which to speak. They were able to acknowledge their desires and to use their dreams and their art to realize their own identity. . . . And at the end of the book their lives take on other dimensions. . . .
>
> That's why I chose to use the New Testament motif of resurrection. After his resurrection, Jesus appears to those who want to see him. Vision is a kind of life. The women of the convent in Paradise are not deified, but after death they appear to those who want to see them, just as the risen Christ appeared to his disciples. It's bigger than nostalgia. The person who has the vision, converses with it, becomes larger than themselves. The language of these passages in the novel is not just lyrical, but transitional, as between two realities.[31]

Thus, Morrison suggests that love of God must be constantly renewed in our current context in our everyday relationships. We cannot hand God on to others any more than we can hand on love or faith. To live is to experience God's love again and again in the activities of our daily lives.

*　　　*　　　*

Morrison was a national exemplar of freedom in letters; President Barack Obama, an admirer of her novels, awarded her the Presidential Medal of Freedom in 2012. Ever since the 1993 Nobel Award, her influence had grown internationally as well. The Louvre Museum in Paris invited her to curate a series of special exhibits on the theme of *The Foreigner's Home* in 2006. She used this opportunity to raise questions of power and access across the globe. In Paris, she extended a platform and audience to numerous immigrant artists, slam poets, and others—especially those from Francophone countries—who would not otherwise have been invited into such an auspicious setting. She was beloved in Mexico, and visited Mexico City—where Gabriel García Márquez had written *One Hundred Years of Solitude*—with theologian and anthropologist David Carrasco, who introduced her to the rich mythology of the Aztecs.

In her final decade, Morrison was asked to speak to theologians and to express the vision of her moral imagination as the Ingersoll Lecturer at Harvard Divinity School in 2012 and as Harvard University's Norton Lecturer in 2016. The first of these visits, a symposium organized by Carrasco, culminated in *Goodness and the Literary Imagination*, an edited collection inspired by Morrison's lecture title to which scholars of religion, history, and culture contributed. Her Norton Lectures were published as *The Origin of Others*, introduced by Ta-Nehisi Coates, in a fitting tribute from a leading writer of the next generation. In these lectures Morrison reveals not only the cruel and jarring results of the "othering" of Black people in slavery, but even the "othering" she experienced within her own family, when as a child she overheard her very imposing and very dark-complected grandmother MacTeer pronounce her and her sister Lois as having been "tampered with" because of their light-colored skin. These publications echo the theological themes woven through Morrison's work all along: a foundational commitment to dialogue and dignity, a belief that the most maimed human being is worthy of our understanding, that within each human being is the possibility of redemption. According to Nick Ripatrazone, "Morrison said it is a sense of 'transcending love' that makes 'the New Testament . . . so pertinent to black literature—the lamb, the victim, the vulnerable one who does die but nevertheless lives.'"

*   *   *

The last time I saw Toni Morrison in person was at a gathering of Morrison scholars in the banquet rooms above the Oberlin Inn. We met in the fall of 2013 to celebrate the establishment of the Toni Morrison Society's archives at Oberlin College,[32] and Morrison joined us in her wheelchair after the Society's brunch, generously offering to answer any and all questions from members present. Morrison spoke about her novel-in-progress set in the midst of the challenges of the immediate present, which would be published as *God Help the Child*, her last work of fiction. She took questions about her previous work, including her unpublished play, *Dreaming Emmett*. At one point she forgot the name of a town in one of her books and joked, "Too many books," which brought immediate protest from her audience. Speaking more personally, she gave a highly entertaining account of meeting Barack Obama on stage when he awarded her the Presidential Medal of Freedom. In a confidential tone that invoked the phrase "quiet as it's kept," she described his "nice man's hands," bringing chuckles from her audience. "My niece tells me I said, 'Watch out for my hair' when he put that thing over my head. . . . Then he bent down and whispered in my ear—two sentences . . . and I can't remember for the life of me what he said."

In her concern with social life and the social construction of reality, Morrison committed herself to standing in the flow of time as both descendant and ancestor, the ancestor not only of a family line but of a literary culture. She still speaks to us through her work and example. I'm grateful that she recorded all of her novels as audiobooks so that we can still literally hear her voice. Throughout my adult life I've claimed Morrison as mentor, and now ancestor, of my imaginative life, one who prompts me to consider the communities in which I participate as reader and writer—to probe the stories that have birthed me and the language legacy I leave for future readers—and to show me what is possible. Her theology of lived experience, her desire to discover the holy in the everyday, is something to which I aspire: to show up for myself and others, to find what connects me to the world and to nourish those connections, to always be open to new perspectives in the search for truth, to meet others where they are, to discover my roots as I continue to grow, to be curious and full of laughter as I work toward justice and joy, stewarding the gifts I have been given to contribute to the larger whole.

Jack Egan

(1916–2001)

Jack Egan, 1971; photo courtesy of the University of Notre Dame Archives

LIFE WITH THE PARISH

*Jack Egan and a Chicago Neighborhood's Fight
for Housing Justice*

Daniel P. Rhodes

He arrived at Presentation Catholic Church in the winter of 1966. And yet, "arrived" is not really the right word, for as his friends and fellow priests tell it, Cardinal Cody effectively "sent [him] to pasture" at the parish with the hopes that it might kill him.[1] The move was as ice cold as the frost that smarts the city that time of year, a strong signal from the newly installed archbishop that he would tolerate no rivals among his vicars. Moving Fr. John Jack Egan to Presentation was intended to be a statement.[2]

He never expected a move like this. Egan, affectionately called Fr. Jack, was a key leader in Chicago Catholic circles. At the time, he was the head of the dynamic archdiocesan Office of Urban Affairs and was beloved across the city even beyond the Catholic community for his work on lay ministry, interfaith collaborations, and issues of urban crisis. Small-boned and balding, Fr. Jack had a fair and speckled complexion that betrayed his Irish lineage. He spoke with a nasal voice, a result of his slightly cleft lip. He wasn't a commanding presence, and he didn't seek attention. But he was confident, energetic, and dynamic in his own way. Though not inherently rebellious or activistic, he somehow often found himself on the edge of things—something many Catholics in the city had grown to love about him. Not a mischief-maker by nature, he was, however, a bit of a risk taker and familiar with controversy.

Only a few months before being relegated to Presentation, Fr. Jack marched arm in arm with Reverends C. T. Vivian and Ralph Abernathy at Selma. When a photo of the three men landed on the front page of the *Chicago Daily News*, Jack became an icon for Catholic progressives in the city, legitimating Catholic involvement in the civil rights movement.[3] For many, he was a sign of the new winds of Vatican II beginning to blow open windows of the church, a figure of the new ecumenical and socially conscious faithful engaging the needs and wounds of the world.[4] But it also made him a target of those who looked leerily at the pace of change and the disruption of order.

A complicated figure, Cardinal Cody was an archbishop keen to maintain control. Before coming to Chicago, he had made a name for himself as something of a liberal in New Orleans when he ordered the integration of parochial schools and even excommunicated staunch segregationists.[5] Nevertheless, he cherished authority. New to the archdiocese, he wanted Fr. Egan—along with the other lay-activating priests in the city—to learn that, as his subordinates, their power came through and from him. He perceived anyone with another power base, particularly any priest, as a threat and a troublemaker.[6] When he arrived in Chicago, he was interested in neither collaboration nor coming to understand the vibrant strain of lay activism its priests had cultivated. Thus, among his first actions as archbishop was to put people in their place: and this meant reappointing Egan to the large, destitute, Black parish in order to keep him quiet by overwhelming him with duties.[7] For Fr. Jack, still fragile from a heart attack a few years earlier, it seemed like it might be the end. But he graciously and obediently accepted this assignment.

Though he had served years before in a parish just a few blocks north, the area had changed drastically.[8] From his rectory windows, Egan looked now upon a neighborhood demographically transfigured. Only fifteen years earlier the parish was nearly entirely white. Now it was completely Black.[9] Once-vibrant storefronts were now vacant and falling into disrepair, and unemployment was pervasive.[10] Riding on the massive wave of Black migrants fleeing the Jim Crow South for the "warmth of other suns" in the urban North, the population of North Lawndale had skyrocketed, making it one of the most densely populated places in the city.[11] Its schools were underequipped and overcrowded; truant young people wandered past the church on weekdays, kicking the trash that littered the streets. Crime was high, and violent crime was spreading throughout the parish. Its population was growing increasingly poorer, darker, younger (over half were under fifteen years old), and sicker, all results of the segregation and isolation pinching larger numbers of Black citizens into dire conditions.[12] White working-class families had left for the newly constructed suburbs, taking the stability of modest wealth and social access with them. The middle-class Black families left behind seemed powerless to curb these trends. What Egan found was a neighborhood in quick, almost calculated, decline.

Presentation Catholic Church sat in the northeast corner of the neighborhood, near what is now Homan Square, once the location of the Chicago-based Sears and Roebuck's headquarters, where it had witnessed and weathered multiple transitions. Founded in 1898 to tend to the growing population of Irish Catholics, the parish was also home to a convent of the Sisters of Charity of the Blessed Virgin Mary (BVM), who ran the parish school and, during its heyday, many of its ministries. Built in a Spanish Renaissance style, the ornate parish bell towers kept watch over the neighborhood's working-class residents. Just five miles straight west of the iconic structure of Willis Tower (previously Sears Tower) and the art deco façades of the Chicago Board of Trade and the city's Lyric Opera House of the downtown Loop, the parish had served as a kind of way station and haven for immigrant communities seeking to gain a foothold in the city.[13] Following the Irish, it was

Polish and Russian Jews who relocated to the neighborhood in the early twentieth century.[14] By the 1950s, Black migrants squeezing into the segregated city were replacing the predominantly Jewish population.

As the Black population increased, the parish Egan inherited suffered the same disregard and marginalization of its new inhabitants. Broken glass strewn across the streets reflected broken and barred-up windows. Crumbling sidewalks lined potholed roads. Uncollected trash piled up in its alleys and avenues due to the neglect of city services. The trash brought rats and roaches, so common in the dilapidated apartments and homes that children from the neighborhood frequently misidentified the rodents for teddy bears. Speaking to the extremity of conditions, at least one little boy was reported to have been gnawed to death by the vermin as he slept in his crib.[15] The gross disrepair of the dwellings led to rampant lead poisoning from leaching pipes and chipping paint. Nowhere else in the city were more welfare recipients aggregated in one place; over one-third of the neighborhood's residents received public aid. Those lucky enough to be employed were paid on average only two-thirds what the city's white families earned.[16] Since the neighborhood was controlled by white outsiders, the residents had no representation and no recourse within City Hall. Disrespect and discrimination were ever-present. And the pressure of these forces suffused the neighborhood with a volatile mixture of shame and rage that regularly erupted in violence. Just a few months before Egan arrived at Presentation, a three-day uprising ended only after police had injured 65 residents and arrested 104 others.[17] While Jack had a history of working with Chicago's Black community leaders, he gained a whole new racial education at Presentation, one that took him out of the high ideals of the church's social and theological pronouncements and into the gritty experience of his new flock.[18]

The condition of the church building upon his arrival was nearly as hopeless as the surrounding community. Three-quarters of the church's families had left for good, and the parish had a mere $382 in reserves.[19] Peeling paint speckled the walls. The furnace was constantly breaking down, and the church basement was squalid.[20] The church had grown increasingly isolated and cloistered in on itself, its doors closed to the community and a wrought-iron fence constructed around it for security. Cardinal Cody must have known when he sent Fr. Jack there that it was a place with little to no pulse.

At first, Fr. Jack was both frightened and heartbroken, and as a result, he was tempted to embrace an authoritative and administrative personality. But years of experience with community organizing, the Christian Family Movement, and the Young Christian Students' and Young Christian Workers' movements soon kicked in, leading him to take a more collective and cooperative approach.[21] Though the problems in Lawndale loomed large, its community—like Egan's own bank of relational connections—was not bereft. The key was locating their assets, unlocking them, binding them together, and marshaling them against the forces of injustice and discrimination.

At Presentation, the exiled Egan learned his own welfare was bound up with that of the surrounding community (Jer. 29:5-7). This knowledge shaped his ministry. "Before Jack came," one young volunteer observed, "there was this tight little group of white people who had this exclusive community. Some privileged black people came in to go to school. Some came to church," but the place really "was an island unto itself." Yet, as Jack's biographer Margery Frisbie confirms, "when Jack came, he opened the windows. He opened the doors. He planted flowers. He pulled down the wrought-iron fence with the gate that intimidated visitors."[22] He invested in the community and invited the community in. "He was an artist at listening," one parishioner said.[23] At Presentation, he relearned the work of the priesthood and of justice. The people of Lawndale and Presentation taught him not to be their champion, but to be their companion. They taught him to discover the gospel anew in the reality of their lives as they struggled against the racist and exploitative forces of American society.[24] And it profoundly shaped him. As he recalled later, "I'm living with black people for the first time in my life. Archbishop Cody couldn't have given me a greater gift. I don't think he thought of it that way. I think he thought he was getting rid of me." He concluded, "Archbishop Cody had an unbelievable power of underestimating people."[25]

Since the Roman Catholic Church was one of the most powerful institutions in the city, it was not to Fr. Jack's advantage to be at odds with Cody. Still, he had other affiliations in the city, including his deep friendship with the acerbic and controversial community organizer Saul Alinsky. Though the mayor had warned him not to fraternize with this "kind" of people,[26] Fr. Jack was the main link in a powerful partnership between Alinsky's Industrial Areas Foundation and the archdiocese prior to Cody's arrival. Alinsky taught the idealistic Egan tactics and strategy, helping him realize that the collar and some sentimentality would change nothing. Egan taught Alinsky, who fancied himself the Machiavelli of the underdog, that the poor and marginalized had real convictions they were unwilling to sell simply for a crude "win," that their sincere faith was not merely to be instrumentalized.[27] Alinsky's tactics and relational emphasis taught Fr. Jack how to create a parish with power and purpose, to work not from the halls of power down but from the bottom up.

The heart of Jack's ministry at Presentation was people, and in addition to his own deep interest in the families of the parish and the neighborhood, he relied on a broad network of both volunteers and leaders to begin to build connections with the neighborhood residents.[28] Jack was fortunate to have the assistance of Peggy Roach, an extremely talented lay activist who became the iron core of Jack's work, keeping it steady, firm, and focused.[29] With the two of them at the helm, the place became a buzzing hub of people and activity. Chicago was still chock-full of Catholic progressives, champing at the bit to get their hands dirty in real service. He also never passed up a good idea. To meet the budget crisis, volunteer Ann Coe Pugliese suggested to Jack that they organize a "Friends of Presentation" campaign, which was soon drawing $4,000 per month in gifts from his contacts across the city. With volunteers, he printed and mailed a monthly newsletter to his mailing list of 1,500 allies. A swarm of supporters cascaded into the parish. Parish leaders and the BMV sisters at Presentation put this flood of help to work, launching a clothes closet, a local food pantry, carpentry classes, a drum and bugle corps, and a library, and bolstering the parish school.[30]

As was the case in other Chicago parishes impacted by segregation, the kids became the heart of the community, the point of dynamic intersection between the Catholic sisters, the priests, and Egan's army of volunteers and the neighbors surrounding the church. With public schools in Lawndale massively underfunded, overcrowded, and understaffed, many concerned parents saw parochial schools like Presentation as their only real option.[31] Soon, a web of Presentation school-associated ministries took off: summer camps for neighborhood kids, a Head Start program, a breakfast program that worked with members of the Black Panther Party, summer school classes for elementary students, street movies, home visits, and even adult education classes and discussion groups.[32]

Fr. Jack took a creative and unconventional approach to meeting the pastoral needs of his new large and underresourced parish. Always keen to see the opportunity for leadership development and practical education, he visited six area seminaries, offering to provide real urban-ministry training opportunities for seminarians willing to come help at Presentation. Sixty priests in training responded to his appeal. In organizing fashion, he assigned each of them a micro-parish of one square city block, initiating what he called "Operation Saturation." "You're to get to know every person in every house or apartment," Jack instructed them. "You're to find out who is ill; who is out of work; who has housing problems; whose kids aren't in school. At the end of the day, you're to report to me on every problem you uncover. We'll discuss then what we are going to do about it."[33] The objective was to renew the parish by reconnecting with the surrounding community, and to regenerate trust and mutuality.

One of those that responded to Egan's call was Jack Macnamara. Macnamara was a Jesuit in training who'd grown up in the northern suburb of Skokie. Egan described Macnamara as extremely bright and "always angry for the right reasons," and Macnamara became enamored with the work.[34] In the summer of 1967, he moved to the neighborhood and worked with Egan to launch the Presentation Church Community Organization Project.[35] They began with a focus on young people, organizing basketball games for the local kids. After learning about the residents' frustration with the pervasive trash problems in the community, Egan and Macnamara led the youth in a "dump-in," an action where they piled excess garbage collected from the neighborhood on the front steps of City Hall.[36] The city quickly moved to ensure that regular trash collection came through Lawndale. In another instance, the two men mobilized young people frustrated that there was no playground to conduct a "play-in," busing the kids to the parks and playgrounds of the mayor's all-white Bridgeport neighborhood. Afterward, Lawndale got its playground nearly overnight.[37] Slowly, the community began to consolidate and to discover its collective power.

The most significant and enduring action of the parish also began that summer. Through a listening campaign organized to build trust with the community and to identify needs, Macnamara came in contact with Ozirea Arbertha. Arbertha was a widow who lived with her four children and her mother in a two-flat building not too far from the church. Like many African Americans moving into the city, she'd struggled to find housing. She commuted three hours each day to her job as a postal worker on the South Side, where she earned a solid annual income of $5,800. Her mother earned an additional $3,400 a year as a nurse's aide. Yet even with a gross income of over $9,000 a year, the family was in financial crisis. "If we just didn't have this big house payment every month," she relayed to Macnamara through tears, "I think I could make ends meet." Learning that they were paying $240 a month in mortgage on the building, Macnamara was gobsmacked. His own middle-class family had struggled to pay their $108 mortgage payments on an only slightly higher income. Something was grossly amiss, something he reported to Egan.[38] Fr. Jack remarked, "You know, I think there's a different way they sell houses out here."[39]

That was an understatement. As the two men soon discovered, Macnamara had stumbled upon one of the worst-kept secrets in segregated Chicago: the exploitative reality of contract sales.

A decade earlier, Egan had led activists in a doomed crusade for integrated housing when the city and the University of Chicago pushed to relocate newly settled Black residents living on the periphery of the campus. Nothing, he learned then, roused the ire of public officials, business executives, and local residents quite like the issue of integrated housing.[40]

At the time, his public position on the issue of housing even ostracized him from his fellow clerics, a particularly painful experience for him. "You had no business there because you are a priest," one priest and mentor chastised. "This is not your role, the role of the priest, to question the university," he continued. "You are just plain wrong, you had the privilege of the best possible training on the role of the laity. . . . You're a disgrace to the Roman Catholic Church and the priesthood."[41] "I never felt more lonely in my life," Jack recalled.[42]

But this time, in Lawndale, the stakes were even greater. As he and Macnamara would discover, the "race tax" imposed through segregation and contract buying expropriated between $3 billion and $4 billion of wealth from the vulnerable Black community in just two decades.[43] Per homeowner, these residents paid over $71,000 more than their white counterparts, and did so under conditions that precipitated immense stress and anxiety.[44]

The same year Fr. Jack came to Presentation, Martin Luther King Jr. moved his family to a dilapidated third-floor flat at 1550 South Hamlin Avenue in Lawndale, just a few blocks from the parish, launching his campaign on housing conditions. At the time, Chicago was the nation's second-largest city, and as King memorably commented, it was maybe even more racist and violent than the deep South.[45] Blacks in search of housing were often the target of violence, terrorism, and intimidation.[46] With no recourse against racial prejudice, they were forced to inhabit isolated pockets of grossly substandard housing, creating a Black Belt that stretched across the South Side and West Side—a feature still visible in the city today. Slumlords extracted overpriced rents for apartments and homes with faulty plumbing, no working heat, and chunks of plaster falling off the walls. And there was little to no recourse for Blacks living under these extreme conditions. The best Egan could manage for his parishioners were small, isolated gains—as when one West Jackson Boulevard tenant, with Egan's help, led a temporary rent strike against a local slumlord.[47] Just as King discovered, the lucrative system of housing discrimination was deeper and more intransigent than Fr. Jack could have imagined.

The rise of the Black slums was precipitated by a mass exodus of white residents from the city to the newly emerging suburbs. This was the result of a new mortgage program from the Federal Housing Administration (FHA) that offered low-cost, federally insured home loans to over two million whites abandoning the nation's major cities.[48] Black citizens, however, were not eligible for these FHA loans. Instead, they were subject to a complex system of prejudiced policy practices known as redlining in which the FHA refused to insure home loans to African Americans and, moreover, refused to insure any mortgages (to whites or Blacks) in neighborhoods where African Americans were present.[49] The FHA's very own *Underwriting Manual* spelled these terms out quite baldly, stating that neighborhoods where the majority of school kids were Black were undesirable and unstable, thereby making home loans too risky to insure.[50] Effectively, Black neighborhoods were circumscribed by FHA officers in red, indicating that the program that made it possible for multitudes of white working-class citizens to purchase their first home with low down payments, low monthly payments, and reasonable interest rates was not available to Blacks.

FHA policies, as a result, basically encouraged and reinforced a system of plunder known as "blockbusting." Described by legal expert Richard Rothstein, "Blockbusting was a scheme in which speculators bought properties in borderline black-white areas; rented or sold them to African American families at above-market prices; persuaded white families residing in these areas that their neighborhoods were turning into African American slums and that values would soon fall precipitously; and then purchased the panicked whites' homes for less than their worth."[51] Buying artificially cheap as a result of this panic peddling, real estate speculators could then demand high prices from African Americans desperate for housing.

As Fr. Jack and Macnamara were learning, contract selling was the final profiteering piece of this complicated puzzle, and Lawndale was an acute site of such exploitative practices. Properties sold to Black residents moving into the neighborhood garnered on average an 84 percent markup from what speculators paid. Moreover, overpricing was not the only predatory element of the practice. Contract sales were also constructed such that the buyer accumulated no equity in the home, transferring ownership only after the entire sum and interest had been paid. Random fees were often charged and assessments levied. If the buyer missed a single payment or even if a payment was late, the seller could evict the buyer and keep the house to resell again—something that frequently happened.[52] It was a vicious arrangement that sucked a massive amount of wealth out of the Black community.

Nearly every building in the eight-block area of Lawndale was sold on contract at vastly inflated prices, yielding a windfall of profits that padded the pockets of a complex array of real estate and business players.[53] As Fr. Jack and Macnamara learned more, they realized that such a massive scam required a bigger and more broadly organized response. Macnamara organized a meeting, inviting area residents in January of 1968 to the basement of Presentation to learn about the contract system and to see what they might do about it together. Eight families showed up; none of them wanted to talk after Macnamara made his presentation detailing the scheme. As Macnamara recounted, "They didn't want to tell even each other that they bought on contract." Furthermore, he surmised, how did they know that this white Jesuit-in-training was not just another pale crook out to loot their community?[54] Silence reigned until Ruth Wells cautiously began to tell her story.

Wells told them that she was wrangling with Moe Forman, one of the most notorious contract sellers in Chicago. A few months earlier, Forman had added an arbitrary fee of $1,500 to Wells's already-inflated monthly payment, and he was threatening to put her family out on the street if they didn't pay up. For nearly ten years, Wells had never missed a payment on her two-flat, a building the block-busting Forman purchased for $13,500 and sold to them for $23,000. After having made extensive repairs to the structure, including a new bath, kitchen, roof, wiring, back porch, fencing, front steps, and sidewalk, Wells was deflated to learn the value of her home was now a mere $14,750. Wells told the assembly in the parish hall how she had consulted with Egan and Macnamara and decided to confront Forman and stick up for herself. She recounted how Fr. Jack, Macnamara, and one of the nuns from the parish accompanied her to Forman's downtown office on a frigid December day.

She'd been praying before the meeting with Forman, she said. "I wanted to know if I was wrong. If I was wrong I would not return to this man, but if I was right I would like to go ahead and fight this thing to the bitter end." Confirmation of her view came, Wells continued, when she demanded to see a copy of her insurance policy and he passed a copy across the table. "His hand began to quiver like a leaf in the wind," she recalled. "I thought, 'Somebody done touched him and let him know. He's feeling something he's never felt before: *guilt!*' He's all trembling and shaking, really upset. And I thought to myself, 'I didn't upset him, but I know *who* did.'" Though Forman refused to remove the fee, Wells, Egan, and the others were able to pressure him into cutting $1,000 from the contract balance.

Having finished her story, Wells asked the others in the Presentation parish hall "if any of them was in the same boat."[55] "Once she told her story," Macnamara recalled, "you couldn't shut anybody up." At the next meeting the Contract Buyers League (CBL) was born.[56] By April, five hundred people were attending CBL's Wednesday night meetings, and by November that number had doubled to over one thousand, spurred on by a larger confrontation with Joe Forman and his company. Forman was unprepared and completely caught off guard by, as Wells merrily put it, "All these black folk knowing the answers. And all these white folk living in Lawndale where he don't think it's safe for a white man to go." Under pressure, he eventually agreed to renegotiate his other contracts as more traditional mortgages, generating "a million-dollar victory" for the young organization.[57]

Still, the opposition was immense, including City Hall, the real estate industry, the title companies, and the mafioso-like sellers. As Jack's faithful assistant Peggy Roach recalled, "Contract buying was a tough issue that demanded tough action."[58] People attempting to expose and correct the lucrative practice had been killed.[59] It was clear that more victories would not come so easily or quickly. But CBL's members were intensely committed, and a group of relentless community leaders, supported by Presentation, took up the mantle of the organization.

CBL's leaders included Clyde Ross, Charlie Baker, Henrietta Banks, and Ruth Wells, whom they affectionately referred to as the Rosa Parks of Lawndale.[60] They galvanized the community into picket lines at contract sellers' homes, infuriating the neighbors in the all-white neighborhoods and embarrassing the sellers' families. They led protests at the headquarters of participating banks and the downtown office of the FHA. For businesspeople who'd secured their consciences on the distorted American values of the integrity of contracts and the fairness of market pricing, these tactics were maddening.[61]

The powers standing behind contract sales were further incensed by the religious backing the organization received from Egan's Presentation parish. CBL was deeply immersed in spirituality and Christian practices of prayer, reading Scripture, singing, and even preaching—so much so that several participants nearly equated the meetings with church services.[62] As one parish participant described it, "CBL was a perfect fit of faith, thought, and action working together efficiently for justice in the neighborhood."[63] Furthermore, it maintained Egan's commitment to interreligious cooperation. Eschewing anti-Semitic sentiments so prevalent around it, CBL worked hard to forge strong relationships with the liberal Jewish community of the city. This basis in faith sustained CBL when their early progress stalled. As sellers dug in, the organization's funds began to deplete, and as Charlie Baker put it, they were "losing faith in the white man who says the legal system can be changed . . . [and] in those who say that justice can be achieved within the framework of the law." But the spiritual nature of CBL meetings continued to uplift and encourage the group. The hope and faith engendered there eventually gave rise to a new, more aggressive strategy called "the big holdout."[64]

Strategizing at their office in the parish basement, leaders discerned that their only point of leverage was in the power of their payments. So together, backed by the pledge of Fr. Jack's support, they planned a strike, hoping to hit the sellers where they'd feel it most—in the pocketbook. The risks were huge. As one observer put it, it could lead to "the spectacle of thousands of black men, women, and children being evicted from their homes as winter approaches." But it might also break the back of the unjust economic system, especially as new members joined and CBL spread across the neighborhoods of the Black Belt.[65] Prepped with antieviction teams, they launched their payment strike on December 1, 1968. Over six hundred families withheld their mortgage payments. Initially, the atmosphere among participants was electric. One member commented that folks "got a real kick out of not paying those crooks another cent till we [got] our renegotiations."[66] Soon the holdout was making national news. But as the notoriety of the campaign rose, so did the fury of the sellers.

By spring, a brutal legal fight began, and it stretched through the summer as a captivated nation tracked the Apollo 11 mission to the moon. As the fight dragged into the fall, evictions ramped up, and CBL attorneys searched for an angle to limit the forcible entry and eviction statute. In a society where the law decisively favored property owners—particularly white property owners— they faced a steep uphill battle. But their resolve held, fueled by anger at the sellers' cruelty. Charlie Baker cast the battle—and the power of the united strikers—in biblical terms: "If a thousand people get together and do one thing, who is going to stop them? It's like when Moses was leading the people away from Pharaoh. As they were going through the desert, the people were mumbling that it was a trick. . . . [But] they got to the other side and the sea fell back on Pharaoh. The same thing happens today. All you got to do is believe. If you all stick together, there's not a thing the real estate man can do."[67] Clyde Ross, Baker's coleader, drove home the point in an impassioned speech of his own, declaring, "They've cheated us about much more than money. . . . We've been cheated out of the right to be human beings in this society."[68] Stalwart in their refusal to cede, CBL received an unanticipated lifeline in the form of a $250,000 gift from the local Jesuits to post bonds for those appealing their eviction rulings.[69] As winter and the one-year mark of the strike approached, both sides were entrenched, and battle lines were drawn.

A late November court ruling against CBL's strikers gave landlords the green light to proceed with evictions on those still holding out, setting the scene for a series of public confrontations between CBL and contract sellers. On December 11, movers arrived at Elizabeth Nelson's home on the South Side to remove her things. It was a poor choice of target, as the media covering the conflict conveyed. Nelson was a widow caring for nine children, eight of whom were orphans of her late sister. She worked nights so she could watch the kids during the day. Nevertheless, the company holding her contract insisted on eviction. "I've paid too much money just to walk off and leave here like this. I have too many children to be set out in the street with no place to go," she told reporters on the scene. "The only way we'll get anything for the colored people is to fight for it; we want fair prices like anyone else." Within a few hours, CBL's grassroots network mobilized, assembling a group of members to move all of Nelson's belongings back into her home. This public act of resistance won her and her family a short-term reprieve, as the owners backed off for the Christmas holiday, recognizing what a public relations disaster it would be to proceed further at that time.[70] But it was clear that the balance was tilting against CBL.

More attempts to evict others prompted Fr. Jack to call on the federal courts to halt them.[71] In turn, sellers upped the ante by compelling the Cook County sheriff to enforce the eviction of 101 contract buyers who were withholding their payments. At early dawn one day near the end of January, as a snowstorm engulfed the city, Sheriff Joseph Woods brought two hundred outfitted deputies to oversee the eviction of Mr. and Mrs. Jonnie Moss. Moss was a hardworking family man who'd held a job with Borden Ice Cream for seventeen years, and Mrs. Moss worked two jobs to help meet their contract payments. They joined with CBL and the payment holdout because, as Jonnie put it, they were "tired" of the injustice of contract sales. They had overpaid nearly $7,000 for their home and had no equity despite having put down $3,500 for the property and having paid on it for nearly a decade. Once the Mosses began withholding payments, the owner charged them with illegally squatting in their own home.[72] As movers and deputies descended on their property, a heartbreaking and chaotic scene unfolded. They dragged the family's furniture out of the home, throwing it on the snow-covered lawn. Movers dumped the family's plastic nativity scene in the bushes. Deputies chased their dog out into the yard and forced the family out to the street, fomenting the ire of neighbors and the assembled CBL contingent.[73]

A confrontation ensued, as the crowd of increasingly agitated spectators swelled to over two hundred, most of them CBL activists, with Fr. Jack among them. When jumpy guards fired two shots from inside the Mosses' home, it seemed the infuriated crowd might riot. Finally, the tension broke when the overwhelmed officers abandoned the property. A newspaper photographer captured an image of a jubilant Egan amid the crowd carting the Mosses' belongings back into the house.[74]

Similar scenes played out through the remaining winter and into the spring, as an onslaught of evictions escalated the call to renegotiate. As the base of CBL, Egan's parish gained a reputation among city officials, sellers, realtors, and law enforcement as an incubator for radicals. CBL's calculated resistance pushed the cost of eviction for the city, county, and state beyond reasonable defense.[75] Yet, with the law on the side of the sellers, Egan's and CBL's power was severely limited. Finally, cornered by the obscenity of pervasive evictions and the imminent possibility of violence erupting from frustrated community members, the mayor intervened to broker a deal between CBL and one of the major contract sellers. CBL's cause was also bolstered by a fortuitous Illinois Supreme Court ruling on April 15 regarding the limits to forcible entry and detainer. The court decision reversed a precedent that excluded "matters not germane" directly to the eviction proceedings, constricting the evidence and arguments plaintiffs could enter. In contrast, the court ruled that issues surrounding the validity of the contracts along with the usurious, fraudulent, and predatory practices surrounding them could be included in considerations of the rights of the victims.[76] As a result, the sellers found themselves on slightly less certain ground. Yet, there was no clear, universal victory for either side, as technicalities in the ruling set limitations on its application. Uncertainty on both sides, subsequently, led some CBL members and contract sellers to sense that their best option was to compromise, something that created tension in the CBL organization between those looking to settle and those wanting to hold out for a more complete victory.[77] Facing even more lengthy legal disputes and ongoing threats of eviction, on July 1, 1970, CBL members ended their strike with mixed feelings.[78] There would be no neat conclusion to CBL's fight.

In the end, CBL won the renegotiation of over 450 contracts. Jack Macnamara estimates that the average savings on each of these was roughly $13,500 per family, a total of just over $6 million. Though these savings certainly made a difference for the residents who received them, the total was only a drop in the bucket compared to what was legally stolen. Still, there were less tangible victories. Those residents unable to get their contracts renegotiated were able to take some control and exert power as part of the community. They talked back to the contract sellers and realtors and were supported in doing so by a church community.[79] CBL members gained self-respect, and they discovered the support and boldness that come with a storm cloud of fellow witnesses discontent with injustice.

*   *   *

In the time Fr. Jack Egan was there, Presentation became a place of wild hospitality and diverse connections as well as a buzzing hive of activity. As one volunteer recounts, "One room symbolized it for me. On the second floor of the rectory was a room called the common room and after people finished working at the end of the day, people'd go up there and meet and have a drink. . . . When you first came, you signed the wall. [I remember] there were these four walls completely filled with signatures." Signatures wallpapered the room, where the names of national luminaries such as Bobby Kennedy, Dorothy Day, Daniel Berrigan, and Saul Alinsky were etched next to those of local community activists like Sam Flowers and Roberta Fair.[80] For the commencement in June of 1969, the schoolchildren selected comedian and civil rights leader Dick Gregory, only recently released from jail, to give the address.[81] This once-declining parish was now a crossroads of Catholic activists and radicals, a raucous hub of community involvement and organizing. It became an invigorating institution for the community, a spring of living water.

Fr. Jack continued to foster this kind of lively, participatory ministry in subsequent positions at the University of Notre Dame and then at DePaul University. As one of Jack's disciples put it, he convinced an entire generation of Catholic students to get involved and not to merely sit on the sidelines. He was always thinking of ways to bring more people into service and into the fellowship of activity, even while in exile himself.[82]

Egan died on May 19, 2001. His obituary appeared in the *National Catholic Reporter* on June 1 across the page from his "last testament," an article he wrote calling for the ordination of women and married men into the Catholic priesthood.[83] He instructed mourners to bring balloons to his funeral. To the end, he understood his role as priest, a role he took very seriously, to be the elevation of the people. In a hierarchy characterized by privilege, honor, superiority, and conformity, Egan stood out not by disobedience but in his desire to see others raised up. In Lawndale, Egan learned that this was not merely a one-way street, for the people also taught him what it meant to be a priest amid a city riddled with divisions, bigotry, and exploitation. Out of death could always come life.

Presentation parish is now closed, its sanctuary razed in 2013. At the corner of West Lexington Street and South Springfield Avenue, the remains of its boarded rectory and school sit amid a community still struggling with generational segregation, exploitation, divestment, and exclusion. Plagued by desertion and deterioration, Lawndale's potholed streets cry out for a reckoning. And the people who have homed here, those passed, many in diaspora, and those making it day to day, bear in mind and body the hard history of this place. Were one to rate Jack Egan's life and ministry on a scorecard of wins and losses, it likely would tilt to the latter. But immediate outcomes are not always the calculus of the kingdom, just as its prophets are rarely honored in their hometowns (Mark 6:4).

Even amid such challenges, a new hope inspired by Fr. Jack's ministry and initiated by some of his organizing descendants is taking shape. "Reclaiming Chicago," a new neighborhood campaign for the construction of affordable, single-family homes has been launched, building on prior, smaller reconstruction efforts. Its goal is to transform two thousand city-owned vacant lots into owner-occupied residences. At the helm of this campaign is a powerful coalition of Black-led institutions and neighborhood groups long rooted in Lawndale. The work of these neighborhood residents is being supported by United Power for Action and Justice, a county-wide, nonpartisan, and broad-based community organization founded in 1997 as an affiliate of the Industrial Areas Foundation network with a large grant from the archdiocese that had been leveraged by Fr. Jack. With the not-so-modest goal of "Reclaiming lost equity for Lawndale . . . 1000 homes at a time!" they've already obtained a public commitment from Mayor Lori Lightfoot for the first 250 city-owned lots along with $5.3 million in city funding. This is the first step in a plan to build two thousand affordable homes on the West and South Sides, beginning with one thousand in Lawndale. Private and state funds totalling $22 million have also been procured for low-interest loans to make these homes available.[84] It's an ambitious plan for revitalization in one of the nation's most violent and troubled areas.[85] There's still so much to be done, but Egan would have loved it.

SARAH PATTON BOYLE

(1906–1994)

Sarah Patton Boyle, with Rev. Robert L. Taylor (left) and Wyatt T. Walker (far right), praying during a demonstration in Richmond, January 2, 1959; used with permission from the *Richmond-Times Dispatch*

Ghostwriting the South into Integration

The Consuming Saintly Obsession of Sarah Patton Boyle

Lauren F. Winner

She signed them S. L. Patton, or Sarah Lindsay, or Sarah P. Boyle. She wrote as Mrs. Roger Boyle Jr. and S. Lindsay Patton. "By keeping these names in rotation I could print an awful lot of letters to the editor without seeming to take over the page," she explained to the editor of the *Norfolk Virginian-Pilot*, ten days after he'd published a letter in which Boyle proclaimed "distress . . . that so few voices publicly defend the Negro people at this time."[1]

Of Virginius Dabney, the editor of the *Richmond Times-Dispatch*, she asked, "Is it permissable [*sic*] to send in two letters under different names? I could use my maiden name, or a pen name which I regularly use for pot boilers, or an entirely different and unrecognizable name." She helpfully enclosed a card listing the options. She asked him to check his preference and get the card back to her.[2]

When Dabney rejected one of her letters, deeming it too radical (the letter "would be an invitation to Ku Kluxers . . . [and] would start a terrific controversy and make matters worse than ever"),[3] Boyle typed a hot page back, disingenuously asking that Dabney not "take what is to follow as an argument with [him] concerning [his] practice," then insisting that "*The conspiracy of silence is creating far more trouble than it is averting*" and suggesting that "a little . . . controversy would [not] do any harm."[4] Dabney has his limitations, which become all the clearer as the 1950s roll on, but if you read enough of his correspondence with Boyle in 1951 and 1952, you begin to think him saintly simply for replying to her.[5] You begin to think of angina when you imagine his receiving yet another letter, return address Mrs. Roger P. Boyle, Charlottesville, Virginia.

This was in the very early phase of Sarah Patton Boyle's civil rights work, when she still believed that most white people in Virginia thought as she now did. Later, after enough snubbings from white friends, after a cross burned on her lawn, after members of the Citizens' Council sent an ambulance to her house in the middle of the night—"We got a call to come to this address and pick up the mangled or dead body of Mrs. Boyle"—she came to see otherwise. But this was when she still held "faith . . . that people are wonderful," when she still expected "of people goodness which they failed to manifest."[6]

*　　　*　　　*

Her father, an Episcopal priest, directed the American Church Institute, which oversaw the schools the Episcopal Church ran for "Negroes." Other than that connection to race work, nothing in Patty Boyle's childhood among (as she put it in 1962) "the best people" predicted her epistolary assault on Virginia's newspapers. Her memoir, *The Desegregated Heart*, told versions of the stock stories that other elites of the segregated South (and their historians) tell when discussing childhood: there were the kindly servants, whom Patty "loved . . . with the unobstructed outgoingness of a child. . . . I took joy in belief that I gave them joy, and comfort in the thought that they loved me." There were the instructions when she turned twelve: the cook and the farm hand were now to call her "Miss Patty," and she was no longer allowed to "play with, even talk to, colored children any more except graciously to greet them or inquire about their welfare." There was, at every turn, the choreography of "the Code": "you must always be polite and gentle with Negroes, you must talk a little down to them, as to a young child, using a tone of condescension, even an accent reserved for them.... You were supposed to store in your memory their quaint sayings taking special care to remember accurately their dialect, mispronunciations and misuse of big words. These made charming anecdotes." If, for some reason, you were sending a letter to a Negro college president, you must not put "Mr." on the envelope—use of the honorific "would embarrass him to death."[7]

These "rules of the Southern way of life" ensured that Sarah Patton Boyle behaved as a typical member of her class for forty years, through her marrying a man who taught drama at the University of Virginia, through the birth of two sons, through countless Sundays in Episcopal churches, through the employment of various "girl[s]" to wash the dishes and clean the apartment.[8]

But then Boyle began to notice what she had not noticed before, and the Code began to seem less inviolable, less natural. The first noticing had to do with discrimination not against "Negroes," but against Jews; she met first one, and then a second young Jewish man, each of whom spoke to her of the barriers they faced. This acquaintance with anti-Semitism unsettled Boyle. She read Milton Steinberg's *The Making of the Modern Jew*, which showed her some of the "suffering brought upon a vivid, gifted people through other peoples' persistent exercise of prejudice, misinformation and faulty generalizations." Boyle was "shaken" by her reading. "Something in me seemed struggling to get free. I had a strong feeling that this problem was mine, that I had a job to do in connection with it."[9]

Another disquieting noticing came via the radio. Norman Thomas was "making one of his recurrent bids for the presidency," and Boyle chanced upon a broadcast from the Socialist Convention Headquarters. The speaker she heard "was a Southern Negro," but she added, "I noted uneasily that I wouldn't have known it had he not said so." Not only was the diction and cadence of the man's speech surprising to Boyle; the content was another revelation. The man said that the platform at the socialist convention was the first time in his life that he had "known human dignity." Those words pressed at Boyle and came very close to breaking the spell of her "indoctrination."[10]

The socialist and the Jews showed her something—or, better, they cleared away some brush so that she might be able to see. And then, when Boyle was forty-four, the event she later identified as "the turning point in her life": an African American lawyer named Gregory Swanson was admitted to the University of Virginia Law School. The night her husband came home and announced that "Next fall we'll probably have our first Negro student," Boyle looked up through the clearing. As soon as she heard her husband's prediction, she "felt lighter." She went on, "Although I hadn't known it, my chest had been in a plaster cast and now was sawed free. . . . I was enriched by the very thought of a Negro student at the University."[11]

Boyle determined to welcome Swanson to Charlottesville. She wrote him a letter—by the time she recalled that 1950 letter in *The Desegregated Heart*, she could see the condescension of her earlier noblesse oblige, the racism that saturated even her gesture of welcome. Yet, even so, the letter was a start: "'Dear Mr. Swanson,' I began, feeling queer and proud. This was the first time I had ever addressed a Negro as Mister. Something old and rigid had given way."[12]

Eventually, Boyle and Swanson met. By that time, Boyle, who'd been an occasional contributor to *Ladies' Home Journal* and other women's magazines for years, had written an article called "We Want a Negro at UVA," which she aimed to publish in *Reader's Digest*. She asked Swanson to "Read it ruthlessly for errors." She thought Swanson "would just love" the article. He did not:

> We sat opposite each other at a small table. . . . He couldn't,
> I was sure, fail to be touched as well as pleased by the way I had
> written it without a single concession to inherited prejudice.

Expressionless, he read it through. Then, without raising his eyes from the page he said, "And you intend to publish that?" A slight tremor in his voice moved me and I answered. . . . "Please don't feel grateful, Gregory. I feel privileged to help." He looked up then. If I had been standing, I would have stepped back. His eyes were the incarnation of hostility, fury. "I suppose I can't stop you. Still, I wish you would refrain from printing that kind of thing about me—at least while I'm at the University." He rose, turned, walked through the door and down the Rotunda steps without glancing at me again.[13]

Boyle was, to put it plainly, devastated. And confused. Seeking to understand Swanson's reaction, she wrote to T. J. Sellers, a local Black newspaper editor, and asked him to read and criticize her article. Sellers took her inquiry at face value and replied, noting, *inter alia*, that "In paragraph one [Boyle] had referred to slavery, a tactless habit of white southerners, with whom the mere sight of a Negro seemed to conjure up nostalgic recollections of those good old days," and that throughout the article she had depicted Swanson and his family as "'quiet easy-going' people with 'not a trace of defiance' against a system which had made intolerable their own lives and the lives of others of their race."[14]

Boyle felt "indignant"—but she was desperate to learn, and soon enough, she persuaded Sellers to give her essentially a private tutorial in American history and sociology, schooling her in "all the facts which had been omitted from my education." "The T. J. Sellers Course for Backward Southern Whites," she calls it in her memoir.[15]

One of Sellers's first lessons was dictional: Boyle's commonplace usage to the contrary, "Southerner" didn't mean "white Southerner."

It may have been during [our] first lesson that I commented on his Yankee accent, and asked if he were from the North.

"Oh, no, I'm a Southerner," he said.

If he had thrown a cup of water in my face, I couldn't have been more surprised. A Southerner! Never had I heard a Negro thus designated. Southerners were white. Sellers was a Southern Negro, not a Southerner.

But of course he was a Southerner really, I hastily told myself, proud of my ability to adjust to shocks.

He seemed to read my thoughts. A natural actor, with unerring skill he injected a note of courtliness into the tone of his urbane voice, and added:

"Yes, I'm a Virginia gentleman."

The cup this time held ice water, but I denied myself a gasp and would not look away from his face. The edges of my eyes noted his faultless, immaculate attire. Measuredly, I replied:

"I'm glad, because Virginia gentlemen are getting rather rare."

. . . By concentration, within a few weeks I was able to compel myself to stop saying "both Southerners and colored people" and to say instead "both white and colored Southerners," though for several years if I used the word "Southerners" alone I always meant white Southerners, and even now I often slip into this habit.[16]

The *Washington Post* recently ran an opinion piece by B. L. Wilson called "I'm Your Black Friend, but I Won't Educate You about Racism. That's on You," in which the author wrote: "A lot of black friends have been getting phone calls from white friends lately. Sometimes they are from people we haven't heard from in years, or know only in passing from work—people who have usually been too busy for us. They want to talk about race and what we can do about it. Who better to explain racism to white people than black people? I'm afraid that didactic model is not going to work."[17]

*   *   *

Her study with Sellers changed Patton, eroding ingrained prejudices, clearing more brush, until one weekend in May 1951. "I knew I must decide, definitely and finally, whether or not I would fight in the Negro's battle for equality. . . . I made my decision on a Friday night . . . and all day Saturday I was sick within. The Southern code muttered in my ear."[18]

Saturday turned to Sunday, and on Sunday, Boyle went to church. In her memoir, there's a lovely play between individual and community, lone believer and *ecclesia*: what happens in church confirms her Friday night decision; church authenticates, or maybe completes, her seemingly solo choice. The opening processional was hymn 536 (Boyle would have been singing from the hymnal the Episcopal Church adopted in 1940)—not Isaac Watts or Charles Wesley, but a more recent hymn, written by Englishman Charles Bax, lamenting World War I: "Turn back O man, forswear thy foolish ways," the hymn began, but Patton barely noticed the words until she came to the third and last stanza: "Earth shall be fair, and all her people one." "It seemed a benediction on the course I had chosen," she said. So, too, the hymn before the sermon, hymn 519, a setting of five stanzas of abolitionist poet James Russell Lowell's "Verses Suggested by the Present Crisis" (Lowell had in mind the War with Mexico and the attendant debate about the expansion of slavery in the United States). "Once to every man and nation, / Comes the moment to decide." Theodore Evans took up the theme in his sermon: "if you decide on the basis of love for your fellow man and of a desire to do what is right," Boyle remembers him saying, "you may be sure that you chose according to His will."[19]

That month she began her letter-to-the-editor campaign.

*   *   *

When Boyle failed to persuade the *Richmond Times-Dispatch* to publish endless letters signed with variations of her maiden and married names ("all letters of a critical nature have to be signed with the name of the author," Dabney had explained to her; "I should think that anything you would write on the race problem would come under that category"),[20] she hatched a new idea: she would organize white men and women with similar views into a brigade of letter writers.[21] Even had editors been willing to end-lessly publish letters by one devoted writer, Boyle realized that "the more my name appears the less weight it will carry until fi-nally everybody will end up by saying 'Oh that's just Patty Boyle shooting her mouth off again!'"[22] So she scoured newspapers, contacted those who had written a single letter supporting inte-gration, and urged them to write more. She rang up sympathetic acquaintances who'd never dreamed of writing to a paper and pro-posed they try their hand. The aim: to flood the papers with mis-sives from white people protesting segregation. Boyle needed as many people as possible to write, or at least sign, pro-integration letters to the editor.

She gave fellow letter writers tips: "I can't over-emphasize the importance of always making it *clear that you are white*," she explained to Marjorie N. Cherry of Buckroe Beach. Criticisms of segregation wouldn't have much impact on white readers if the readers assume the writer is "colored." Of course, the truth is the truth, "no matter who said it. But coming from a white person it has a wollop of emotionality which it lacks from a Negro."[23]

And if her friends were willing but not capable—if they weren't confident writers—she'd draft the letters herself and affix their sig-natures. In all, some nineteen people let her write letters in their names. By September, she had placed "29 letters in defense of the Negro," and Boyle was confident that, "As soon as I can get some other writers to functioning and line up a few more signers, this campaign will be able to make itself felt in real earnest."[24]

Realizing that were she to draft dozens of letters a week she would inevitably begin to repeat this or that turn of phrase, Boyle began to recruit other ghostwriters. She created an elaborate handwritten chart to sync letter-drafters, signatories, and newspapers. One of her correspondents was John Whetzel, a like-minded Danville-based launderer whom she'd only known for about ten minutes, and who was dying of ALS. The letter Boyle wrote to Whetzel after he told her of his "fatal nerve disease" is remarkable.[25] First, with a near manic energy, she devotes a page to urging Whetzel to pray for healing. "All you need is sufficient faith to open the channel up to God. . . . I want you to know that I know that you can heal yourself and that I shall not be the least surprised to learn that you have done so. I don't think your work here is finished . . . I need you. The Negro people need you." And then, having hectored him to pray his way to health, Boyle invited Whetzel to join her team of epistolists. He could write letters from his sickbed, perhaps? He could "locate one or two other persons" to sign letters he or she might draft. He could "take over the typing, mailing out, and checking to see if they are printed."[26] What is more remarkable? That she asked this of a dying man, or that, in his last months, despite the "paralysis . . . affecting his vocal cords" and making it difficult to dictate correspondence, he accepted the invitation?[27]

Boyle also tried to recruit Lillian Smith. This was about two years after *Killers of the Dream* had clinched Smith's reputation as the most insightful white analyst of the rot at the center of the South. Boyle had never met Smith but, unsurprisingly, admired her with an admiration verging on awe. Writing to Smith at the summer camp for girls she ran with her partner Paula Snelling, Boyle cast her vision of flooding southern newspapers with letters by white southerners sympathetic to integration. Insisting that the plan was "a child of your brain," she asked Smith to join her in drafting letters to be signed by others. "Let's try it," she urged Smith. "What have we got to lose?" Smith gracefully evaded the invitation. "Your idea of letters is so good; so *really good*," she wrote, before stiff-arming Boyle. Her health prevented her from taking part.[28]

Perhaps Boyle's campaign seems, from the distance of seventy years, quixotic and naïve. But I think it is remarkable. Boyle believed, it seems, that she could ghostwrite the South into integration.

*   *   *

Before her retirement from civil rights work in the late 1960s, Patty Boyle gave a lot of speeches. She led a get-out-the-vote drive for a referendum on the establishment of a public housing authority. Deeming the church where she'd experienced that liturgical confirmation of her call to civil rights too slow on race matters, she left and began attending Charlottesville's predominantly Black Trinity Episcopal Church. She served on the Episcopal Church's national advisory committee on intergroup relations. She testified, in 1958, in an NAACP (National Association for the Advancement of Colored People) suit against Virginia. She marched in the March on Washington, and she was arrested, in St. Augustine, Florida, during a 1963 SCLC (Southern Christian Leadership Conference) protest of a segregated motel. She seemed to find the arrest thrilling.

But she was first a writer.

The potboilers she'd mentioned to Dabney were articles written under the name Patty Patton, pieces like "How Far Can You Stretch a Dollar,"[29] written to keep her mind lively[30] and generate income when the children were young and her husband was busy teaching drama at the university (and though she pooh-poohed them once she got political, Boyle kept publishing such bagatelles at least through the mid-1950s: the same month that school officials in Charlottesville and Arlington were petitioning the Fourth Circuit Court of Appeals to reverse orders requiring school desegregation, Patty Patton urged readers of *Parents' Magazine and Family Home Guide* to "make your child welcome in the kitchen" just as soon as "he shows an interest in food preparation").[31]

The occasional potboiler notwithstanding, once she joined "the integration struggle," most of Boyle's writing was devoted to "the struggle of right and wrong,"[32] to voting, to "intergroup communications," to insisting that white "Southerners Will Like Integration" (to use the title of the *Saturday Evening Post* article that brought her to national attention, and brought her especial local opprobrium; the headline-writer, it's worth noting, had not the benefit of Sellers's lesson). *The Desegregated Heart* found black and white readers, all over the country; having devoted herself to writing it, Boyle then devoted herself to learning the mechanics of making money publishing books, and to beginning to write, in fairly short order, her second book, a practical guide for black and white people seeking to understand and get to know one another. (She never did publish the ill-fated article she'd shown Swanson.)

And all those letters to the editor.

*   *   *

In the last decade of his life, Pascal obsessively pursued the idea that a certain theoretical understanding of grace was the right one. He wrote about it almost fanatically, and it destroyed parts of his life, leading to his being censured by ecclesial authorities and to the loss of some of his intimate associates.

Or think of Søren Kierkegaard, possessed by the task of showing how Hegel is wrong, of eviscerating Hegel's systematization, his insistence on occupying a perspective that is not given by the first person but is rather somewhere else. Think of Kierkegaard writing endlessly his desire that the world, the Christian world, and the gospel be available, and writing, writing, writing his certainty that Hegelianism won't let you have those things, that Hegelianism gives you only a thesis and an antithesis instead.

For many years—the years in which my only real acquaintance with Sarah Patton Boyle was a copy of *The Desegregated Heart*, plucked from a used bookstore on Elliewood Avenue and half-read on my shelf—I assumed that if one were to class her with the saints, one would probably find her alongside other activists, with Will Campbell and Dorothy Day and maybe even Norman Morrison, race traitors and class traitors, people who allowed their convictions about who their neighbors were to make their lives strange.

But more and more I see her saintliness as participant in that long tradition of Christian writers who were obsessed by an idea, and who followed that obsession with their pen (often pseudony-mously, as it turns out).

Consuming obsession occupies a significant place in the Christian saintly tradition. Most of us aren't thus obsessed. It's rare that someone accords a single thing all seriousness and focus, and makes it truly central to the ordering of life. Most people do this and that, never coalescing around a single center. And when those of us who aren't thus coalesced see someone who is, we often admire her and learn something from her, and feel disconcerted and slightly horrified. Consuming saintly obsession is admirable because it's a kind of clarity, and a kind of love, and the church always needs people who love in just that way; if there were no such people, there'd be much that we wouldn't see. Saints of consuming obsession repeatedly and emphatically give voice to an understanding of what counts. In Pascal's case, what counts about grace. In Boyle's case, what counts about racist discrimi-nation. Saints of consuming obsession show off what they see, to the church and to the world: I'm going to tell you again, they say, and again and again, and here again just a little differently. Most of us are more dilute, likely to address or attend one thing for a little while, and then go on to something else; the church needs those people, too, of course, and their habit of being has much to commend it. It's a habit of being that can, sometimes, make space for raising a child while earning a salary. It's a habit of being that runs local churches. It can make space for avocation. For the altar guild. But what it cannot offer is the remorseless drumbeat that clarifies and directs.

*   *   *

In time, her optimism, her confidence that the majority of white southerners supported integration, her belief that (as she put in a letter to fellow letter-to-the-editor writer Lorna Mansfield) a small army of letter writers would give confidence to those scared to speak out, and soon there'd be a large army, and before too long, the resistance of those few white Virginians truly committed to segregation would be overcome—in time, that optimism was destroyed.

It wasn't simply that James Jackson Kilpatrick was taking to the pages of his *Richmond News Leader* to expound the idea of "interposition," or that an Episcopal church in Patton's own Charlottesville was offering its Sunday school classrooms for all-white study so that the public school could close rather than integrate. More intimate than all this public sinning were the many friends who had disappointed Patty Boyle. Friends who'd sworn they shared her views no longer invited her to parties, and wouldn't make eye contact if they saw her in town. Trying to raise money for the Virginia Council on Human Relations in the mid-1950s, Boyle approached a friend who'd often "privately boosted" Boyle's confidence and cheered her on. He had also recently undertaken a $50,000 renovation of his home. Boyle asked him to spend several hundred dollars on Council memberships. "Leaning forward on a thousand-dollar couch, he murmured: 'We just can't afford it darling. How I wish we could!'" Surprised but undaunted, Boyle proposed the twenty-five-dollar membership category, then the five-dollar category. "'Not even that, honey. You see with the new addition and all—But don't think we aren't *with* you. You *know* how we feel.'"[33]

Perhaps even more galling was the stunning rapidity with which fair-weather friends who'd utterly shunned Boyle suddenly softened toward her as soon as the Charlottesville city schools integrated with relative calm in September 1959. "I've thought of you and prayed about you so often in these months. Can't we get together? I've so much to tell and ask you." "You'll never know what you meant to me through all this. You saved my faith in the South." "You spoke for us all. I didn't feel I ever had to say anything, because you said everything that needed to be said—*so beautifully*." Were these men and women sincere? Boyle thought they probably were. "Whatever they had done or not done a few months ago, they *meant* what they were saying now." But Boyle was unmoved by her erstwhile friends' warm gestures. She had become too internally impoverished to care. "In 1950, I had many inner mansions—built of the loftiness of man, the mellow loveliness of Dixie, the steadfastness of friends, my own capacity to give and take. Nothing remained of all this now."[34]

When reading Boyle's descriptions, in *The Desegregated Heart*, of the friends she had once judged reliable and steadfast, I think of nothing so much as of Job. Perhaps Boyle will have friends again, but she comes to believe that she has vested too much hope in human capacity and human goodness, that she was mistaken to look to human beings rather than to God for enduring love, and that she would now make the grounding of any loves she might give or receive not the unsteadiness of human love, but rather the God who is love and who will store up her loves "where moth and rust do not corrupt."[35]

*   *   *

It's no surprise that she spent herself, that her work became her exhaustion. If reporters are to be believed, throughout the 1950s and early 1960s, Patton "worked an average of 18 hours a day writing, traveling, and speaking."[36] Boyle's own accounts of her exhaustion are inflected, of course, with the presumptions of her social class and her gender: "Dear Elizabeth," she wrote in Oc-

tober 1955, to Mrs. J. Waites Waring, who by then had left South
Carolina for New York. "I really ought to move North. For there's
no Southern leisure in my life anyhow. I just go from one pressure
to another just like a Yankee. But after all if you have two children,
a husband and crusade and no maid and try even to do the family
laundry and try to keep up church and civic activities (feeling that
a strong tie-in with other things helps the crusade along) you just
don't have time for the letter writing you would like to do or even
for the reading either."[37] Or, the month before: "I must leave on
the 6 a.m. train to speak at the NAACP in Gloucester tomorrow,
getting home at 1:10 a.m. next day, so must get my house and ice-
box in order to leave the family."[38]

I imagine that reading the mail she daily received was, in a
different way, exhausting—an exhaustion born not of busyness but
of navigating the following:

- the five-page letter penned in blue ink by a Mrs. Hunter
  Bourne of Ashland, Virginia, comprising mostly Bible verses
  (these include Genesis 10:5 ["By these were the isles of the
  Gentiles divided in their lands; every one after his tongue,
  after their families in their nations"] and Deuteronomy 7:1
  ["All communion with the nations is forbidden"]), and ending "You must be a Catholic and the Bible is not your sole
  source of information?")[39]
- the hateful, hateful purple mimeographed faux application
  for the NAACP: Address (If living in car, give model, make
  and tag number) . . . GIVE APPROXIMATE ESTIMATE
  OF INCOME From theft, From Relief/Unemployment . . .
  PLACE OF BIRTH (Check One) CHARITY HOSPITAL [or]
  FREE Public Hospital WOULD YOU BE WILLING: Serve
  as DIRECTOR OF FORD FOUNDATION DIRECTOR OF
  URBAN LEAGUE UNITED NATIONS[40]
- "Please what kind of a woman are you, who calls herself a Southern white woman, and at the same time a pro-integrationist?"[41]

Boyle was courageous in the face of anger and threat. When the cross was burned on her lawn, she grabbed her thirteen-year-old-son and said, "Look! They're burning a cross for Mother. Isn't it beautiful?"[42] Of the letters, she said that having received them, she could not put them out of her mind when she saw an ostensibly polite middle-class segregationist.[43]

It was exhausting, too, to pursue the commitments of a non-Manichean approach to politics—that's my gloss, not a term (as far as I'm aware) that Boyle uses: threading through Boyle's correspondence is a refusal to see even the struggle for civil rights as a struggle of the wholly righteous battling the wholly corrupt. Boyle suggests there's something fatiguing in the capacity to see flaws and foibles in one's comrades, and in the capacity to see something other than corruption in one's foes. Again, she wrote to Waring:

> If only there were real white and real black. I mean in right and wrong. . . . If only those who oppose [integration] were altogether wrong, instead of just 90% wrong. If only all who support integration did so for worthy reasons, and all who oppose did so for unworthy reasons. If only all these things were so, how much less weary one would become in the struggle for what one believes. I shouldn't complain though, for I really think that the issues of right and wrong are about as clearly marked in this particular struggle as they ever are. Yet it is true that I think one's tiredness results more from the dim than from the opposition even here. One has no sooner gathered momentum for a resistless charge then suddenly the line between the right and wrong disappears altogether, and one must halt and search until it is clearly seen again. If only the opposition were entirely wrong all the time, how simple the fight would be.[44]

Perhaps the exhaustion of seeing one's opposition as not "entirely wrong all the time" is why there's so little such sight today.

*   *   *

Boyle was, in the estimation of historian Jennifer Ritterhouse, "the most outspoken white integrationist in Virginia."[45] But she hasn't been much remembered. Which is curious, given that Charlottesville has always been a town obsessed with its own memory of itself—the grain of that obsession is different since 2017, but not the fact of it.

In 2001, Boyle was one of eight locals, living and dead, designated a "bridge builder." The designation earned her a small plaque on the Drewary J. Brown Bridge on West Main Street.[46] That was around the same time a historical marker was erected on Preston Avenue, summarizing the shameful history of *Buck v. Bell* (Carrie Buck, one of the forced sterilized, was born in Charlottesville and is buried near here), and around the same time another black-and-white marker went up in honor of Georgia O'Keefe, who stayed in her mother's rented house on and off for a few years around World War I and taught some art classes at the university. Eight years earlier, I'd left Charlottesville for college. I left knowing what *Buck v. Bell* was all about, and there was a poster of an O'Keefe iris tacked to the wall of my childhood bedroom (in a house on a street named after a Revolutionary War battle, so I knew, too, about Howe's victory over Washington at Brandywine Creek). I must have read, in high school, King's letter from Birmingham Jail, where he includes Boyle in a list of six white writers whom he deemed useful to the movement. But I don't recall ever having heard of Patty Boyle during my childhood.

Perhaps that's because, to borrow Ritterhouse's phrasing, Boyle's piety, her detailed narration of the ways her experience working for civil rights tarnished her faith in human beings but transformed her faith in God, "makes for unfamiliar and even uncomfortable reading for secular audiences in the post-civil rights era."[47]

Or perhaps she's not much remembered because, in the end, Boyle didn't accomplish very much—which can be said of most white southerners in the movement; the story of the movement's victory, or, to borrow from historian David L. Chappell, what made civil rights move, was by and large the action of African Americans, and when the actions of white southerners like Virginia Foster Durr or P. D. East did help the movement, they helped largely because of African Americans' strategic and savvy exploitation of white southerners' gestures.[48] Maybe we don't, beyond that plaque on the bridge, remember Boyle because her achievements, in the end, were slight.

A few months ago, the book club at my church—a largely white congregation, in a small town in Piedmont North Carolina—read *The Desegregated Heart*. This was during COVID, the book club met on Zoom, and it was a small crowd—me and a half-dozen or so congregants. One of them, an artist who had led the town to remove its Confederate monument a year before, said he thought the book was not really about what Patty Boyle found in her activism. It was about, Will said, what she lost. "What are you willing to be a fool for?" Will asked, and of course the measure of the Holy Fool is never what she accomplishes.

In 1957, James McBride Dabbs, the race liberal from South Carolina, lamented, in a letter to Boyle, that he hadn't had a cross burned on his lawn, as she had. But Dabbs was enough of a Christian to criticize his own metric: "Oh, well, no one ever knows just what effect he has; our job is to go ahead and do the best we can. As Robert Frost said, 'Something has to be left to God.'"[49] Which is to say: when you read someone who bears witness, what's important is not that the writer you're reading accomplished something, but that her witness gives you clarity about what's really going on. Maybe Boyle was a great success, if what counts as success is doing what the biblical prophets did—just saying some true things, regardless of the effect their proclamation did (or didn't) have on their auditors, because bringing the message is what they were called by God to do. "What I really have in mind," Boyle wrote to the editor of the *Norfolk Virginian-Pilot* in 1951, "is a campaign for truth."[50]

In 1965, she divorced. In 1967, she left civil rights work: "racial conflict" was "no longer my field of endeavor," she explained to one interlocutor.[51] The "Black Power approach"—an approach she thought had many flaws—did not have space for her. In a letter to Sellers, she adverted to Ecclesiastes: "there's a time to speak and a time to be silent. I'm glad that when it was time to speak, I spoke."[52]

When I suggest Patty Boyle didn't accomplish very much, I don't mean to damn her with faint praise. I only mean to suggest the limits of consequentialist reasoning, the limits of judging what we do by what it achieves. What she did was tell the truth, over and over, about the harm and injustice of segregation and of other forms of racism. Over and over—God gave her some things to say, and she said them.

Ramon Dagoberto Quiñones

(1935–)

Ramon Quiñones; photo courtesy of the Chandler Museum

JESUS IS MY COYOTE

Padre Ramon Dagoberto Quiñones and
the Sanctuary Movement

M. Therese Lysaught

I sat transfixed by the homily. It was my first visit to St. Therese of the Little Flower Catholic Church in South Bend, Indiana. The parish, the pastor was explaining, was in the middle of a serious discernment process. As a community, they were deliberating on whether or not they would receive and shelter Central American refugees who were fleeing brutal civil wars. He encouraged his parishioners to attend discussion groups after Mass, to study the question, to pray about it. In a month, they would vote on whether to become a . . . "sanctuary" church. I had never heard of *this*. They were going to decide . . . as a parish? I had never seen *that*. The congregation would welcome refugees to live in their buildings and care for and accompany them twenty-four hours a day, each parishioner risking at minimum a five-year prison term and $2,000 fine? I had never *encountered* people who were willing to go to jail for their faith. Would I ever be?

As I listened to that homily on December 2, 1985, Padre Ramon Dagoberto Quiñones sat eighteen hundred miles away in the US district courtroom in Tucson, Arizona. In his customary place next to his colleague Doña Maria, he wasn't wearing his usual gray suit over his clericals. Instead, he was dressed in black. So was she. So were their nine American friends, all codefendants in the "Sanctuary Trial."[1] And all their attorneys. And many spectators. All wore the color of mourning in remembrance of the four church women who were raped and assassinated by a Salvadoran government death squad at the beginning of the Salvadoran civil war, five years prior to that very day. Together, their living human bodies formed a bold statement in fabric that wordlessly proclaimed the reason they were on trial: "*Nuestras hermanos y hermanas son presente!*"

EL SANCTUARIO

When Padre Quiñones put on his collar that fateful morning four years earlier, June 6, 1981, he expected his day to be no different from any other day. He would say Mass, attend to parish business, chat with parishioners, feed the hungry, welcome refugees, visit prisoners—in other words, live the gospel as he had done since he was ordained twenty years earlier. He chuckled remembering his first parish, Saint Martin de Porres, up the road in Hermosilla. Back then he had celebrated the Eucharist in a vacant lot! That was before the Second Vatican Council. He had still worn his cassock every day. The long, hot robe made motorcycle rides to parishioners' homes a challenge, to be sure—but they could hear in advance that the priest was arriving!

Padre Ramon had served at El Sanctuario Nuestra Senora de Guadalupe—one of the largest and loveliest churches in Nogales, Sonora, Mexico—for almost two decades now. Its white, stucco façade—blindingly bright in the intense sun—shone like the beacon that any church named for La Virgen should. With the indispensable help of parishioners like Doña Maria del Socorro Pardo de Aguilar, the church fed dozens of children every day in its large gleaming kitchen as well as so many people without anywhere to live, whose numbers had mushroomed along with the multiplying *maquiladoras*, birthed in the early 1980s under Reagan and Thatcher's destructive new world of neoliberal economics. People came from such long distances to work in those squalid factories, uprooted from their land, their homes, their communities. They lived in cardboard shacks, with no running water and no electricity. Who could live on four dollars per day, let alone feed a family? He was happy to welcome them.

On top of that, there were the refugees. A mere three miles lay between El Sanctuario and her sister parish, Sacred Heart Catholic Church, across the border in Nogales, Arizona. And between them sat a major point of entry between Mexico and the United States. For almost three decades, refugees and would-be immigrants had passed through the area with regularity. But after 1980, when the Salvadoran National Guard assassinated Archbishop Romero, civil war erupted in El Salvador, and the brutality in Guatemala devolved into genocide, what had been a trickle of refugees from Central America became its own *rio grande*. They were arriving at an alarming rate, mostly on foot, and all in desperate need. They described unimaginable atrocities in their home countries: the torture, the threats, the killings, the persecution. The women, especially, recounted their harrowing journeys. For many, Nogales, Mexico, marked their last stop on the trek to seek asylum in the United States.

At first, it was simply a matter of giving them refuge for a few days—a place to wash, to eat, to rest, to sleep, to pray. Other Mexican churches did the same thing. But the migrants seemed particularly drawn to El Sanctuario. Perhaps its simple adobe style reminded them of their homes. Perhaps it was their deep love for La Virgen. Whatever the reason, they flocked to Padre Ramon's church. On any given night, they would be tending to up to forty people.

Or perhaps it was Padre Ramon himself, who found obvious joy in providing refugees shelter on their journey. He smiled, made jokes, and provided a space of light and friendship and a word of peace and prayer on their sojourn. As they stumbled wearily through the arched church entrance, his dark eyes danced in welcome behind his black-rimmed aviator-shaped glasses. Though not particularly outspoken, he conveyed an energy and vitality with his wiry frame. His dark hair—short on the sides, combed up with a hint of a pompadour—assured them they had landed at a place of order and style. "It is my priestly duty," he had often told Doña Maria, "to help the persecuted and house the homeless."[2] Yes, serving them was a duty—but it was also a gift to him. In serving them, he was serving Jesus.

But it had evolved into so much more. For one thing, the Mexican government began colluding with the Americans to block his guests from entering the United States. Shocked, Padre Ramon told Doña Maria, "The US Immigration Service will not accept applications for asylum from Salvadorans and Guatemalans. The American officials pick up the telephone and call Mexican authorities who very quickly pick up the trusting refugee and take him to a Mexican jail for deportation."[3] Mexican agents even arrested refugees before they got to the border. No wonder the federal prison on the outskirts of town—El Centro de Prevencíon y Readaptacíon—overflowed with Central Americans, none of whom had committed a crime.

On his weekly visits to prison, the priest could see their desperation. Busy saying Mass for Mexican prisoners, he never had enough time to minister to the Central Americans. And there were so many. The sight overwhelmed him each week: over two dozen men jammed into a 30-square-foot cell, hungry, traumatized, dreading their imminent deportation. Doña Maria began coming along to help. She brought food along with her comforting presence and helped him counsel the prisoners on how to get across the border undetected.[4] Padre Ramon often told his friends that he was no liberation theologian—just a traditional parish priest who served the poor, because serving the poor *is* the Christian tradition. Liberation theologian or not, he was a balm for the prisoners. Above the pain and squalor of their dismal cell, one prisoner had scratched a simple message high on one of the walls, speaking for them all: "Viva Padre Quiñones."[5]

SOLIDARITY

Viva he still did. That December day in the courtroom, Padre Quinones's codefendants were worried about him, particularly about
his heart trouble. He repeatedly assured them that he was fine.
He was only forty-nine. Could they not see how relaxed he was?
True, driving fifty-five miles from Nogales to Tucson every day,
and then driving fifty-five miles back, was getting a little old. But
it was harder on his old blue Ford than it was on him.

He had made this drive every day since the trial started on October 22, and they told him that the proceedings might drag on
until June. He took some comfort in knowing that he didn't have
to be here—he was here by choice. His attorney told him that as
a Mexican citizen, he could have ignored the indictment, stayed
in Nogales, and not even been arrested. His own government had
no quarrel with him. But Padre Ramon knew he had done nothing
illegal, and he wanted to prove that in a court of law. If he didn't
participate in the trial, he told Doña Maria, "I would feel like I
would have to petition the US government every time I wanted to
feed this person or provide lodging for that person, to guide this
one or support that one."[6] So there he was, every day, up at 5 a.m.,
visiting his parishioners in the morning, driving to Tucson for the
trial, back by 7 p.m. for Mass and other church matters. At least
he was in bed by 11 p.m. Thankfully, the US government provided
an interpreter so that he and Doña Maria could follow the court
proceedings every day.

More than seeking to prove he'd done nothing wrong, though,
Padre Ramon was here for his friends, for the church. They were
just regular people of faith—clergy and priests and nuns and
laypeople—ordinary Christians who had responded to a crisis.
And for the priest and his *compañeros*, one of the most beautiful
things about the sanctuary movement was that it wasn't Christians acting as individuals. It was churches acting as churches—as
Christ's body alive and active in the world. Welcoming sojourners

and strangers and refugees, *as church*; tending to their needs, *as church*; learning from our brothers and sisters who are not first and foremost Mexicans or Anglos or Salvadorans or Guatemalans, but who—with us—are part of Christ's body that crosses all borders. *This* was one of the most important truths of the sanctuary movement: that spurred by the face of Christ in the faces of those fleeing violence and persecution, the church, especially the church in the United States, had rediscovered itself, *converted* to the gospel, and acted in the world as church![7]

As Saint Paul wrote, if one member of the body suffers, all suffer (1 Cor. 12:26). So for Padre Ramon, avoiding arrest and the trial was not an option. Instead, he was here, in this Tucson courtroom, sitting proudly with his codefendants Doña Maria, Jim Corbett, Rev. John Fife, Sister Darlene Nicgorski, Phillip Willis-Conger, Peggy Hutchison, Fr. Tony Clark, Mary K. Doan Espinoza, Nena MacDonald, and Wendy LeWin. Together, they faced seventy-one federal charges; together, they witnessed to the truth; and together, they bore the costs and joys of following Jesus in a world filled with contempt for refugees and immigrants.

Los Dos "Padres"

Padre Quiñones was just the person Jim Corbett was looking for that hot morning on June 6, 1981. A Quaker goat rancher from Arizona, Corbett had begun helping Central American refugees in the United States earlier that year. Like most people, Corbett fell into the work when he picked up a refugee alongside the road and listened firsthand to his personal story.[8] Though initially drawn into the work for humanitarian rather than justice reasons, Corbett and others quickly discovered that the US Immigration and Naturalization Service (INS) was effectively refusing to grant asylum to Salvadorans and Guatemalans. Corbett witnessed INS agents brazenly destroy asylum applications. He heard allegations that Central Americans "voluntarily" withdrew their applications—at gunpoint. Before Corbett could even visit refugees, the INS forcibly relocated them to detention centers far from any legal assistance.

Frustratingly, all Corbett's efforts to work within the "justice" system—to post bonds, provide legal assistance, give food and shelter to refugees while they applied for asylum—were fruitless. While most refugees from countries with "communist" governments were granted asylum, almost all from El Salvador and Guatemala were deported back to their countries.[9] This seemed gravely to violate both the US 1980 Refugee Act and international law. Salvadorans and Guatemalans were refused asylum on the grounds that they were simply "economic" refugees. "Economic"? Corbett knew that well over ten thousand Salvadorans had already been killed before their civil war had even started. Refugees they found in fields and along roads spoke of horrifying atrocities. For them, deportation meant certain death—not because of any political affiliation, but simply because they were poor or indigenous or catechists and the oppressive regime wanted to send a message of terror to those communities. Corbett and his allies all knew the real reason—the United States was "indirectly" supporting the Salvadoran and Guatemalan regimes through its foreign policy and active military assistance. To provide asylum would be an implicit confession that our government was supporting regimes that were slaughtering their own people.

Corbett soon realized that if asylum-seeking refugees were simply going to be deported, what they needed was not legal aid but help eluding capture at the border. For a while, he had been driving to Nogales, Mexico, picking up refugees, and smuggling them across the border to his house in Tucson—"the Corbett Inn," as he and his wife jokingly called it. But he needed someone on the Mexican side to help with the effort. When a friend mentioned Padre Quiñones, Corbett knew he had found his man.

And so, Corbett now stood in Padre Quiñones's office.

As it turned out, this mild-mannered priest needed something too—help at the local prison with Central American refugees. Now the solution had walked into his office. This wiry white American with an unkempt goatee who towered over him by at least a head would accompany Padre Ramon and Doña Maria on their weekly prison visits, posing as a Catholic priest so the guards would let him in.

For the next two years, after passing through the gauntlet of prison gates and personnel, while Padre Quiñones said Mass, "Padre Jaime" and Doña Maria met with the Central Americans—he with the men, she with the women—advising prisoners on matters such as how to avoid Mexican immigration authorities if they attempted their journey again; how to avoid US INS officials; how to pass as Mexican; and how to understand their legal rights in the United States. So many just wanted help contacting their families in the United States or their home countries, a task Doña Maria and Corbett helped with happily.

Did the trio plan to start a modern-day underground railroad? "Plan" might be too strong of a word, but bit by bit they laid the next rails of a line that had already run for a decade from churches in El Salvador and Guatemala to El Sanctuario and her sister parishes in Nogales.[10] They simply added the next station: Sacred Heart Church in Nogales, Arizona, run by Padre Ramon's friends Fr. Tony Clark and Mary Espinoza, the parish's coordinator of religious education.

Here's how it worked: Padre Quiñones and his parishioners would continue to provide refugees with food and shelter, but they would now be more intentional about helping them evade capture at the border. Where were the holes in the border fences? How might they look, speak, and sound more like a Mexican? Parishioners would leave their photo ID border passes at the church so that refugees who resembled them could use them to cross the border and pass as Mexicans. If they made it past the INS agents, they knew how to reach Sacred Heart. From there, Corbett and Clark would take over, again giving them shelter, food, and legal advice, returning the IDs to El Sanctuario to be used again, and transporting them to churches in cities across the United States and Canada.

But on that sunbaked afternoon in June 1981, who could have imagined how explosively this railroad would expand? They didn't even have a second church on the US side. At least, not yet.

SANCTUARY

The defendants' black attire that morning in court not only voiced solidarity for the four murdered churchwomen and all the Salvadorans and Guatemalans who had died under these same repressive regimes. It was also one of the few ways they had to testify to the reasons for their sanctuary work. Federal District Judge Earl H. Carroll, who sat at his perch overseeing the courtroom, gave them few other options. He had ruled that the defendants could not present any evidence or arguments about their religious and humanitarian justifications. When Padre Quiñones's attorney William Risner attempted to interject this information, Carroll accused him of making "inflammatory remarks" and silenced him.

How do you defend yourself when you're not allowed to present reasons for your actions? The defendants were banned from using most words related to faith or religion. Religion, they were told, was just a "pretext" for their political goals. The attorneys literally had to ask Carroll if they could refer to Padre Ramon as "Father" or to Darlene as "Sister," or if they had to call Southside Presbyterian a "building" rather than a "church." Beyond being ridiculous, didn't this violate that much-hailed First Amendment in the United States that was supposed to allow people to freely speak about and practice their religious beliefs?

One thing that united Padre Quiñones with his colleagues was how deeply their work was grounded in their faith. Matthew 25 tells us very clearly to feed the hungry, give drink to the thirsty, clothe the naked, shelter the homeless. As you did it for the least of these, you did it for me, Jesus says. He and his friends believed that their faith prevented them from simply standing by while people were dying. "Charity," Padre Ramon told Risner, "does not require any documentation."[11]

Even more, the sanctuary defendants were motivated by God's particular concern for refugees stated repeatedly through-out the Hebrew Scriptures. As they built the movement, Leviti-cus 19—where God tells Israel, as part of a longer version of the Ten Commandments, to love the *gerim*, the resident aliens—was frequently on their lips: "When a foreigner resides among you in your land, do not mistreat them. The foreigner residing among you must be treated as your native-born. Love them as yourself, for you were foreigners in Egypt. I am the LORD your God."[12] At the heart of the Christian biblical tradition is the memory that we were once refugees . . . but God accompanied us. So we, too, are to love strangers and treat them *no differently* than those in our own communities.

Though Padre Ramon and his *compañeros* weren't permitted to tell this story in court, sanctuary itself dates back to Israel's ear-liest memories. Numbers, Deuteronomy, and Joshua repeatedly discuss "cities of refuge," established for anyone who had acci-dentally killed someone, to give them safety while the community deliberated on their case. Although varying in its specifics, this an-cient practice was carried forward through Christian history, rec-ognized in Roman law, medieval canon law, and English common law, with churches, and sometimes bishops' houses, monasteries, hospitals, and even cemeteries, being considered places where the law stopped at the door. For these were holy places, places of God's presence, places of *sanctitas*. Thus, churches were sanctuaries in two intertwined senses—as places of refuge (safety) because they were first places of God's presence (sanctity), and as places where people came to worship and find shelter in the Lord who saves. For the law to enter these holy places and violently arrest someone was to desecrate these spaces.[13]

Elizabeth I in England ended sanctuary in the 1600s, but Padre Ramon knew that in his own Catholic tradition it had persisted through the 1983 Code of Canon Law. So for three thousand years churches had provided safety for people who had potentially *done* wrong. But even more, for innocent people in harm's way—such as Salvadorans and Guatemalans who were *victims* or potential victims of violence and wrongdoing—churches and religious communities had long served as safe havens. Historical examples abound. For example, churches played a huge role in the abolitionist underground railroad in the United States, helping one thousand to five thousand slaves per year to escape, transporting them to safety, and providing food, shelter, and at times legal assistance between 1830 and 1860. Led by pastor Andre Trocme during World War II, French Huguenots in Le Chambon, France, hid from the Nazis over three thousand Jewish children who would certainly have been sent to death camps. And in 1967, Arlington Street Unitarian Church in Boston provided sanctuary for three hundred Vietnam War draft resisters, quickly being joined by other congregations.

For all these reasons, refugees from Central America sought help from churches in their own countries. But then, in a horrific new historic twist, the long-honored border at the church door was violated. Their governments started killing priests and nuns, desecrating churches, and killing people who sought refuge there. So the refugees sought sanctuary at churches in Mexico—El Sanctuario and others . . . and now at churches in the United States.

But the accused couldn't mention any of this information about sanctuary and the Christian tradition during their trial. Even worse—they were prohibited from breathing a word about the political conditions in Central America, the terrible human rights abuses perpetrated by the Salvadoran and Guatemalan governments on their own citizens, or the role the United States was playing in funding those governments.[14] That critical testimony, too, had been barred. The attorneys and witnesses were prohibited from using the words "refugee," "torture," "killed," "terror," and "death." *Nor* could they mention international refugee law, constitutional rights, immigration procedures, or even the defendants' understanding that they were acting lawfully per the 1980 Refugee Act and the United Nations accords on refugees.

Yet these were the precise reasons that Padre Ramon and his friends had risked their lives and their liberty. Their faith brooked no other response. As the Good Samaritan picked up the wounded man at the side of the road, they could not turn away from their Central American sisters and brothers whom they literally found on the side of the road. So what if there was a "border" between El Sanctuario and Sacred Heart? Today the road to Jericho runs between Palestine and Jordan—maybe the Samaritan had carted the injured man across a border too. Sure, the Samaritan used a donkey rather than Corbett's rickety pickup truck, but he took him to an inn, a shelter, where he could be healed, cared for, safe. What if the Samaritan had had to care for not one injured man but hundreds of men, women, and children?

What if the inn ran out of space, the way Corbett's house rapidly did? In 1981, when the sanctuary providers started this work, they quickly needed more safe havens. As true Samaritans find a way out of no way, Corbett knocked on many church doors—and he finally found one that opened: Southside Presbyterian Church in Tucson, Arizona.

La Declaración

Southside Presbyterian Church was nothing like El Sanctuario. The scraggly neighborhood in which it was located was dotted with movie-set cacti, weeds, and rusty playground equipment.[15] When Padre Quiñones first visited Southside, a huge sign stood in the yard outside the small blue and white stucco building proclaiming: "Este es un sanctuario para los oprimidos de Centroamérica!" [This is a sanctuary for the oppressed of Central America!]. Clearly, he thought, no one was attempting to hide what they were doing.

John Fife, pastor at Southside, was a natural ally for Corbett. He had gotten involved in this issue in 1980 when a coyote left twenty-five Salvadoran refugees in the desert outside Tucson in the blistering summer heat. Half had died. The survivors were brought to local churches for help. Fife and his church friends were aghast at their stories of atrocities, and then they were shocked when the INS arrested the survivors and tried to deport them to the places where these atrocities had occurred! Being Christians, they tried to help. They raised bond money and bonded the refugees out of detention. They set up the Tucson Ecumenical Council, which had raised a lot of money to keep paying these bonds and other legal defense bills. They organized a weekly prayer vigil and even worked on what Fife called "legislative, judicial and corporate strategies." One was particularly creative—they organized shareholder resolutions to get all US commercial airlines to refuse to accept Salvadoran deportees on their flights. And it worked.

But ultimately, they couldn't stop the deportations. In 1981, the INS had deported over fifteen thousand Salvadorans back to what Fife called "the death squads." Then, at a prayer vigil, Fife met Corbett. Corbett had already discovered that legal strategies weren't very effective. In partnership with Padre Quiñones, he had started sheltering refugees at his own place in Tucson, but he needed more room. So he asked Fife if Southside would take them. Typical Fife—he took it to the church elders, and they deliberated and prayed over it. The congregation finally agreed (with only two abstentions). No doubt Corbett's impassioned declamation swayed them: "We can take our stand with the oppressed or we can take our stand with organized oppression, we can serve the Kingdom of God or we can serve the Kingdoms of this world—but we cannot do both. . . . When the government itself sponsors the crucifixion of entire peoples and then makes it a felony to shelter those seeking refuge, law-abiding protest merely trains us to live with atrocity."[16]

Energized by success, Corbett took the proposal to several other churches in Tucson. And on March 24, 1982—the second anniversary of Romero's assassination—Southside Presbyterian and a half-dozen congregations in Tucson, Berkeley, Milwaukee, Chicago, and other cities publicly declared that they would be "sanctuaries" for refugees from Central America. They even held a press conference and read aloud a letter they had sent to the US government: "We are writing to inform you that the Southside Presbyterian church will publicly violate the Immigration and Nationality Act Section 274(a). We have declared our church as a 'sanctuary' for undocumented refugees from Central America. . . . We believe that justice and mercy require that people of conscience actively assert our God-given right to aid anyone fleeing from persecution and murder. The current administration of the United States law prohibits us from sheltering these refugees from Central America. Therefore, we believe that administration of the law is immoral as well as illegal."[17] From then on, they were "the sanctuary movement"! Southside began housing up to two dozen refugees per night—pretty impressive for a church with maybe 160 members. They fed and tended to malnourished children. Doctors from the congregation provided medical care for those who had been tortured. They taught English, gathered food, welcomed the refugees into their homes for dinners and hospitality, worshiped with them, listened to them, and learned what was going on in their countries of origin.

Other churches across the country began housing people too, or helping them move along this new "underground railroad" transporting people to Chicago, Philadelphia, New Hampshire, San Francisco, Portland, and even Canada. None of them could have foreseen that, by 1990, over five hundred churches with thousands of congregants would publicly—*publicly*—declare that they too were sanctuaries, would shelter some 500,000 thousand refugees.[18] Many more churches would serve as "secondary sanctuaries," providing material support to the five hundred.[19]

The Legalities

Ordinarily, few things could dim Padre Quiñones's cheery demeanor, but Judge Carroll was one. That December morning, Carroll was, as always, eyeing the defendants with contempt. He was clearly biased against their cause. He'd made disparaging remarks about Latinos, and apparently owned stock in Central American and Peruvian mining companies, as well as a bank that regularly hired undocumented refugees. The lawyers had tried repeatedly to get him disqualified from the case, without success. For Padre Quiñones, the judge's behavior completely refuted the common Latin American opinion that US justice couldn't be corrupted.

This whole trial raised so many questions for the passionate priest. For instance, as he queried Risner: "How could Dona Maria and I be indicted for violating US laws for something we supposedly did in our own country? We have never been accused of any wrongdoing in Mexico. Our work has been open, lawful, and necessary."[20]

And what of this selective prosecution? A myriad of folks in the southwest United States transported undocumented immigrants. That was widely known. Farmers transported border crossers to work in their fields every day. Wealthy women picked up undocumented women to clean their houses. If people did this to make money or to maintain their social status, it was okay, but if they did it because of their faith, they're a criminal? Padre Ramon chafed at the hypocrisy. "The US government, in its strange alliance with the court, has shown all the symptoms of a desire to punish certain persons who, because of their Christian vocation, become a danger to the politics of the country," he asserted.[21]

But could the government do that—could it infiltrate churches and bug their gatherings and worship services? Didn't this violate the United States' alleged commitment to the separation of church and state? What "evidence" the INS had against them came from informants that had infiltrated their work. The defense lawyers were very excited about what they kept calling "constitutional questions" regarding these informants. Apparently, the INS had never gotten a warrant, but apparently you needed one in the United States to send a spy into a place—particularly into a church! And even stranger, this was the first time the US government had sent wired informants into churches. Could that possibly be constitutional?

The sanctuary activists also firmly believed that they were *not* violating the law, *not* engaged in civil disobedience. On the one hand, the Americans were exercising their First Amendment rights—to enact their faith by assisting people fleeing terror. Like Padre Ramon, they believed that their faith required them to feed, clothe, and shelter those in need. Period. On the other hand, yes, the Immigration and Nationality Act at 8 USC 1324 said that it was "unlawful for an individual to knowingly assist a person *unlawfully present* in the United States." But the sanctuary participants firmly believed that according to constitutional law, international law, and US law, the refugees were lawfully present in the United States, so they had every legal right to engage in a public, recognized religious ministry to refugees. For, according to a different section of that same law—8 USC 1101 (a)(42)—"a refugee qualifies for political asylum in the US if it can be established that he or she, owing to a well-founded fear of persecution for reasons of race, religion, nationality, membership of a particular social group or political opinion, is unwilling to avail himself of the protection of that country."[22] Membership in a particular social group that was being targeted for death—the poor, indigenous, or innocent bystander—that wasn't enough? This was all grounded in the 1951 UN Convention and 1967 Protocol Relating to the Status of Refugees. In fact, in May 1981, before Padre Quinones had even met Corbett, the UN High Commissioner on Refugees specifically stated that "El Salvadoran refugees, as a group, meet the requirements for refugee status."[23]

Thus, from the defendants' perspective, international law was on their side. In assisting these Central Americans, they were not acting illegally. But, again, they couldn't mention any of this. They were not allowed to make their own case. So if the courts don't let you present your arguments, what do you do? Christ was silent before Pilate. They'd be silent too. They had decided, with their lawyers, that none of them would take the stand, and that they would not call any witnesses in their defense. Darlene didn't think this was a very good idea. But Corbett had said, "We won't be able to tell the truth, even in part"—so why pretend? And maddeningly, every time some bit of truth was about to emerge, Carroll dismissed the jury from the courtroom.

Thus, in lieu of words, their black attire in the courtroom on that December day represented their religious, humanitarian, and legal arguments. Sister Darlene summed it up well: "We are doing just what they did. We have not been physically raped or killed by our government. But for many of the same deeds for which these four women were brutally killed, our homes have been searched, our churches bugged, our prayer services infiltrated, and our activities criminalized."[24] They had, in the words of German theologian Dorothee Sölle, "become illegal on behalf of the illegal ones." On their behalf, they were crying out prophetically against US support of "specific policies of death and terror."[25] But mostly they were just trying to save innocent people from being viciously killed.

And amusingly, God was proving to be a God of justice—the government's case was so weak! The defendants and, in fact, the whole sanctuary movement, had been very public about their work. The churches and synagogues that participated in the movement had publicly declared themselves as sanctuaries. Best of all, Jesus Cruz—the prosecution's "key witness"—had made a mess of his testimony. Apparently, he had been a professional coyote prior to working for the INS. *He himself* had *already* been convicted of smuggling people. Apparently, he had also violated US gun laws *while* he was working for the INS, might have failed to report all his INS income on his taxes, and was a known perjurer! Of course, if he could lie to a priest, why wouldn't he lie in the courtroom? Padre Ramon and his codefendants were almost entertained listening to Cruz's testimony—it was so full of contradictions and what Corbett had called "sleazy details," that most of his testimony so far had been suppressed. How could the use of US government agents in Mexico "not be an obvious violation of our national sovereignty?" Padre Ramon silently asked.

Doña Maria had been very suspicious when Cruz had shown up at El Sanctuario, so eager to help. But who would have expected a man named "Jesus" to be a US government informant?

La Serpiente

Jesus Cruz was stout, a decade older than Padre Quiñones, a ring of hair circling his balding head. He appeared one day at the priest's office, with a *truckload* of oranges, tangerines, and grapefruits for the needy. He declared that he sympathized with the sanctuary movement and wanted to volunteer. Cruz also was both a Mexican and a US permanent resident, which he said gave him a distinct advantage in helping people cross the border.

Cruz had already worked on eight or nine immigration stings for the US government. If he hadn't accepted this assignment, they had threatened to send him back to prison or back to Mexico—or both.[26] In March 1983, when the US government officially launched Operation Sojourner, they got lucky. Corbett was working in the United States, so Padre Quiñones was again shorthanded at the prison. He needed another "priest" to continue to counsel the Central Americans. Cruz arrived just at the right time.

Doña Maria's colleagues in Tucson shared her suspicions. But Corbett convinced them to give Cruz and his partner, Salamón Graham, the benefit of the doubt. He'd read a study, he said, that 20 percent of informants are converted by the groups they infiltrate, and they had made a commitment to be as public and transparent as possible. And Cruz was a star volunteer. He helped lots of refugees sneak through holes in the border fence. He ferried envelopes with immigration documents among various parties. He accompanied immigrants as they impersonated Mexicans at the Nogales checkpoint. He drove dozens of Central Americans to Phoenix, Tucson, Santa Fe, Albuquerque, and Los Angeles. Those long drives were especially good for long conversations. Cruz was a good listener, getting the Anglos and migrants to open up, share their stories, and let him know their operations. Unbeknownst to the refugees and activists, Cruz was recording it all.

Cruz's friends back in Florida would have laughed to see how "religious" he had become. He had been going to Mass, even saying the rosary with the communities. His most clever move was joining the Bible studies. Jim Oines, pastor at Alzona Lutheran Church in Phoenix, had started a Bible study for the refugees because he thought it would be the best way to help them develop a sense of community. They loved it. So did Cruz, who attended at least once a month, but for different reasons. The refugees really thought of Cruz as a friend—and often asked him for rides home. Thus, he learned where they all lived.

This growing trust opened the door to meetings of the inner circle. Here the sanctuary activists usually discussed and debated logistics of smuggling larger groups of Central Americans or what cars to use—things like that. Cruz found these sanctuary people—and their meetings—strange. Fife had been clear that no one was "the leader." The activists claimed that the movement was decentralized, grassroots, spiritual. But Cruz was baffled as to why these Christians risked doing jail time for helping Central Americans—for *free*? At least Villalon and Salvidar—with whom he *would* be in jail if he weren't wearing a wire—made money smuggling people. What he was doing wasn't much different from the work he did for those guys as a coyote. But now he was a government coyote with a microphone, and he had every conversation—every dinner, car trip, Bible study, planning meeting, heck, even a prayer service—on tape. A hundred hours of tape. James Rayburn, INS chief investigator at the Phoenix office, was very well pleased with his informant's work.

THE VERDICT

On July 1, 1986, the verdict came in: GUILTY. Father Quiñones, Doña Maria, and five of his coconspirators.

It came as a shock. To the defendants, the media, and clearly the jury too. But what other outcome could be expected, given how Carroll restricted the trial and the jury instructions? After sitting for twenty-three long weeks, the jurors had deliberated for nine days. As the verdicts were read, one juror cried. Another went home to throw up. Still another declared: "These were good people—we didn't want to convict them." Their feelings were summed up by an observer from Ohio: "I got a sense that they are really ordinary people. They are not gods or saints. They're just ordinary people who acted."[27]

Of all people, Corbett was acquitted. Ironically, it seems he was in Mexico networking when Cruz taped most of the sanctuary meetings.

Learning of the tapes, Padre Quiñones felt betrayed. He had considered Jesus to be his friend. "I have felt pain today. I would like to be Christ," he told Doña Maria with a sly grin, "and give him a kiss in retribution for the kiss Judas gave Christ."[28]

For Padre Ramon, guilty on one count of conspiracy, one misdemeanor, and innocent of two felony charges. But it was all just symbolic. In the end, all their sentences were suspended, and they were given five years of probation. He would be back in Mexico that night—doing the exact same thing. He had already begun raising $12,000 to build a two-story extension on El Sanctuario so he could house twice as many people. A priest, a Christian—he had always acted in accord with his religious canons—no sham verdict was going to change that. "It is the mission of the church to help the poor and needy and these charges against me aren't crimes in Mexico,"[29] he noted. He did find one vocation-related value in the whole ordeal: "I believe that I had to give witness to my calling, even if it means to risk persecution. This is my calling."[30]

Was the verdict "the death knell for the sanctuary movement," as Donald M. Reno, the US attorney who prosecuted the case, proclaimed?[31] Not at all. The seeds planted by Padre Ramon and his *compañeros* bloom even today. And the work is more necessary than ever. Although it's hard to imagine, the situation is arguably worse for the refugees at the US/Mexican border now than it was in the 1980s. Those trying to escape the violence that continues to plague Central America now meet more strident government atrocities in the United States—children ripped from their families and kept in cages; Trump's border wall; more stringent crackdowns on immigrants throughout the United States; endless deportations.[32] Since 2013, at least 130 deported Salvadorans had been disappeared, tortured, or killed.[33]

In response, in 2007, the New Sanctuary Movement emerged, and a new network of some four hundred to eight hundred sanctuary congregations has blossomed. Even more powerfully, the biblical notion of sanctuary cities has been resurrected—to date some two hundred cities in the United States have declared themselves to be sanctuaries for immigrants and undocumented people.[34] This movement challenges us today to hear the words of Holocaust survivor Elie Wiesel:

> One can live a mile away from the border, and it's not a mile, it's a lifetime. . . . I could never understand and I cannot un-

derstand now how those people in Switzerland, who were free, could remain free and eat in the morning and at lunch and at dinner while looking at the other side, at occupied France. . . . Good and evil were separated by a man-made frontier. Any frontier is man-made, and yet, on one side people died, and on the other, they went on living as though the others didn't die.[35]

Every member of this new movement today, whether they know it or not, follows in the footsteps of Padre Ramon and his friends, who fearlessly and joyfully embodied Jesus, the ultimate coyote, the one who crossed the unbridgeable border to ferry each human person—including each of us—to a new land, God's kingdom of wholeness, healing, and *shalom*.

NOTES

FOREWORD

1. Dietrich Bonhoeffer, *Letters and Papers from Prison*, ed. Eberhard Bethge (New York: Simon & Schuster, 1997), 297.

2. Bonhoeffer, *Letters and Papers from Prison*, 383.

3. Friedrich Nietzsche, *"The Twilight of the Idols" with "The AntiChrist" and "Ecce Homo,"* trans. Antony M. Ludovici (London: Wordsworth, 2007), 129.

4. Bonhoeffer, *Letters and Papers from Prison*, 383.

5. Søren Kierkegaard's vertiginous *Fear and Trembling* was a book Bonhoeffer carried with him during these years, and I have sometimes regarded this passage as a revision of the propulsive Kierkegaardian notion of the instant, as Bonhoeffer observed in *The Cost of Discipleship*. When Jesus calls a person to come and follow, Bonhoeffer said, Jesus calls the person to come and die. "The bridges are torn down, and the followers simply move ahead. A call to discipleship thus immediately creates a new situation."

6. Bonhoeffer, *Letters and Papers from Prison*, 279.

7. Dietrich Bonhoeffer, *Sanctorum Communio: A Theological Study of the Sociology of the Church*, Dietrich Bonhoeffer Works, vol. 1, ed. Clifford J. Green, trans. Reinhard Krauss and Nancy Lukens (Minneapolis: Fortress, 1998), 157.

8. Dietrich Bonhoeffer, *Ethics* (New York: Simon & Schuster, 1995), 62.

9. Curtis Mayfield, cited in "People Get Ready: The Impressions,"

accessed February 16, 2022, http://www.coveredbybrucespringsteen.com/viewcover.aspx?recordID=350.

10. Curtis Mayfield, cited in "People Get Ready: Song Inspired by March on Washington Carries Enduring Message," Terry Gross, Fresh Air Interview, NPR, August 26, 2003; "500 Greatest Songs of All Time," *Rolling Stone*, 2003.

11. Dietrich Bonhoeffer, *London: 1933–1935*, Dietrich Bonhoeffer Works, vol. 13, ed. Keith W. Clements, trans. Isabel Best (Minneapolis: Fortress, 2007), 284.

12. Bonhoeffer, *Letters and Papers from Prison*, 157.

13. Bonhoeffer, *Ethics*, 62–63.

14. Bonhoeffer, *Letters and Papers from Prison*, 13.

15. Bonhoeffer, *Letters and Papers from Prison*, 383.

FLORENCE JORDAN

1. Thomas Chisholm, "Great Is Thy Faithfulness" (Hope Publishing, 1923).

2. The italicized parts of the chapter are fictionalized moments of an imagined day in Florence Jordan's later life. While attentive to spatial and historical realities, creative license has been taken. The notion of constructing around a single day has been borrowed most closely from Tish Harrison Warren's book *Liturgy of the Ordinary: Sacred Practices in Everyday Life* (Downers Grove, IL: InterVarsity Press, 2016).

3. As C. S. Lewis memorably puts it: "the cross comes before the crown, and tomorrow is a Monday morning." C. S. Lewis, *The Weight of Glory* (New York: HarperOne, 2001).

4. Dietrich Bonhoeffer, *Life Together* (London: SCM, 2015).

5. Eugene Peterson, *A Long Obedience in the Same Direction* (Downers Grove, IL: InterVarsity Press, 2000).

6. *Louisville Courier-Journal*, April 18, 1922; *Louisville Courier-Journal*, October 28, 1923; "Louisville Society," *Louisville Courier-Journal*, February 24, 1935. *Louisville Courier-Journal* clippings provided by Southern Baptist Theological Seminary archive. Special thanks to Adam Winter for digitizing and sending.

7. "Activities Announced," *Louisville Courier-Journal*, November 4, 1928.

8. Dallas Lee, *The Cotton Patch Evidence* (Americus, GA: Koinonia Partners, 1971), 17.

9. Lee, *The Cotton Patch Evidence*, 15.

10. Florence Jordan, interview by Vicki Ragsdell, Southern Baptist Theological Seminary Archive, March 18, 1986, http://hdl.handle.net/10392/4087.

11. Florence Jordan, interview.

12. Florence Jordan, interview.

13. Lee, *The Cotton Patch Evidence*, 17.

14. Florence Jordan, "The Witness That Counted," *Round Table*, Summer 1984, 2–7, http://karenhousecw.org/RadicalismOvertheLongHaul.htm.

15. Florence Jordan to Clarence Jordan, Clarence L. Jordan Papers, MS 756 1:10, Hargrett Rare Books Library, University of Georgia, Athens, GA (hereafter MS 756).

16. "Weddings: Kroeger-Jordan," *Louisville Courier-Journal*, July 26, 1936.

17. Lee, *The Cotton Patch Evidence*, 20.

18. Influential in this was Clarence's professor at Southern Seminary, Edward A. McDowell Jr., who related the Greek New Testament to social issues and encouraged students to address Christianity toward racial injustices, even taking Clarence to a meeting of the Southern Interracial Commission. Jordan later commented that this experience was a "turning point" in his life, saying, "it seemed to bring into the open feelings which had lain, like molten lava, within the inner recesses of my heart." Tracy Elaine K'Meyer, *Interracialism and Christian Community in the Postwar South* (Charlottesville: University Press of Virginia, 1997), 29.

19. Florence Jordan to Ken Corson, August 10, 1976, Clarence L. Jordan Papers, MS 2341 2:8, Hargrett Rare Books Library, University of Georgia, Athens, GA (hereafter MS 2341).

20. Lee, *The Cotton Patch Evidence*, 17.

21. Lee, *The Cotton Patch Evidence*, 20. Sampey reversed this decision after a student protest. The Simmons students ate in the dining hall in the end, due largely to Florence's courage.

22. MS 756 1:11, quoted in K'Meyer, *Interracialism and Christian Community*, 32.

23. Clarence Jordan, quoted in David Morgan, "Alongside Us Caucasians," *Biblical Recorder*, November 6, 1940, 10; K'Meyer, *Interracialism and Christian Community*, 34.

24. W. C Boone to Frank Leavell, October 20, 1941, MS 756 1:14; K'Meyer, *Interracialism and Christian Community*, 34.

25. MS 756 1:11, quoted in K'Meyer, *Interracialism and Christian Community*, 33.

26. MS 756 24:4, quoted in K'Meyer, *Interracialism and Christian Community*, 34.

27. Ruth 1:16 ESV.

28. MS 2341 3:8.

29. Clarence Jordan to Fe, November 20, 1939, MS 756 1:11.

30. Lee, *The Cotton Patch Evidence*, 33.

31. This idea is based on an oft-repeated quote from missionary Jim Elliot: "he is no fool who gives up what he cannot keep to gain what he cannot lose." *Journals of Jim Elliot*, ed. Elisabeth Elliot (Ada, MI: Revell, 2002), 174.

32. Lee, *The Cotton Patch Evidence*, 33.

33. MS 2341 3:8.

34. Lee, *The Cotton Patch Evidence*, 30.

35. They considered "population, ratio of blacks to whites, income, soil types, tenancy, climate, spiritual resources, and so on." Lee, *The Cotton Patch Evidence*, 32; K'Meyer, *Interracialism and Christian Community*, 39.

36. Koinonia newsletter, September 23, 1942, MS 756 2:3.

37. Ps. 16:5 ESV.

38. Clarence Jordan to Florence Jordan, November 14, 1942, Koinonia Farm archive; Clarence to Florence, November 15, 1942, Koinonia Farm archive.

39. Clarence Jordan to Florence Jordan, November 18, 1942, Koinonia Farm archive.

40. Clarence Jordan to Florence Jordan, December 7, 1942, Koinonia Farm archive.

41. Clarence Jordan to Florence Jordan, December 7, 1942, Koinonia Farm archive.

42. Clarence Jordan to Florence Jordan, November 15, 1942, Koinonia Farm archive.

43. Clarence Jordan to Florence Jordan, November 18, 1942, Koinonia Farm archive.

44. Joyce Hollyday, "The Dream That Has Endured," *Sojourners* 8, no. 12 (1979).

45. Koinonia Newsletter, 1942, MS 756 2:3.

46. K'Meyer, *Interracialism and Christian Community*, 47; Lee, *The Cotton Patch Evidence*, 45.

47. Florence Jordan, interview.

48. Hollyday, "The Dream That Has Endured."

49. Jim Jordan, email to author, January 24, 2020.

50. Isa. 61:11.

51. There is some dispute about the date of this. Tracy K'Meyer says April 4, 1951, while Dallas Lee places the event earlier, in 1950. Clarence

and Florence Jordan, Howard and Marion Johnson, Gil Butler, Ora and C. Conrad Browne, and Norman Lory join in 1950/1951; in 1954: Harry and Allene Atkinson, Billie Nelson; in 1955: Iola Eustice, Margaret and Will Wittkamper; in 1956: Christian Drescher and Marguerite Reed.

52. Jim Auchmutey, *Class of '65: A Student, a Divided Town, and the Long Road to Forgiveness* (New York: Public Affairs, 2015), 11.

53. Robert Steed, "Two Weeks at Koinonia," *Catholic Worker* (1957).

54. Jim Jordan, email to author, January 24, 2020.

55. Lee, *The Cotton Patch Evidence*, 71.

56. Nelson to Florence Jordan, October 2, 1954, MS 756 3:1.

57. Jim Jordan, email to author, January 24, 2020.

58. Nelson to Florence Jordan, October 2, 1954, MS 756 3:1.

59. Florence Jordan, quoted in Koinonia newsletter, 1960, Koinonia Farm archive.

60. Koinonia newsletter, Spring 1982, Koinonia Farm archive.

61. Clarence Jordan to Florence Jordan, December 7, 1942, Koinonia Farm archive.

62. Lee, *The Cotton Patch Evidence*, 75.

63. Luke 12:11.

64. Lee, *The Cotton Patch Evidence*, 77.

65. Jim Jordan, email to author, January 24, 2020.

66. Ira B. Faglier to Clarence Jordan, August 9, 1950, MS 756 2:13; Lee, *The Cotton Patch Evidence*, 77–78.

67. Lee, *The Cotton Patch Evidence*, 78.

68. Jim Jordan, email to author, January 24, 2020. Despite their sadness, the expulsion came as something of a clarifying relief. As the 1951 newsletter stated: "We rejoice in the clarity that it brings to us regarding our witness on this element of the gospel. Our witness is no longer divided. We are now whole-heartedly committed to complete brotherhood across all barriers with no other commitments to compromise our witness." Koinonia newsletter, January 12, 1951, MS 756 2:14; Rom. 6:5 ESV.

69. Florence Jordan, "The Witness That Counted."

70. Jim Jordan, "Growing Up at Koinonia," *Christianity Today*, March 9, 2005, https://www.christianitytoday.com/ct/2005/marchweb -only/32.0a.html; Teresa Mansfield, quoted in Ansley Quiros, *God with Us: Lived Theology and the Freedom Struggle in Americus, Georgia, 1942-1976* (Chapel Hill: University of North Carolina Press, 2018), 31.

71. "Florence Jordan," Spring 1982, Koinonia Farm archive.

72. Little is known publicly about this, and Florence doesn't write

about it herself (understandably). Initially, I presumed this pregnancy to have resulted in a miscarriage, but both Jim Auchmutey and Katie Long seem to refer to a newborn child. In an email, Lenny Jordan seems to confirm this, writing of his mother's experience "losing a child after me." Lenny Jordan, email to author, January 31, 2020.

73. Norman Long and Katie Long to Florence Jordan, February 16, 1955, MS 756 3:2; Job 1:21.

74. Auchmutey, *Class of '65*, 83.

75. MS 2341 2:9.

76. Jim Jordan, "Growing Up at Koinonia."

77. K'Meyer, *Interracialism and Christian Community*, 86.

78. Lee, *The Cotton Patch Evidence*, 130.

79. Auchmutey, *Class of '65*, 52.

80. Florence Jordan, "The Witness That Counted."

81. Auchmutey, *Class of '65*, 55.

82. Florence Jordan, "The Witness That Counted."

83. Florence Jordan, "The Witness That Counted."

84. Howard and Marion to Clarence and Florence Jordan, September 15, 1965, MS 756 6:12.

85. Auchmutey, *Class of '65*, 64.

86. Florence Jordan, interview.

87. Lenny Jordan to Florence Jordan, July 7, 1972, MS 756 8:5.

88. Florence Jordan, untitled speech, date unknown, Koinonia Farm archive.

89. Scott Russell Sanders, *Staying Put in a Restless World* (Boston: Beacon, 1994).

90. As Florence put it: "Clarence read his Greek New Testament always. He could read it like we read English. It was the Greek of the everyday people, the koine Greek, not the classical. And so he translated just as he read it, using modern equivalents." Hollyday, "The Dream That Has Endured"; MS 2341 1:14.

91. Matt. 13:23 ESV.

92. Florence Jordan, "The Witness That Counted."

93. Coretta Scott King to Florence Jordan, telegram, October 30, 1969, MS 2341 2:5.

94. Florence Jordan, quoted in K'Meyer, *Interracialism and Christian Community*, 178.

95. Jan Jordan, "Civil Rights and Uncivil Whites," *Faith at Work* 78, no. 4 (1965): 12–17; MS 756 15:6.

96. Ruth 1:17 ESV.

97. "Florence Jordan," Spring 1982, Koinonia Farm archive.

98. Jim Jordan, email to author, January 24, 2020.

99. Jim Jordan, email to author, January 31, 2020.

100. Koinonia Newsletter, Spring 1982, Koinonia Farm archive.

101. Ps. 92:13–14 ESV.

102. Ruth Field, "Remembrance of Florence," Koinonia Farm archive.

103. Mary Lathbury, "Day Is Dying in the West," 1878; Lenny Jordan, email to author, January 31, 2020.

104. Annie Dillard, *The Writing Life* (New York: Harper & Row, 1989), 32.

105. Martin Luther King Jr., "I Have a Dream Speech," 1963; many think that King was consciously invoking Koinonia Farm with this line.

106. Warren, *Liturgy of the Ordinary*, 84.

107. Warren, *Liturgy of the Ordinary*, 35.

108. Florence Jordan to John Gabor, July 17, 1959, MS 756 6:1.

BRUCE KLUNDER

1. The only scholarly account that gives Klunder and his work more than a passing reference is Nashani Frazier, *Harambee City: The Congress of Racial Equality in Cleveland and the Rise of Black Power Populism* (Fayetteville: University of Arkansas Press, 2017).

2. Mrs. Bruce W. Klunder, "My Husband Died for Democracy," *Ebony*, June 1964, 32, in Folder 1, Box 1, Reverend Bruce Klunder Collection (RBKC), Western Reserve Historical Society, Cleveland. Bruce Klunder, "A Death and Life Matter," August 1963, typescript sermon in possession of author.

3. Robert E. Strippel to W. Evan Golder, March 12, 1974 (first and fourth quotes). "Once More Let Death Mark a New Beginning," *Intercollegian*, May 1964 (second and third quotes), Robert W. Clarke to friends, April 1964. All in Folder 1, Box 1, RBKC.

4. This brief biographical material is gathered from several sources, primarily the letter of Strippel to Golder, March 12, 1974, and "Once More Let Death Mark a New Beginning," RBKC.

5. Mrs. Bruce W. Klunder, "My Husband Died for Democracy."

6. Bruce Klunder used the phrase "iron ring" to describe the plight of Black Clevelanders in his sermon, "A Death and Life Matter."

7. For a detailed explanation of how federal housing programs benefited whites and not Blacks, see Thomas L. Sugrue, *Sweet Land of Liberty:*

The Forgotten Struggle for Civil Rights in the North (New York: Random House, 2009), 52–53.

8. "Race and Poverty: A Joint Report of the Regional Church Planning Office and the Office of Religion and Race," May 1964, Folder 215, Box 10, Inner City Protestant Parish Papers, Western Reserve Historical Society.

9. Frazier, *Harambee City*, 82.

10. Kimberley L. Phillips, *Alabama North: African-American Migrants, Community, and Working-Class Activism in Cleveland, 1915–45* (Urbana: University of Illinois Press, 1999), 159.

11. Frazier, *Harambee City*, 81–82.

12. For a detailed description, see Frazier, *Harambee City*, 83.

13. Frazier, *Harambee City*, 83.

14. Frazier, *Harambee City*, 83–84.

15. Frazier, *Harambee City*, 86–89. These events can also be followed in the *Cleveland Press* and *Call and Post* throughout January 1964.

16. Frazier, *Harambee City*, 92–93.

17. Frazier, *Harambee City*, 94.

18. Bonnie Remsberg and Charles Remsberg, "What Four Brave Women Told Their Children," *Good Housekeeping*, n.d., 152, Folder 1, Box 1, RBKP.

19. Mrs. Bruce W. Klunder, "My Husband Died for Democracy."

20. Bruce Klunder, "A Death and Life Matter."

21. Program for the Memorial Service for the Reverend Bruce William Klunder, 1937–1964, Folder 2, Box 1, RBKP; *Cleveland Press*, April 10, 1964, A-4.

22. Mrs. Martha Symms to Editor, *Cleveland Plain Dealer*, April 10, 1964, crank letters file, Reverend Harry Taylor Papers (RHTP), Church of the Covenant, Cleveland.

23. A. F. Hecker to Harry B. Taylor, June 10, 1964, crank letters file, RHTP.

24. Thomas M. Hatch to Mr. Benedict R. Schwegler, n.d., Bishops Office files, Archives of the Episcopal Diocese of Ohio, Cleveland.

25. Writer and recipient unidentified, n.d. (c. April 1964), crank letters file, RHTP.

26. Unidentified writer to unidentified paper, n.d. (c. May 1964), crank letters file, RHTP.

27. Mrs. E. R. Neill to unidentified paper, n.d. (c. May 1964), crank letters file, RHTP.

28. *Church Life Magazine*, Episcopal Diocese of Ohio, April 1964, 4.

29. Minutes of Advisory Committee Meeting, May 7, 1964, Office of

Religion and Race, folder 215, box 10, Inner City Protestant Parish Papers, Western Reserve Historical Society.

30. Taylor to Dr. Arthur W. Mielke, April 29, 1964, folder 359.33, RHTP.

31. Author unidentified to Taylor, n.d. (April 1964), folder 359.33, RHTP.

32. Margery (Mrs. Thomas) Bletcher to Mrs. Chambers, n.d. (c. May 1964), folder 359.33, RHTP.

33. Unidentified newspaper, June 1964; *Cleveland Plain Dealer*, June 16, 1964, clippings in container 3, folder 5, Collinwood United Church of Christ Papers, Western Reserve Historical Society.

34. Hadden, *The Gathering Storm in the Churches* (New York: Doubleday, 1969). I have been unable to document the twelve pastors who lost their churches.

35. Frazier, *Harambee City*, argues that Klunder's death divided Black activists more deeply and helped give rise to Black nationalist ideology in Cleveland.

36. Leonard F. Zaller to Mr. Roy Wilkins, May 2, 1966, container 1, folder 3, Greater Cleveland Conference on Religion and Race Papers, Western Reserve Historical Society.

37. Jordan C. Band to Mr. Howard Burger, November 8, 1968, Container 1, Folder 13, Greater Cleveland Conference on Religion and Race Papers.

38. Mrs. J. H. Morris to Mr. Henry Donahower, April 18, 1968, Folder 78, Box 3, Karl F. Bruch Jr. Papers, Western Reserve Historical Society.

39. Brief information about the Hough Riots, as they came to be known, can be found at "Hough Riots," *Encyclopedia of Cleveland History*, accessed January 17, 2022, https://case.edu/ech/articles/h/hough-riots. See also Todd Michney, "Race, Violence, and Urban Territoriality: Cleveland's Little Italy and the 1966 Hough Uprising," *Journal of Urban History* 32 (2006): 404–28.

Tom Skinner

1. "Urbana Now," conference program, December 1970, Urbana, id344553, Collection 300 Records of InterVarsity Christian Fellowship, CN/300, Box 68-6, Billy Graham Center Archives.

2. Tom Skinner, "The U.S. Racial Crisis and World Evangelism," InterVarsity Urbana Student Missions Conference, Urbana-Champaign,

December 1970, https://urbana.org/message/us-racial-crisis-and-world
-evangelism.

3. Skinner, "The U.S. Racial Crisis and World Evangelism."

4. *Urbana &* 1, no. 6 (April 1, 1971), Urbana, id344553, Billy Graham
Center Archives.

5. Bill Pannell, interview with author, November 8, 2017.

6. Appleton to Alexander, January 9, 1971, Urbana, id344553, Billy
Graham Center Archives.

7. E. Brandt Gustavson, memo from Moody Broadcasting Department. April 14, 1971, Urbana, id344553, Billy Graham Center Archives.

8. John Perkins, telephone interview with author, September 11, 2020.

9. See Carolyn Renée Dupont, *Mississippi Praying: Southern White
Evangelicals and the Civil Rights Movement, 1945–1975* (New York: New
York University Press, 2013); Peter Slade, *Open Friendship in a Closed
Society: Mission Mississippi and a Theology of Friendship* (Oxford: Oxford
University Press, 2009), for more history and background on Southern
Presbyterians and the formation of the PCA; and Stephen R. Haynes, *The
Last Segregated Hour: The Memphis Kneel-Ins and the Campaign for Southern
Church Desegregation* (Oxford: Oxford University Press, 2012).

10. African American Ministries–Presbyterian Church in America,
https://aampca.org/.

11. Charlotte Graham, "Mission: Reconciliation," *Jackson Clarion-
Ledger*, October 16, 1993, 5D.

12. Slade, *Open Friendship*, 79.

13. Lecrae, "The Pains of Humanity Have Been Draining Me,"
Huffington Post, October 26, 2016, huffpost.com/entry/i-declare-Black
-lives-matter_b_5808be36e4b0dd54ce385412#:~:text=Honestly%2C%20
the%20pains%20of%20humanity,together%2C%20and%20found%20
God%20together.

14. Michael Emerson and Christian Smith, *Divided by Faith: Evangelical Religion and the Problem of Race in America* (London: Oxford University
Press, 2000), 188.

15. Stokely Carmichael was not the first person to use the phrase
"Black power." Author Richard Wright wrote a book called *Black Power*
in 1954. Malcolm X's contribution to the Black freedom struggle served
as a precursor to the Black Power movement of the 1960s and 1970s. The
concept of Black empowerment itself can be traced to Marcus Garvey and
the Universal Negro Improvement Association (UNIA), and, in various
forms, as far back as African contact with colonial America.

16. Martin Luther King Jr., *Where Do We Go from Here: Chaos or Community?* (Boston: Beacon, 2010), 31.

17. Peniel E. Joseph, *Stokely: A Life* (New York: Basic Books, 2014), 116.

18. Tom Skinner, *Tom Skinner Speaks at Wheaton* (Brooklyn, NY: Skinner and Associates, 1969), 21.

19. "'Black Power': Statement by National Committee of Negro Churchmen," *New York Times*, July 31, 1966, E5.

20. Ron Potter, phone interview, October 17, 2017.

21. Carl Ellis Jr., telephone interview with author, October 25, 2017.

22. Carl Ellis Jr., telephone interview.

23. "What Went Down at Urbana '67—Urbana '70 Black Student Promotional," *Vimeo*, InterVarsity Christian Fellowship, accessed November 18, 2017, vimeo.com/42230364.

24. "What Went Down at Urbana '67?"

25. "What Went Down at Urbana '67?"

26. *The Narrative of the Life of Frederick Douglass, An American Slave, Written by Himself* (Overland Park, KS: Digireads; originally published, 1845), 105.

27. Martin Luther King Jr., "Letter from a Birmingham Jail," April 16, 1963.

28. Skinner, "The U.S. Racial Crisis and World Evangelism."

29. Kate King and Maria Armental, "Musician Recalls Brother, Whose Beating Sparked '67 Newark Riots," *Wall Street Journal*, July 12, 2017, https://www.wsj.com/articles/musician-recalls-brother-whose-beating-sparked-67-newark-riots-1499903836.

30. Jonathan P. Hicks, "This Day in Black History: July 20, 1967," BET, July 20, 2014, https://www.bet.com/news/national/2012/07/20/this-day-in-Black-history-july-20-1967.html.

31. William Pannell, phone interview with author, November 8, 2017.

32. See King, *Where Do We Go from Here*, chap. 2, "Black Power."

33. Skinner, "The U.S. Racial Crisis and World Evangelism."

34. Here Skinner echoes Martin Luther King Jr.'s assertion that the three great evils facing society were racism, poverty, and militarism—a concept he had been speaking about publicly since at least 1967. Whether the similarity was conscious or coincidental is unknown.

35. Advertisement, *Bridgeport Post*, February 4, 1967, 5.

36. Skinner, *Tom Skinner Speaks at Wheaton*, 21.

37. Advertisement, *Bridgeport Post*, February 4, 1967, 5.

38. Tom Skinner, *Black and Free*, rev. ed. (Maitland, FL: Xulon, 2005), 56.

39. Skinner, *Black and Free*, 74.

40. Skinner, *Black and Free*, 76.

41. Skinner, *Black and Free*, 83.

42. Skinner, *Black and Free*, 91.

43. Emerson and Smith, *Divided by Faith*, 117.

44. For more on the white evangelical "colorblind" approach to racism, see Jesse Curtis, *The Myth of Colorblind Christians: Evangelicals and White Supremacy in the Civil Rights Era* (New York: NYU Press, 2021).

45. Pat Morley, telephone interview with author, September 9, 2020.

46. "Patrick Morley, Founder & Executive Chairman," Man in the Mirror, accessed January 18, 2022, https://maninthemirror.org/patrick -morley-executive-chairman/.

47. Morley, telephone interview.

48. Morley, telephone interview.

49. Slade, *Open Friendship*, 53.

50. Lee Paris, telephone interview with author, September 11, 2020.

51. Paris, telephone interview.

52. See Kristin Kobes Du Mez, *Jesus and John Wayne: How White Evangelicals Corrupted a Faith and Fractured a Nation* (New York: Norton, 2020), and Beth Allison Barr, *The Making of Biblical Womanhood: How the Subjugation of Women Became Gospel Truth* (Grand Rapids: Brazos, 2021), for more about the patriarchy and misogyny characteristic of much of evangelicalism in the United States.

53. "About Us," Skinner Leadership Institute, accessed January 18, 2021, https://www.skinnerleaders.org/about-us.

54. Juliana Menasce Horowitz and Gretchen Livingston, "How Americans View the Black Lives Matter Movement," Pew Research Center, July 8, 2016, https://www.pewresearch.org/fact-tank/2016/07/08/how -americans-view-the-Black-lives-matter-movement/.

Rachel Carson

1. Mary McCay, "Rachel Carson," in *Encyclopedia of Religion and Nature*, ed. Bron Taylor (New York: Continuum, 2005), 269–71.

2. Jill Lepore, "The Right Way to Remember Rachel Carson," *New Yorker*, March 19, 2018, 1, https://www.newyorker.com/magazine/2018 /03/26/the-right-way-to-remember-rachel-carson.

3. Kelsey Juliana, in Mallory McDuff, "My Students Show Me How Climate Action Is Better Than Despair," *Sojourners*, October 23, 2018, https://sojo.net/articles/my-students-show-me-how-climate-action -better-despair.

4. Jill Lepore, in Steven Valentine, "Rachel Carson Dreams by the Sea," *The New Yorker Radio Hour*, April 17, 2020, https://www.wnycstudios.org /podcasts/tnyradiohour/segments/rachel-carson-dreams-sea-rerun.

5. Linda Lear, *Rachel Carson: Witness for Nature* (New York: Holt, 1997).

6. Olga Huckins, in Terry Tempest Williams, "One Patriot," in *Rachel Carson: Legacy and Challenge*, ed. Lisa Sideris and Kathleen Dean Moore (Albany: State University of New York Press, 2008), 21.

7. Rachel Carson, *Silent Spring* (New York: Houghton Mifflin, 1962), dedication page.

8. Carson, *Silent Spring*, 103.

9. Sandra Steingraber, "The Fracking of Rachel Carson," *Orion Magazine*, 2012, https://orionmagazine.org/article/the-fracking-of-rachel-carson.

10. Carson, *Silent Spring*, 1–3.

11. Carson, in Lear, *Rachel Carson*, 393.

12. Carson, *Silent Spring*, 15.

13. Carson, *Silent Spring*, 15–17.

14. Carson, in Lear, *Rachel Carson*, 395.

15. Robert Kennedy, in Lepore, "The Right Way," 14.

16. McCay, "Rachel Carson," 269–71.

17. Lear, *Rachel Carson*.

18. McCay, "Rachel Carson," 270.

19. Priscilla Coit Murphy, *What a Book Can Do: The Publication and Reception of "Silent Spring"* (Amherst: University of Massachusetts Press, 2005), as cited in Eve Andrews, "Teen Girls Took Over the Climate Movement: What Happens Next?" *Grist*, January 1, 2020, https://grist.org/climate/teen-girls-took-over-the-climate-movement-what-happens-next/.

20. *New York Times*, in Lear, *Rachel Carson*, 482.

21. Rachel Carson, "Women's National Press Club Speech," cited in *Lost Woods: The Discovered Writings of Rachel Carson*, ed. Linda Lear (Boston: Beacon, 1962), 201.

22. Carson, "Women's National Press Club Speech," 203.

23. *CBS Reports*, "The Silent Spring of Rachel Carson," April 3, 1963.

24. *CBS Reports*, "The Silent Spring of Rachel Carson."

25. Carson, in Lear, *Rachel Carson*, 442.

26. Lear, *Rachel Carson*.

27. Lepore, "The Right Way," 2.

28. Carson, in Lepore, "The Right Way," 2.

29. Rachel Carson, "The Real World around Us" (address to Theta Sigma Phi sorority of women journalists, 1954), in Lear, *Lost Woods*, 160.

30. Lear, *Rachel Carson.*

31. Lepore, "The Right Way to Remember Rachel Carson."

32. Lear, *Rachel Carson.*

33. Lear, *Rachel Carson*, 14–15.

34. Lepore, "The Right Way to Remember Rachel Carson."

35. US Fish and Wildlife Service, "Rachel Carson Biography," last updated February 5, 2013, https://www.fws.gov/refuge/rachel_carson/about/rachelcarson.html.

36. Rachel Carson, "Undersea," 1937, in Lear, *Lost Woods*, 9–11.

37. Lear, *Rachel Carson*, 212.

38. Martha Freeman, ed., *Always, Rachel: The Letters of Rachel Carson and Dorothy Freeman, 1952–1964* (Boston: Beacon, 1995).

39. Maria Popova, "The Monarchs, Music, and the Meaning of Life: The Most Touching Deathbed Love Letter Ever Written," *Marginalia* (formerly *Brain Pickings*), January 13, 2017, www.brainpickings.org/2017/01/13/rachel-carson-dorothy-freeman-letters/.

40. Rachel Carson, "Two Letters to Dorothy and Stanley Freeman," 1956, in Lear, *Lost Woods*, 169.

41. Rachel Carson, in Paul Brooks, *The House of Life: Rachel Carson at Work* (Boston: Houghton Mifflin, 1972), 9.

42. Rachel Carson, *The Sense of Wonder* (New York: HarperCollins, 1956).

43. Robert Fuller, *Wonder: From Emotion to Spirituality* (Chapel Hill: University of North Carolina Press, 2006).

44. Carson, *The Sense of Wonder*, 15.

45. Carson, *The Sense of Wonder*, 98–100.

46. Richard Louv, *Last Child in the Woods* (Chapel Hill, NC: Algonquin, 2008).

47. Carson, *The Sense of Wonder*, 57.

48. Carson, "The Real World around Us," 163.

49. Rebecca Solnit, "Why Climate Action Is the Antithesis of White Supremacy," *Guardian*, March 19, 2019, https://www.theguardian.com/commentisfree/2019/mar/19/why-youll-never-meet-a-white-supremacist-who-cares-about-climate-change.

50. Carson, *The Sense of Wonder*, 59.

Allan M. Tibbels

1. Saundra Saperstein, "Sandtown Typical of Urban Blight," *Washington Post*, July 2, 1980, B1, 2.

2. Dietrich Bonhoeffer, *Ethics*, trans. Reinhard Krauss, Charles C. West, and Douglas W. Stott, Dietrich Bonhoeffer Works, vol. 6 (Minneapolis: Fortress, 2005).

3. Camilo José Vergara, *American Ruins* (New York: Monacelli, 1999).

4. Matthew Desmond, *Evicted: Poverty and Profit in the American City* (New York: Crown, 2016).

MARY PAIK LEE

1. Mary Paik Lee, *Quiet Odyssey: A Pioneer Korean Woman in America* (Seattle: University of Washington Press, 1990), 7.

2. Lee, *Quiet Odyssey*, 12, 14.

3. Mary Paik Lee, in conversation with Sonia Sunoo, 1977, Sonia Sunoo Oral History Series, Korean American Digital Archive, Korean Heritage Library, University of Southern California (USC), Los Angeles, CA (hereafter, Lee, USC interview).

4. Idk man, "Silence Will Not Save You. Your Degree Will Not Save You. Your Indifference Will Not Save You. Your Colorblindness Will Not Save You," *Twitter*, November 25, 2014, twitter.com/beenblackedout /status/537295515579199488?s=20.

5. Lee, USC interview.

6. Lee, USC interview.

7. Lee, USC interview.

8. Lee, USC interview.

9. Lee, USC interview.

10. Lee, *Quiet Odyssey*, 23.

11. Lee, *Quiet Odyssey*, 23.

12. Lee, USC interview; Lee, *Quiet Odyssey*, 54.

13. David K. Yoo, *Contentious Spirits: Religion in Korean American History, 1903–1945* (Stanford, CA: Stanford University Press, 2010), 9.

14. Lee, *Quiet Odyssey*, 54–55, 57; Lee, USC interview.

15. Lee, *Quiet Odyssey*, 50–51.

16. Yoo, *Contentious Spirits*, 12.

17. Lee, *Quiet Odyssey*, 134.

18. Lee, *Quiet Odyssey*, 94.

19. Lee, *Quiet Odyssey*, 95.

20. Lee, *Quiet Odyssey*, 95.

21. Lee, *Quiet Odyssey*, 95–96.

22. Lee, *Quiet Odyssey*, 100, 105.

23. Lee, *Quiet Odyssey*, 103, 128.

24. Lee, *Quiet Odyssey*, 128, 134.

25. Lee, *Quiet Odyssey*, 113, 128.

26. Lee, *Quiet Odyssey*, 116.

27. Delores Williams, *Sisters in the Wilderness: The Challenge of Womanist God-Talk* (New York: Orbis, 1993).

FLANNERY O'CONNOR

1. Sally Fitzgerald, ed., *The Habit of Being: Letters of Flannery O'Connor* (New York: Farrar, Straus & Giroux, 1979), 572.

2. Flannery O'Connor, "Revelation," in *Flannery O'Connor: The Complete Stories* (New York: Farrar, Straus & Giroux, 1971), 506.

3. O'Connor, "Revelation," 508.

4. Fitzgerald, *The Habit of Being*, 97.

5. Andalusia is Flannery O'Connor's farm and homeplace in Milledgeville, Georgia. It is now a Flannery O'Connor museum, open to the public.

6. Fitzgerald, *The Habit of Being*, 103.

7. Fitzgerald, *The Habit of Being*, 11–12.

8. Benjamin Alexander, ed., *Good Things out of Nazareth: The Uncollected Letters of Flannery O'Connor and Friends* (New York: Convergent, 2019), 110.

9. Alexander, *Good Things out of Nazareth*, 109.

10. Brad Gooch, ed., *Flannery: A Life of Flannery O'Connor* (New York: Back Bay Books, 2009), 319.

11. Gooch, *Flannery*, 53, 258.

12. Alexander, *Good Things out of Nazareth*, 225.

13. Fitzgerald, *The Habit of Being*, 402.

14. Fitzgerald, *The Habit of Being*, 573.

15. Gooch, *Flannery*, 132.

16. See for example, Fitzgerald, *The Habit of Being*, 74, 270, 298, 506.

17. Fitzgerald, *The Habit of Being*, 506.

18. Fitzgerald, *The Habit of Being*, 456.

19. Gooch, *Flannery*, 308.

20. Gooch, *Flannery*, 253.

21. Gooch, *Flannery*, 124.

22. Gooch, *Flannery*, 90.

23. Gooch, *Flannery*, 90.

24. Gooch, *Flannery*, 347.

25. Fitzgerald, *The Habit of Being*, xviii.

26. I am especially thankful to Lauren Winner, who suggested that I make my struggle the theme of this chapter.

27. To cancel someone—usually a celebrity or other well-known figure—means to stop supporting, patronizing, or celebrating the work of that person. The reason for cancellation usually is due to the person in question having behaved or spoken in an objectionable or unacceptable way. See https://www.merriam-webster.com/words-at-play /cancel-culture-words-were-watching.

28. Paul Elie, "How Racist Was Flannery O'Connor?," *New Yorker*, June 15, 2020, https://www.newyorker.com/magazine/2020/06/22/how -racist-was-flannery-oconnor.

29. Elie, "How Racist Was Flannery O'Connor?"

30. Alexander, *Good Things out of Nazareth*, xvii.

31. Angela Alaimo O'Donnell et al., *Letter in Protest of the Cancelling of Flannery O'Connor*, July 31, 2020, https://angelaalaimoodonnell.com /letter-in-protest-of-the-cancelling-of-flannery-oconnor/.

32. Alexander, *Good Things out of Nazareth*, 4.

33. Flannery O'Connor, *A Prayer Journal* (New York: Farrar, Straus & Giroux, 2013), 38, 18, 21.

34. O'Connor, *A Prayer Journal*, 19.

35. O'Connor, *A Prayer Journal*, 23.

36. O'Connor, *A Prayer Journal*, 11.

37. O'Connor, *A Prayer Journal*, 17.

38. Fitzgerald, *The Habit of Being*, 389.

39. Fitzgerald, *The Habit of Being*, 503.

40. Fitzgerald, *The Habit of Being*, 458.

41. Fitzgerald, *The Habit of Being*, 387.

42. Fitzgerald, *The Habit of Being*, 242.

43. Flannery O'Connor, *Mystery and Manners*, ed. Sally Fitzgerald and Robert Fitzgerald (New York: Farrar, Straus & Giroux, 1961), 181.

44. Fitzgerald, *The Habit of Being*, 352.

45. O'Connor, *Mystery and Manners*, 124, 81.

46. O'Connor, *Mystery and Manners*, 27.

47. O'Connor, *Mystery and Manners*, 184.

48. Fitzgerald, *The Habit of Being*, 395.

49. O'Connor, *Mystery and Manners*, 226.

50. Alexander, *Good Things out of Nazareth*, 302.

51. Fitzgerald, *The Habit of Being*, 367.

52. O'Connor, *Mystery and Manners*, 115.

53. O'Connor, *Mystery and Manners*, 112.

54. Please note that I am in no way justifying the horrors and degradation of racism, nor do I ever want to suggest that racism is a good thing because it allows grace to happen. What I am posing instead is this theological question: Given that the tragic ugly horror of racism exists, where—if at all—does God's grace occur within it?

55. Once O'Connor even signed a personal letter that she wrote to friend Maryat Lee, "Mrs. Turpin." See Fitzgerald, *The Habit of Being*, 579.

56. Flannery O'Connor, "A Good Man Is Hard to Find," in *Flannery O'Connor: The Complete Stories*, 133.

PETE SEEGER

1. Pete Seeger, *The Incompleat Folksinger*, ed. Jo Metcalf Schwartz (New York: Simon & Schuster, 1972), 271.

2. John Lewis and Michael D'Orso, *Walking with the Wind: A Memoir of the Movement* (New York: Simon & Schuster, 1998), 356; Charles Fager, *Selma, 1965: The March That Changed the South*, 2nd ed. (New York: Charles Scribner's Sons, 1974), 151.

3. Roy Reed, "Alabama March Passes Midpoint; Sore Feet and High Spirits in Evidence at Camp," *New York Times*, March 24, 1965.

4. "You Can't Write Down Freedom Songs," *Sing Out!* 15, no. 3 (July 1965), in *Pete Seeger: In His Own Words*, ed. Rob Rosenthal and Sam Rosenthal (Boulder, CO: Paradigm Publishers, 2012), 121.

5. Pete Seeger, "Some Songs of the Selma Marchers," *Broadside*, no. 57 (April 10, 1965): 4; Seeger, *The Incompleat Folksinger*, 110.

6. When *Life* wrote a feature article on Seeger a year earlier, they noted his working clothes: "He . . . looks rather like a nervous garage mechanic—until he unslings his guitar." Bruce Paisner, "A Minstrel with a Mission," *Life*, October 9, 1964, 61.

7. Toshi Seeger's photographs of the march illustrate the liner notes of Pete Seeger, Len Chandler, The Freedom Voices, *WNEW's Story of Selma*, LP (Folkways Records, 1965), https://folkways.si.edu/wnews-story-of -selma/african-american-spoken-american-history-struggle-protest /music/album/smithsonian.

8. David Dunaway, in his biography, has the Seegers joining the march on Wednesday, March 24: David King Dunaway, *How Can I Keep from Singing? The Ballad of Pete Seeger*, 2nd ed. (New York: Villard, 2008), 293.

And Alec Wilkinson follows suit: Alec Wilkinson, *The Protest Singer: An Intimate Portrait of Pete Seeger* (New York: Knopf, 2009), 92. Allan Winkler makes no attempt to give dates for the Seegers' presence at the march: Allan M. Winkler, *"To Everything There Is a Season": Pete Seeger and the Power of Song*, New Narratives in American History (Oxford: Oxford University Press, 2009), 110–12. However, after piecing the evidence together and corresponding with David Dunaway, we both agreed that Pete and Toshi most likely joined the march in Lowndes County in the afternoon of Tuesday, March 23, and left the march in the afternoon or evening of Wednesday, March 24. When Dunham interviewed Seeger, Pete clearly stated, "We just joined it for the last two days." But then he also said, "We flew out, and on the next day read it in the paper. We had to catch a plane before the march actually reached Montgomery, so we weren't there for either the beginning or the end." David King Dunaway, "Interview Transcript. Pete Seeger Interviewed by David Dunaway, Dec 15, 1977," The David Dunaway/Pete Seeger Interviews Collection 1977, Box 1, Folder 14, American Folklife Center, Library of Congress, Washington, DC. In a piece for *Broadside* that Seeger dated "Wednesday, March 24, 1965," he wrote of the "songs heard during the past day and a half," which clearly places him on the march that Tuesday. Seeger, "Some Songs of the Selma Marchers," 2. This is supported by a contemporary account of the march that describes a sleeping Pete Seeger in the camp on Tuesday night (March 23). Renata Adler, "The Selma March," *New Yorker*, April 10, 1965, https://www.newyorker.com/magazine/1965/04/10/letter-from-selma.

9. Dunaway, "Interview Transcript" (December 15, 1977); Pete Seeger, "Interview," ed. Joseph Mosnier, Civil Rights History Project, July 22, 2011, Library of Congress, https://www.loc.gov/item/afc2010039_crhp0039. Seeger recalls leaving from Montgomery airport. Assuming this is where they flew in, Pete and Toshi would have been driven east down the highway toward Selma, meeting the marchers in Lowndes County sometime in the afternoon of March 23. In an article written that summer, Seeger says "three hundred foot-weary but light-souled people stopped for a rest." This might suggest that he and Toshi joined the marchers before they arrived at their campsite; Seeger, "Some Songs of the Selma Marchers," 2; "You Can't Write Down Freedom Songs," 121.

10. Roy Reed, "Freedom March Begins at Selma; Troops on Guard," *New York Times*, March 22, 1965.

11. Paul L. Montgomery, "It Was Chilly under Big Top for 350 Tramping through Alabama," *New York Times*, March 23, 1965.

12. Roy Reed, "Rights Marchers Push into Region Called Hostile," *New York Times*, March 23, 1965. Lewis and D'Orso, *Walking with the Wind*, 356.

13. Roy Reed, "Alabama Freedom Marchers Reach Outskirts of Montgomery," *New York Times*, March 25, 1965.

14. Howard Zinn, *SNCC: The New Abolitionists* (Boston: Beacon, 1964), 153–54.

15. Ralph Abernathy, in Henry Hampton, Steve Fayer, and Sarah Flynn, *Voices of Freedom: An Oral History of the Civil Rights Movement from the 1950s through the 1980s* (London: Vintage, 1990), 237.

16. John Lewis, in Hampton, Fayer, and Flynn, *Voices of Freedom*, 237. There were 1,800 Alabama national guardsmen and 2,000 US Army troops protecting the marchers. Lewis and D'Orso, *Walking with the Wind*, 356.

17. Reed, "Rights Marchers Push into Region Called Hostile"; Adler, "The Selma March."

18. Reed, "Rights Marchers Push into Region Called Hostile."

19. "A Letter to My Grandchildren, across the Years," November 30, 1956, in *Pete Seeger: In His Own Words*, 99.

20. Seeger to David Leventhal, October 11, 1963, in *Pete Seeger: In His Own Words*, 113.

21. Seeger to Pat Fry, November 2005, in *Pete Seeger: In His Own Words*, 90.

22. "Letter to My Grandchildren," 102.

23. Dunaway, *How Can I Keep from Singing?*, 54–55. The Communist Party (USA) membership peaked at seventy-five thousand in 1938. Fraser Ottanelli, *The Communist Party of the United States from the Depression to World War II* (New Brunswick, NJ: Rutgers University Press, 1991), 154; "Revelations from the Russian Archives: Soviet and American Communist Parties," Library of Congress, 1992, https://www.loc.gov/exhibits/archives/sovi.html#sova.

24. Pete Seeger, interview by David King Dunaway, March 6, 1977, in David King Dunaway and Molly Beer, *Singing Out: An Oral History of America's Folk Music Revivals* (New York: Oxford University Press, 2010), 83.

25. Dunaway, *How Can I Keep from Singing?*, 88.

26. Ron Eyerman and Andrew Jamison, *Music and Social Movements: Mobilizing Traditions in the Twentieth Century*, Cambridge Cultural Social Studies (Cambridge: Cambridge University Press, 1998), 64.

27. Dunaway and Beer, *Singing Out*, 57.

28. Ronald D. Cohen and James Capaldi, *The Pete Seeger Reader* (Oxford: Oxford University Press, 2013), 48.

29. Doris Willens, *Lonesome Traveler: The Life of Lee Hays* (Lincoln: University of Nebraska Press, 1993), 182.

30. Alan Lomax, *The People's Songbook*, ed. Waldemar Hille (New York: Boni & Gaer, 1947), 6.

31. David King Dunaway, "Program II: Folk Songs and Ballads," in *Pete Seeger: How Can I Keep from Singing?* (PRI, June 30, 2008), https://beta.prx.org/series/31028.

32. Cohen and Capaldi, *The Pete Seeger Reader*, 85.

33. "Union Hoot: The Scabs Crawl In / We Pity Our Bosses Five / Keep That Line A-Moving / Join the Picket Line Today," on *Pete Seeger: The Smithsonian Folkways Collection*, CD (Smithsonian Folkways, 2019).

34. Seeger to People's Songs supporters, January 26, 1948, in Cohen and Capaldi, *The Pete Seeger Reader*, 95.

35. Clancy Sigal, "Pete Seeger, Folk Hero of the Sixties—and the Fifties and the Forties—Is to Sing in London Tonight," *Guardian*, March 7, 1978, in Cohen and Capaldi, *The Pete Seeger Reader*, 209.

36. Pete Seeger, interview with Doris Willens, November 10, 1982, in Willens, *Lonesome Traveler*, 111.

37. Jim Brown, *Pete Seeger: The Power of Song*, DVD (USA: Genius Products [Ingram], 2008).

38. "New Notes on Metropolitan Music," *New Counterattack*, July 30, 1954, 3.

39. Pete Seeger, "Summary of Government Charges," March 30, 1957, in Cohen and Capaldi, *The Pete Seeger Reader*, 129.

40. For a detailed account of this whole episode, see Jesse Jarnow, *Wasn't That a Time: The Weavers, the Blacklist, and the Battle for the Soul of America* (New York: Hachette Books, 2018).

41. Cohen and Capaldi, *The Pete Seeger Reader*, 27.

42. Dunaway, "Program II: Folk Songs and Ballads."

43. Seeger to Woody Guthrie, 1956, in *Pete Seeger: In His Own Words*, 53. It was not until an interview Seeger gave in 1994 after receiving the Kennedy Center Honors that he finally acknowledged his mistake: "I apologize for once believing Stalin was just a hard driver, not a supremely cruel dictator." Marc Fisher, "America's Best Loved Commie: Even a Radical Can Become a National Treasure. Just Ask Pete Seeger," *Washington Post*, December 4, 1994, in Cohen and Capaldi, *The Pete Seeger Reader*, 228.

44. Seeger, "Letter to My Grandchildren," 101. Seeger identified him-

self as a communist for the rest of his life, crafting increasingly careful personal definitions. "At this late age of eighty-two, I call myself a Luxemburgian communist [after Rosa Luxemburg, who rejected Lenin's censorship of the press]. . . . If you don't have freedom of the press . . . inevitably things go from bad to worse." Pete Seeger, interview with Studs Terkel, 2002, in Cohen and Capaldi, *The Pete Seeger Reader*, 48. In 1995, after receiving the Kennedy Center Honors Award, he said, "I still call myself a communist, because communism is no more what Russia made of it than Christianity is what the churches make of it." "The Old Left," *New York Times*, January 22, 1995.

45. Ralph J. Gleason, "A Singer Who Meets You Half Way," *San Francisco Sunday Chronicle (This World)*, July 11, 1965, 43, in Cohen and Capaldi, *The Pete Seeger Reader*, 185.

46. Seeger to Bess Lomax Hawes, "Letter to Bess Lomax Hawes from Crimea," Bess Lomax Hawes Collection (AFC 2014/008), April 21, 1964, Seeger family, 1954–1964, American Folklife Center, Library of Congress, Washington, DC, https://www.loc.gov/resource/afc2014008 .afc2014008_ms2510/?sp=45&r=-0.214,0.1,1.393,0.7,0.

47. Seeger to Bess Lomax Hawes, "Letter to Bess Lomax Hawes from Moscow," Bess Lomax Hawes Collection (AFC 2014/008), May 1, 1964, Seeger family, 1954–1964, American Folklife Center, Library of Congress, Washington, DC, https://www.loc.gov/resource/afc2014008 .afc2014008_ms2510/?sp=74&r=-0.901,0,2.802,1.408,0.

48. Seeger to Bess Lomax Hawes, "Letter to Bess Lomax Hawes from Kiev," Bess Lomax Hawes Collection (AFC 2014/008), April 18, 1964, Seeger family, 1954–1964, American Folklife Center, Library of Congress, Washington, DC, https://www.loc.gov/resource/afc2014008 .afc2014008_ms2510/?sp=71&r=0.365,0.059,0.618,0.311,0.

49. Seeger, *The Incompleat Folksinger*, 155.

50. Collier (1944–2020) grew up in Fort Smith, Arkansas, singing in church. He moved to Chicago when he was seventeen and got involved with the Fellowship of Reconciliation. A pianist, he said, "the guitar came with the Movement." Jimmy Collier, interview by Kerry Taylor, July 2, 1999.

51. Interview, Jimmy Collier by David King Dunaway, July 10, 1978, in Dunaway, *How Can I Keep from Singing?*, 297. Collier described Seeger's influence on him: "Pete Seeger, a real good, close friend of mine when I was young. . . . It was something distant about him, but he . . . could razor focus in on you, and whatever you wanted to do, you would be glad to

do it." Interview of Lynn Adler (SCLC), Elaine DeLott Baker (Council of Federated Organizations [COFO]), Stephen Blum (COFO), Jimmy Collier (SCLC), David Gelfand (SNCC), Charles Love (SCLC), Marcia Moore (SNCC), by Chude Allen, "The Freedom Movement and Ourselves: Looking Back 50 Years Later, Group B," April 5, 2014, https://www.crmvet.org /disc/14chude.htm.

52. Seeger, "Some Songs of the Selma Marchers," 2.

53. A photograph of the tableau appeared in the *New York Times* the next day. Reed, "Alabama Freedom Marchers Reach Outskirts of Montgomery"; Adler, "The Selma March." Thanks to Heather Begarnie for identifying the instrument from a photograph of Seeger playing it. Matt Herron, *Folk Singer Pete Seeger Playing Penny Whistle as Marchers Move toward Montgomery*, Take Stock: Images of Change, March 21, 1965, http://www.takestockphotos.com/imagepages/imagedetail.php ?PSortOrder=25&FolioID=7#.

54. Len Chandler, telephone interview by Peter Slade, October 4, 2019.

55. Len Chandler, "Wallace Said We Couldn't March," 1965, in Seeger, Chandler, The Freedom Voices, *WNEW's Story of Selma*. If you have read this far in the footnotes, you deserve a break: make yourself a cup of coffee and listen to this album on Spotify, https://open.spotify.com /album/1OLg4xKIKlhtL7mZigjx6v.

56. Len Chandler, interview by Julie M. Thompson, June 18, 2018, https://activistvideoarchive.org, Activist Video Archive, https://activist videoarchive.org/archive-library-2/2018/6/18/len-chandler Disc 3.

57. Hampton, Fayer, and Flynn, *Voices of Freedom*, 237.

58. Len Chandler, "Right! Right!," in *WNEW's Story of Selma*.

59. Ellen Harold and Peter Stone, "Guy Carawan," Association for Cultural Equity, accessed September 19, 2020, http://www.culturalequity .org/alan-lomax/friends/carawan.

60. Carawan counted Seeger as a great influence. It was Seeger who, in 1959, suggested Carawan go to Highlander to continue the work left by the tragic death of Zilphia Horton. Seeger, "Some Songs of the Selma Marchers," 2; Candie Carawan and Guy Carawan, *Sing for Freedom: The Story of the Civil Rights Movement through Its Songs* (Sing Out Corporation, 1990), 4.

61. Interview with Miles Horton in Bernice Johnson Reagon, "Songs of the Civil Rights Movement, 1955–1965: A Study in Culture History," ed. Lorraine A. Williams (PhD diss., Howard University, 1975), 76.

62. Sam A. Rosenthal, "A Folksong in Flight: Pete Seeger and the Genesis of 'We Shall Overcome,'" in *We Shall Overcome: Essays on a Great American Song*, ed. Victor V. Bobetsky (Lanham, MD: Rowman & Littlefield, 2014), 23–24.

63. Reagon, "Songs of the Civil Rights Movement," 78; Seeger, *The Incompleat Folksinger*, 112; Pete Seeger, *Where Have All the Flowers Gone? A Singer's Stories, Songs, Seeds, Robberies*, ed. Peter Blood (Sing Out Publications, 1993), 34.

64. Lee Hayes, "A Sermon to Songwriters," *People's Songs*, April 1948, 11.

65. Guy Carawan and Candy Carawan, "Carry It On: Roots of the Singing Civil Rights Movement," in *Freedom Is a Constant Struggle: An Anthology of the Mississippi Civil Rights Movement*, ed. Susie Erenrich (Montgomery, AL: Black Belt, 1999), 146–47.

66. "Whatever Happened to Singing in the Unions," *Sing Out!* 15, no. 2 (May 1965), in *Pete Seeger: In His Own Words*, 89.

67. Seeger, "Some Songs of the Selma Marchers," 2.

68. Seeger, "Some Songs of the Selma Marchers," 2; "You Can't Write Down Freedom Songs," 121.

69. Seeger, "Some Songs of the Selma Marchers," 2. The seventy-eight-year-old John Seeger was at that time developing an "electronic-mechanical melody-grapher" for UCLA to accurately capture that flying bird on a graph. Ann M. Pescatello, *Charles Seeger: A Life in American Music* (Pittsburgh: University of Pittsburgh Press, 1992), 212. "My father was completely into music," Seeger said. "He didn't think anything else in the world was worth thinking about." Pete Seeger, interview with Studs Terkel, 45.

70. "You Can't Write Down Freedom Songs," 121.

71. Adler, "The Selma March."

72. Reed, "Alabama Freedom Marchers Reach Outskirts of Montgomery."

73. Taylor Branch, *At Canaan's Edge: America in the King Years, 1965–68* (New York: Simon & Schuster, 2006), 153.

74. James Orange, "Oh Wallace," in Reagon, "Songs of the Civil Rights Movement," 172.

75. Dunaway, *How Can I Keep from Singing?*, 277; Bernice Johnson Reagon, interview by David King Dunaway, December 7, 1977, in Dunaway and Beer, *Singing Out*, 139.

76. Pete Seeger, "Pete Seeger," *Sing Out!* 15, no. 1 (March 1965): 85, 87, in Cohen and Capaldi, *The Pete Seeger Reader*, 183.

77. Vincent Harding and Rachel Harding, *Bernice Johnson Reagon: The Singing Warrior* (The Veterans of Hope Project at the Iliff School of Theology, 2000); for biographical information, see http://www.veteransofhope .org/veterans/bernice-johnson-reagon/.

78. Reagon, "Songs of the Civil Rights Movement," 139–41; Winkler, *"To Everything There Is a Season,"* 104. Sociologist Dick Flacks draws attention to Seeger's often overlooked "organizational entrepreneurship." Cohen and Capaldi, *The Pete Seeger Reader*, 239.

79. Pete Seeger, *We Shall Overcome: Recorded Live at His Historic Carnegie Hall Concert, 1963*, LP (Columbia, 1963).

80. Seeger described these recording arrangements to David Dunaway. David King Dunaway, "Interview Transcript. Pete Seeger Interviewed by David Dunaway, Dec 14, 1977," The David Dunaway/Pete Seeger Interviews Collection 1977, Box 1, Folder 14, American Folklife Center, Library of Congress, Washington, DC.

81. Howard Zinn, *The Southern Mystique* (New York: Knopf, 1964), 77, in Reagon, "Songs of the Civil Rights Movement," 21.

82. Reagon, "Songs of the Civil Rights Movement," 22.

83. Seeger to Ray M. Lawless, February 18, 1953, in Cohen and Capaldi, *The Pete Seeger Reader*, 116.

84. Reagon, "Songs of the Civil Rights Movement," 22.

85. Andrew Young, *An Easy Burden: The Civil Rights Movement and the Transformation of America* (New York: HarperCollins, 1996), 183.

86. Harding and Harding, *Bernice Johnson Reagon.*

87. Quoted in Warren R. Ross, "Singing for Humanity: The Pete Seeger Saga," *UU World*, 1996.

88. Seeger, *Where Have All the Flowers Gone?*, 56.

89. "Pete Seeger's Session: A Beliefnet Interview with the Great Folk Singer on God, Religion, and Whether Music Can Change the World," *Beliefnet*, August 2006, https://www.beliefnet.com/entertainment/music /2006/08/pete-seegers-session.aspx.

90. Seeger to Archie Green, November 17, 1959, in Cohen and Capaldi, *The Pete Seeger Reader*, 135.

91. Lee Hays, interview by David King Dunaway, May 25, 1977, in Dunaway and Beer, *Singing Out*, 95–96.

92. "Pete Seeger's Session."

93. Seeger, *Where Have All the Flowers Gone?*, 174.

94. "Baccalaureate Address," June 6, 1965, in *Pete Seeger: In His Own Words*, 122–23.

95. Paul Cowan, "Non-Confrontation in Beacon, New York," *Village Voice*, December 16, 1965, 9, 11–12, in Cohen and Capaldi, *The Pete Seeger Reader*, 192.

96. Pete Seeger, "Talk to Teens," *Seventeen*, November 1963, in Seeger, *The Incompleat Folksinger*, 554.

97. He was not alone. John Lewis, the veteran of hundreds of marches and protests, said of the march: "There was never a march like this one before, and there hasn't been one since. The incredible sense of community—of *communing*—was overwhelming." Lewis and D'Orso, *Walking with the Wind*, 359.

98. Seeger, Chandler, The Freedom Voices, *WNEW's Story of Selma*.

99. "Baccalaureate Address."

100. Pete Seeger et al., *Everybody Says Freedom: A History of the Civil Rights Movement in Songs and Pictures* (New York: Norton, 1990), 201.

101. Seeger, *The Incompleat Folksinger*, 112.

102. Seeger, *Where Have All the Flowers Gone?*, 134.

103. Sholom Rubinstein, "Political Songs," *Rainbow Quest with Pete Seeger* (WNJU-TV, 1966), https://archive.org/details/RainbowQuest14.

104. Reed, "Alabama Freedom Marchers Reach Outskirts of Montgomery."

105. Fager, *Selma, 1965*, 158.

106. Donald Janson, "Stars Give Show for Rights March; More Than 10,000 Attend Final Night Program," *New York Times*, March 25, 1965. This is the source of the myth that the stage was made out of coffins. These were actually the large wooden crates used to ship coffins to the funeral home. Lewis and D'Orso, *Walking with the Wind*, 359.

107. Emilie Raymond, *Stars for Freedom: Hollywood, Black Celebrities, and the Civil Rights Movement* (Seattle: University of Washington Press, 2015), 189–95.

108. This chapter is following the assumption that the Seegers departed from Montgomery sometime in the afternoon of March 24 for the reasons given above in note 8. It is possible, but less probable, that they spent another night under canvas and left the morning of March 25. If so, they would have been in Montgomery for the "Night of Stars" concert. I could find no evidence that Seeger performed in the "Night of Stars." He is not listed as one of the performers at the concert at St. Jude's that Wednesday night; Janson, "Stars Give Show for Rights March." I have not seen any photographs of the concert that include Pete Seeger, and I have found no mention of the concert in Seeger's writings and interviews.

It is hard to imagine, if he were there, Seeger not participating in some capacity. If he attended, it is odd that he doesn't mention the concert. It seems a reasonable hypothesis that he was traveling that evening, and he was using his time to write up his folksinger's field report for *Broadside*.

109. Pete brought his banjo—it is visible in Toshi's photographs—though there is no record of him playing it. He proudly shares his own design for the banjo bag in Seeger, *The Incompleat Folksinger*, 377.

110. David King Dunaway, "Interview Transcript. Pete Seeger Interviewed by David Dunaway, July 24, 2000 Follow-Up," The David Dunaway/Pete Seeger Interviews Collection 2000, Box 12, Folder 124, American Folklife Center, Library of Congress, Washington, DC.

111. Seeger, "Some Songs of the Selma Marchers," 2.

I want to thank Julie Thompson at the Activist Video Archive in California and Todd Harvey at the American Folklife Center in DC for their invaluable assistance; David King Dunaway for answering all my questions and digging through his notes; Kerry Taylor for passing along his interview with Jimmy Collier; and Len Chandler for sharing his time and his memories of Pete Seeger and the march from Selma to Montgomery.

TONI MORRISON

1. Betty Fussell, "All That Jazz," in *Conversations with Toni Morrison*, ed. Danille Taylor-Guthrie (Jackson: University of Mississippi Press, 1994), 280–87, here 283.

2. Toni Morrison, "A Slow Walk of Trees," in *Toni Morrison: What Moves at the Margin*, ed. Carolyn C. Denard (Jackson: University of Mississippi Press, 2008), 3–14, here 7.

3. *Toni Morrison: What Moves at the Margin*, 3–14. The essay first appeared in the bicentennial issue of the *New York Times Magazine*, July 4, 1976.

4. *Toni Morrison: What Moves at the Margin*, 4.

5. Edward Moran, "Dick and Jane Readers," in *Encyclopedia.com*, accessed January 20, 2022, https://www.encyclopedia.com/media/encyclo pedias-almanacs-transcripts-and-maps/dick-and-jane-readers.

6. Nick Ripatrazone, "On the Paradoxes of Toni Morrison's Catholicism," Literary Hub, March 2, 2020, https://lithub.com/on-the-paradox es-of-toni-morrisons-catholicism/.

7. Alain Elkann, "The Last Interview," in *Toni Morrison: The Last Interview and Other Conversations* (New York: Melville House, 2020), 160.

8. David Carrasco, "Writing Goodness and Mercy: A 2017 Interview with Toni Morrison," in *Toni Morrison: Goodness and the Literary Imagination*, ed. David Carrasco, Stephanie Paulsell, and Mara Willard (Charlottesville: University of Virginia Press, 2019), 227–28.

9. Ripatrazone, "On the Paradoxes of Toni Morrison's Catholicism."

10. Carrasco, "Writing Goodness and Mercy," 229.

11. Conversation with David Carrasco, October 29, 2021. Morrison developed a friendship at Princeton with David Carrasco, now the Neil L. Rudenstine Professor of the Study of Latin America at Harvard University. From their first meeting in 1991, when Carrasco, then a visiting professor at Princeton, persuaded Morrison to let him sit in on her class, they developed a conversation about religion in Morrison's work. Morrison also engaged him to research the concept of Paradise in African and Afro-Brazilian traditions.

12. "'I Regret Everything': Toni Morrison Looks Back on Her Personal Life," *Fresh Air*, NPR, interviewed by Terry Gross, April 20, 2015, https://www.npr.org/2015/08/24/434132724/i-regret-everything-toni-morrison-looks-back-on-her-personal-life.

13. "'I Regret Everything.'"

14. David Streitfeld, "The Laureate's Song," *Washington Post*, October 8, 1993, https://www.washingtonpost.com/archive/lifestyle/1993/10/08/the-laureatess-life-song/10d3b79b-52f2-4685-a6dd-c57f7dde08d2/.

15. Paul Elie, "The Secret History of *One Hundred Years of Solitude*," *Vanity Fair*, December 9, 2015, https://www.vanityfair.com/culture/2015/12/gabriel-garcia-marquez-one-hundred-years-of-solitude-history.

16. Streitfeld, "The Laureate's Song."

17. Ripatrazone, "On the Paradoxes of Toni Morrison's Catholicism."

18. Zia Jaffrey, "The Salon.com Interview," February 3, 1998, in *Toni Morrison: The Last Interview*, 67–68.

19. Shirley A. Stave, ed., *Toni Morrison and the Bible: Contested Intertextualities* (New York: Lang, 2006), 7.

20. Peter Slade, Sarah Azaransky, and Charles Marsh, eds., *Introduction to Lived Theology: New Perspectives on Method, Style, and Pedagogy* (Oxford: Oxford University Press, 2017).

21. Bill Moyers, "A Conversation with Toni Morrison," in Taylor-Guthrie, *Conversations with Toni Morrison*, 262–74.

22. Anne Koenen, "The One out of Sequence," in Taylor-Guthrie, *Conversations with Toni Morrison*, 67–83.

23. Author interview with Elaine Pagels, October 21, 2021.

24. Of the theological content of their conversations, Pagels recalls, "We didn't talk 'theology' about theologians at all—except for Augustine, Origen, and James Cone, I don't read theology if I can help it—it was about stories, like some of those in *Paradise*, and experiences." Pagels, email to author, October 25, 2021.

25. In 1992, Morrison approached the administration at Princeton with a proposal for developing an Atelier Program, in which visiting artists from different disciplines would collaborate and work together with students in a workshop setting. They supported the proposal and several remarkable collaborations ensued with artists such as Andre Previn, Yo-Yo Ma, and Jacques D'Amboise.

26. See Stephanie Li, "Five Poems: The Gospel according to Toni Morrison," *Callaloo* 34, no. 3 (Summer 2011): 899–914.

27. Willis Barnstone and Marvin Meyer, eds., *The Gnostic Bible* (Boston: Shambhala, 2003), 224–32, here 226.

28. A version of the interview is published in *Toni Morrison: Conversations*, ed. Carolyn C. Denard (Oxford: University Press of Mississippi, 2008), 196–205.

29. The few direct quotes here are reconstructed from memory.

30. *Toni Morrison: Conversations*, 198.

31. *Toni Morrison: Conversations*, 197.

32. All of Morrison's papers are now at Princeton University.

JACK EGAN

1. Margery Frisbie, *An Alley in Chicago: The Ministry of a City Priest*, commemorative edition with new introduction and conclusion by Robert A. Ludwig (Franklin, WI: Sheed & Ward, 2002), 176.

2. Egan was given the title monsignor in 1957 when Cardinal Samuel Stritch was archbishop of Chicago. Monsignor is not a position, but an honorific title for clergy within the Catholic Church bestowed upon those deemed to have provided valuable service to the church or who are acting in a specific capacity within church governance. I refrain from using it in this piece because it is rather unfamiliar to a wider reading audience.

3. Frisbie, *An Alley in Chicago*, 174–76.

4. Frisbie, *An Alley in Chicago*, 169–70.

5. John T. McGreevy, *Parish Boundaries: The Catholic Encounter with Race in the Twentieth-Century Urban North* (Chicago: University of Chicago Press, 1996), 186.

6. Frisbie, *An Alley in Chicago*, 177.

7. Frisbie, *An Alley in Chicago*, 171.

8. Frisbie, *An Alley in Chicago*, 115–16. While rooming in the rectory at Our Lady of Angels in West Garfield Park, Egan had witnessed one of the most tragic scenes in the history of Chicago's Catholic community. A terrible fire at the parish school broke out on December 1, 1958, killing three nuns and ninety-two children and injuring another sixty-six children as they sought to escape the flames and smoke. The school was almost completely destroyed, and Fr. Jack took a leave of absence from his work at the Office of Urban Affairs to serve the parish full time in the months afterward. The episode left a lasting mark on him and his ministry.

9. Frisbie, *An Alley in Chicago*, 172–73.

10. William Julius Wilson, *When Work Disappears: The World of the New Urban Poor* (New York: Vintage Books, 1997), 35.

11. Beryl Satter, *Family Properties: How the Struggle over Race and Real Estate Transformed Chicago and Urban America* (New York: Picador, 2009), 36. She notes that "Between 1940 and 1960, Chicago's black population skyrocketed, from 277,731 to 812,637." The phrase "the warmth of other suns" comes from a poem written by Richard Wright included in a revised version of his autobiography, *Black Boy*, and has been taken as the title of Isabel Wilkerson's beautiful and intimate account of this Great Migration story. See Isabel Wilkerson, *The Warmth of Other Suns: The Epic Story of America's Great Migration* (New York: Vintage Books, 2010).

12. Satter, *Family Properties*, 94. She reports that the population density of the neighborhood in 1960 was 29,000 people per square mile, compared to the city average of 17,000.

13. McGreevy, *Parish Boundaries*, 21. McGreevy recounts that for Catholics the parish was such a prominent and important part of life that most answered the question of "Where are you from?" by giving their parish name.

14. Satter, *Family Properties*, 17–18.

15. Keeanga-Yamahtta Taylor, *Race for Profit: How the Banks and the Real Estate Industry Undermined Black Homeownership* (Chapel Hill: University of North Carolina Press, 2019), 27–28.

16. Satter, *Family Properties*, 170.

17. Satter, *Family Properties*, 169.

18. McGreevy, *Parish Boundaries*, 140. The universal theology articulated within church doctrine with respect to race, McGreevy reports, was often in deep tension with views and actions of Catholics on the ground where racism persisted.

19. Frisbie, *An Alley in Chicago*, 173, 177.

20. Satter, *Family Properties*, 234.

21. Frisbie, *An Alley in Chicago*, 179.

22. Frisbie, *An Alley in Chicago*, 180.

23. Satter, *Family Properties*, 120.

24. John J. Egan Papers, University of Notre Dame Archives, Notre Dame, Folder 1/08, Presentation School, 1967–1970, Egan, "An Open Letter to the Sisters of Charity and the Faculty and Staff," February 5, 1969.

25. Frisbie, *An Alley in Chicago*, 177.

26. McGreevy, *Parish Boundaries*, 194.

27. Sanford D. Horwitt, *Let Them Call Me Rebel: Saul Alinsky—His Life and Legacy* (New York: Vintage Books, 1992), 268–70.

28. Author interview with Kathleen Pelletier Moriarty, November 23, 2020.

29. Satter, *Family Properties*, 235, and Frisbie, *An Alley in Chicago*, 190–91. The story of Peggy Roach's life is relayed in Nicholas A. Patricca, *Peggy Roach: One Woman's Journey, a Nation's Progress* (a publication of the Ann Ida Gannon, BVM, Center for Women and Leadership at Loyola University Chicago, 2015), and any full-length biography of Egan would be grossly incomplete without the robust inclusion of her tireless work with him.

30. Frisbie, *An Alley in Chicago*, 177–78.

31. Matthew J. Cressler, *Authentically Black and Truly Catholic: The Rise of Black Catholicism in the Great Migration* (New York: New York University Press, 2017), 62.

32. John J. Egan Papers, Folder 3/38, letter to Cardinal Cody, November 17, 1967.

33. Frisbie, *An Alley in Chicago*, 178–79.

34. Frisbie, *An Alley in Chicago*, 192.

35. Satter, *Family Properties*, 237.

36. Satter, *Family Properties*, 238.

37. Satter, *Family Properties*, 238.

38. Satter, *Family Properties*, 239. See also, Jerry DeMuth, "How Much Is This House Worth? Chicago Parish Moves to Get House Near FHA Level," *National Catholic Reporter* 4, no. 30 (May 22, 1968): 2.

39. Author interview with John Jack Macnamara, July 12, 2020.

40. Frisbie, *An Alley in Chicago*, 86–88. For more on how this struggle impacted Egan's relationship with Alinsky, see Horwitt, *Let Them Call Me Rebel*, 373.

41. Frisbie, *An Alley in Chicago*, 105.

42. Horwitt, *Let Them Call Me Rebel*, 374.

43. Taylor, *Race for Profit*, 52; Natalie Moore, "Contract Buying Robbed Black Families in Chicago of Billions," NPR (WBEZ), May 30, 2019. Moore's reporting covers a new study conducted by the Samuel DuBois Cook Center on Social Equity at Duke University entitled "The Plunder of Black Wealth in Chicago: New Findings on the Lasting Toll of Predatory Housing Contracts," May 2019, https://socialequity.duke.edu/wp-content/uploads/2019/10/Plunder-of-Black-Wealth-in-Chicago.pdf.

44. Author interview with Jack Macnamara, July 12, 2020. Macnamara was a contributor to the above study and references it in commenting on this figure. The Samuel DuBois Cook Center study calculates the effective race tax associated with contract buying to be $587 per month, or $71,727 over the life of the contract. See "The Plunder of Black Wealth in Chicago," 9.

45. King told reporters in 1966 after the violent attack on Black marchers in Marquette Park, "I've been in many demonstrations all across the South, but I can say that I have never seen, even in Mississippi and Alabama, mobs as hostile and as hate-filled as I'm seeing in Chicago." See Ron Grossman, "50 Years Ago: MLK's March in Marquette Park Turned Violent, Exposed Hate," *Chicago Tribune*, July 28, 2016, https://www.chicagotribune.com/opinion/commentary/ct-mlk-king-marquette-park-1966-flashback-perspec-0731-md-20160726-story.html.

46. Taylor, *Race for Profit*, 79.

47. Satter, *Family Properties*, 227–29.

48. Taylor, *Race for Profit*, 106.

49. Richard Rothstein, *The Color of Law: A Forgotten History of How Our Government Segregated America* (New York: Liveright, 2017), 13.

50. Taylor, *Race for Profit*, 32. Taylor reports that "less than two percent of FHA-insured properties went to non-whites" (35).

51. Rothstein, *The Color of Law*, 95. See also, Taylor, *Race for Profit*, 48.

52. Rothstein, *The Color of Law*, 96. The Samuel DuBois Cook Center study estimates the average markup of contract sales at 84 percent. See "The Plunder of Black Wealth in Chicago," iii.

53. Satter, *Family Properties*, 240.

54. Author interview with Jack Macnamara, July 12, 2020.

55. Satter, *Family Properties*, 243–44.

56. Author interview with Jack Macnamara, July 12, 2020.

57. Satter, *Family Properties*, 245–47.

58. Peggy Roach, *Memoir*, an unedited and unpublished manuscript property of the Ann Ida Gannon, BVM, Center for Women and Leadership at Loyola University Chicago, quoted in Patricca, *Peggy Roach*, 54.

59. Frisbie, *An Alley in Chicago*, 192.

60. Patricca, *Peggy Roach*, 50.

61. Satter, *Family Properties*, 254.

62. Satter, *Family Properties*, 261.

63. Patricca, *Peggy Roach*, 51.

64. Satter, *Family Properties*, 271.

65. Satter, *Family Properties*, 271.

66. Satter, *Family Properties*, 274.

67. Satter, *Family Properties*, 293.

68. Satter, *Family Properties*, 293.

69. Author interview with Jack Macnamara, July 12, 2020.

70. Satter, *Family Properties*, 297–98.

71. Satter, *Family Properties*, 298.

72. Satter, *Family Properties*, 300.

73. Satter, *Family Properties*, 299.

74. Satter, *Family Properties*, 299.

75. Satter, *Family Properties*, 309. The cost per eviction had reached nearly $42,000, Satter reports.

76. Satter, *Family Properties*, 307.

77. Satter, *Family Properties*, 306–8.

78. Satter, *Family Properties*, 311.

79. Author interview with Jack Macnamara, July 12, 2020.

80. Author interview with Kathleen Pelletier Moriarty, November 23, 2020.

81. John J. Egan Papers, Folder 1/08, letter to Mr. and Mrs. Dick Gregory, May 18, 1969.

82. Author interview with Tom Lenz, June 30, 2020.

83. This article, first published in the *Catholic Reporter*, is included in full in Robert Ludwig's conclusion to Frisbie, *An Alley in Chicago*, 320–24.

84. United Power for Action and Justice, "United Power Year End Review," an email summary of annual work sent to UPAJ members and supporters, December 28, 2021. See also Kyle Swenson, "These Chicago Residents Are Trying to Revitalize Their Neighborhood without Gentrification," *Washington Post*, October 22, 2021, https://www.washington post.com/dc-md-va/2021/10/22/these-chicago-residents-are-trying -revitalize-their-neighborhood-without-gentrification/.

85. Linda Lutton, "Community Groups Push a Bold Idea to Revitalize Some Chicago Neighborhoods," WBEZ, July 1, 2020, https://www.wbez .org/stories/community-groups-push-a-bold-idea-to-revitalize-some -chicago-neighborhoods/3ef59336-fb18-4684-90c2-3f354fe5987e.

SARAH PATTON BOYLE

1. Sarah Patton Boyle (hereafter SPB) to Harold Sugg, June 19, 1951, Sarah Patton Boyle Papers (hereafter SPB Papers), Small Special Collections, the University of Virginia; SPB, "Individual white persons should have the courage to speak out," clipping from the *Norfolk Virginian-Pilot*, June 9, 1951.
2. SPB to Dabney, May 10, 1951, Box 23, black notebook, SPB Papers.
3. SPB to Dabney, May 20, 1951, Box 23, black notebook, SPB papers.
4. Dabney to SPB, May 25, 1951, Box 23, black notebook, SPB papers.
5. In fact, he didn't always, per the tart note "To this letter I received no reply" scrawled across the bottom of Boyle's copy of one of her longer missives: SPB to Dabney, n.d., Box 23, black notebook, SPB papers.
6. Sarah Patton Boyle, *The Desegregated Heart: A Virginian's Stand in Time of Transition*, ed. Jennifer Ritterhouse (Charlottesville: University Press of Virginia, 2001), 252, 29, 223.
7. Boyle, *The Desegregated Heart*, 8, 30, 21, 22–27.
8. Boyle, *The Desegregated Heart*, 27, 44–45.
9. Boyle, *The Desegregated Heart*, 47.
10. Boyle, *The Desegregated Heart*, 49.
11. Boyle, *The Desegregated Heart*, 49–52.
12. Boyle, *The Desegregated Heart*, 56.
13. Boyle, *The Desegregated Heart*, 72–73.
14. Boyle, *The Desegregated Heart*, 83–84.
15. Boyle, *The Desegregated Heart*, 102, 127.
16. Boyle, *The Desegregated Heart*, 104.
17. B. L. Wilson, "I'm Your Black Friend, but I Won't Educate You about Racism. That's on You," *Washington Post*, June 8, 2020.
18. Boyle, *The Desegregated Heart*, 123.
19. Boyle, *The Desegregated Heart*, 123–25.
20. Dabney to SPB, May 14, 1951, Box 23, black notebook, SPB Papers.
21. Boyle, *The Desegregated Heart*, 134–35.
22. SPB to J. Whetzel, May 30, 1951, Box 8, folder 16, SPB papers.
23. SPB to Cherrie, September 28, 1951, Box 23, black notebook, SPB Papers.
24. Kathleen Anne Murphy, "Sarah Patton Boyle and the Crusade

Against Virginia's Massive Resistance" (MA thesis, University of Virginia, 1983); SPB to Whetzel, September 14, 1951, Box 8, folder 16, SPB Papers.

25. Whetzel to SPB, May 25, 1951, Box 8, folder 16, SPB Papers.

26. SPB to Whetzel, May 30, 1951, Box 8, folder 16, SPB Papers.

27. Whetzel to SPB, August 3, 1951, Box 8, folder 16, SPB Papers. Boyle, "John Whetzel and Brotherhood" (typescript), page 3, Box 8, folder 16, SPB Papers. John W. Wetzel, "Negro Is Pictured as Awakened, Modern," Box 23, black notebook, SPB Papers.

28. SPB to Lillian Smith, September 9, 1951; and SPD to Lillian Smith, September 16, 1952, SPB Papers (8003-c).

29. "How to Gain Personal Power" (adv.), *New York Times*, March 2, 1941.

30. In a 1998 essay, Joanna Bowen Gillespie, a historian of Episcopal women who befriended Patton several years before her death, reads Boyle's commitment to civil rights as, in part, the finding of purpose in a smart, bored, midcentury housewife. She was a woman of talent with no outlet, Gillespie wrote, a woman for whom "none of the more typical white matron activities"—raising two sons, "dabbling in oil painting," writing chatty articles for *Ladies' Home Journal* and *Vogue*—sufficed. In 1948, two years before her encounter with Swanson, Boyle wrote of her restlessness to a friend in Wisconsin: "I've never been confronted with one full-size job that I thought was worth doing with my full strength. I'm not being used, my energy is not fully consumed. I feel the constant pressure of repressed power. . . . I'm a potential fanatic who has not yet found my cause." Perhaps that's a needful strand of an account of why Patty Boyle did what she did: had she been a man of her class, she would have had a career; instead, she found, or was found by, a cause. Joanna Bowen Gillespie, "Sarah Patton Boyle's Desegregated Heart," in *Beyond Image and Convention: Explorations in Southern Women's History*, ed. Janet L. Coryell et al. (Columbia: University of Missouri Press, 1998), 169.

31. "Two Segregation Appeal Briefs Filed," *Washington Post and Times Herald*, October 1956; Patty Patton, "Make Your Child Welcome in the Kitchen," *Parents' Magazine & Family Home Guide*, October 1956, 105.

32. "Mrs. Boyle Says Love Needed on Race Issue," *New Journal and Guide*, March 30, 1957.

33. Boyle, *The Desegregated Heart*, 266.

34. Boyle, *The Desegregated Heart*, 291–93.

35. Boyle, *The Desegregated Heart*, 304–7.

36. Frank Burleso, "Woman Is Firm in Segregation Fight," *Winston Salem Journal and Sentinel*, March 1, 1964 (in Boyle file at the Charlottesville Albemarle Historical Society).

37. SPB to Waring, October 13, 1955, Box 8, SPB papers.

38. SPB to Waring, September 23, 1955, Box 8, SPB papers.

39. Box 11, folder 2 (miscellaneous correspondence, 1961–1962), SPB papers.

40. Box 11, folder 2 (miscellaneous correspondence, 1961–1962), SPB papers.

41. Box 11, folder 2 (miscellaneous correspondence, 1961–1962), SPB papers.

42. Boyle, *The Desegregated Heart*, 254.

43. Boyle, *The Desegregated Heart*, 240.

44. SPB to Waring, September 23, 1955.

45. Jennifer Ritterhouse, "Speaking of Race: Sarah Patton Boyle and the 'T. J. Sellers Course for Backward Southern Whites,'" in *Sex, Love, Race: Crossing Boundaries in North American History*, ed. Martha Hodes (New York: New York University Press, 1999), 492.

46. *BridgeBuilders, 2001–2016, Charolottesville, VA*, available at CVille-Bridge-Builders-2ndprintrun-8-pages.pdf.

47. Ritterhouse, introduction to Boyle, *The Desegregated Heart*, xix.

48. David L. Chappell, *Inside Agitators: White Southerners in the Civil Rights Movement* (Baltimore: Johns Hopkins University Press, 1994); David L. Chappell, *Stone of Hope: Prophetic Religion and the Death of Jim Crow* (Chapel Hill: University of North Carolina Press, 2004).

49. Dabbs to SPB, January 20, 1957, folder "James McBride Dabbs," Box 8003-c, SPB Papers.

50. SPB to Harold Sugg, Box 23, black notebook, SPB Papers.

51. SPB to Mary Carver, September 23, 1968, Box 21, "Correspondence Preparatory to and in Response to SPB's Radio Interviews and T.V. Appearances," SPB Papers.

52. SPB to Sellers, March 27, 1967, in Boyle, *The Desegregated Heart*, 383.

RAMON DAGOBERTO QUIÑONES

1. In addition to Padre Quiñones and Doña Maria del Sorocco, the other sanctuary trial defendants were John Fife, pastor of Southside Presbyterian Church in Tucson, Arizona; Quaker Jim Corbett; Peggy Hutchison, a Methodist and graduate student at the University of Arizona; Nena MacDonald, a nurse who worked with the movement for two months in the summer of 1984; Philip Willis-Conger, son of former Methodist missionaries to Latin America and director of the Tucson Ecumenical Council's Task Force on Central America; Sister Darlene Nicgorski,

a nun with the School Sisters of St. Francis in Milwaukee, Wisconsin, who had worked in Guatemala in the early 1980s and witnessed atrocities; Fr. Tony Clark, pastor of Sacred Heart Catholic Church in Nogales, Arizona; Mary K. Doan Espinoza, coordinator of religious education at Sacred Heart Church in Nogales; and Wendy LeWin, a lay church worker serving refugees in Phoenix. All told, they were charged with seventy-seven counts of violating US immigration laws, particularly of 8 USC 1324 and 1325 for smuggling, transporting, harboring, aiding and abetting the entry of "illegal aliens" into the United States (see Michael L. Altman, "The Arizona Sanctuary Case," *Litigation* 16, no. 4 [Summer 1990]: 23–26, 53–54). A number of counts were dropped over the course of the trial.

2. Arthur H. Rotstein, "Sanctuary Defendants Profiled, Disposition of Charges with PM-Sanctuary Trial," Associated Press, May 2, 1986.

3. Bill Curry, "INS to Study Claims of Abuse as Sanctuary Sentencing Ends," *Los Angeles Times*, July 3, 1986.

4. Pardo de Aguilar said in Spanish, "As a Catholic woman, I participate actively in actions of the church . . . giving shelter to people who don't have a place to stay. I've given refuge to many people in need." Beth McCorkle, United Press International, February 20, 1985.

5. Miriam Davidson, *Convictions of the Heart: Jim Corbett and the Sanctuary Movement* (Tucson: University of Arizona Press, 1989), 40. Much of this chapter is informed by Davidson's excellent work as well as Robert Tomsho's *The American Sanctuary Movement* (Austin: Texas Monthly Press, 1987); Susan Bibler Coutin, *The Culture of Protest: Religious Activism and the US Sanctuary Movement* (San Francisco: Westview, 1993); and Hilary Cunningham, *God and Caesar at the Rio Grande: Sanctuary and the Politics of Religion* (Minneapolis: University of Minnesota Press, 1995).

6. Jay Mathews, "The Sanctuary Movement Awaits Judgement," *Washington Post*, April 18, 1986.

7. See Jim Corbett, "The Covenant as Sanctuary," *Cross Currents*, Winter 1984–1985, 393–404, and John M. Fife, "The Sanctuary Movement: Where Have We Been? Where Are We Going?" *Church and Society*, March-April 1985, 16–24.

8. Many people involved in the sanctuary movement tell the same story: their life changed when they met a refugee face-to-face, heard the refugee's story. Once they met a real person, they could not just stand by and do nothing. As one Presbyterian pastor in Ohio said: "We're a very conservative group of folks politically. But once we encountered the refugees face to face, we couldn't justify not taking them in." Ellie McGrath, "Religion: Bringing Sanctuary to Trial," *Time Magazine*, October 28, 1985.

9. Central Americans were required to produce "proof" of persecution. Only refugees "fleeing communism" were granted asylum. Visa approval rates for Salvadorans and Guatemalans were about 3 percent, compared to about 60 percent for Iranians, 40 percent for Afghans fleeing Soviet invasion, 32 percent for Poles, 12 percent for Nicaraguans escaping the Sandinistas, and 100 percent for Cubans. In 1983, one Guatemalan was granted asylum in the United States. Robert M. Press, "Is It Safe for Guatemalan Refugees to Return Home?" *Christian Science Monitor*, May 30, 1985; "Sanctuary Movement," University of Arizona Library Special Collections: Tucson. It is estimated that about 500,000 Salvadorans and Guatemalans had sought refuge in the United States by 1991, with only 5 percent being granted asylum; see Collin Tong, "Hopeful Changes on the Border," *Christianity and Crisis*, February 4, 1991, 14–16.

10. This chapter joins the work of Becky Thompson and others in reframing the story of the sanctuary movement. As she notes, "What is deceptive and racially biased about identifying 'the sanctuary movement' with predominantly white congregations is that the lion's share of the work with refugees was done clandestinely by Mexicans in Mexico and Latino and multiethnic communities in the United States who took in and sustained hundreds of thousands of refugees"; see "El Testigo Verdadero Libra Las Almas," in *Disrupting White Supremacy from Within: White People on What We Need to Do*, ed. Jennifer Harvey, Karin A. Case, and Robin Hawley Gorsline (Cleveland: Pilgrim, 2004), 165–66.

11. Edward Havens, United Press International, July 2, 1986.

12. Lev. 19:33–34 NIV. For more on the scriptural practice of sanctuary, see Chad Thomas Beck, "Sanctuary for Immigrants and Refugees in Our Legal and Ethical Wilderness," *Interpretation: A Journal of Bible and Theology* 72, no. 2 (2018): 132–45.

13. For more on the practice of sanctuary in the Christian tradition, see Renny Golden, "Sanctuary and Women," *Journal of Feminist Studies in Religion* 2, no. 1 (1986): 131–51, and Cunningham, *God and Caesar*, 68–101.

14. The atrocities occurring in Central America in the 1970s–1980s and the US involvement in them have been extensively documented. Between 1980 and 1991, approximately 1 million Central Americans crossed the US border seeking asylum. In El Salvador, the military had killed over 10,000 people by 1980; during the Salvadoran civil war, which lasted from 1980 to 1992, over 75,000 Salvadorans were killed, an estimated 95 percent of those deaths being perpetrated by government forces. In Guatemala, where the civil war lasted from 1960 to 1996, it is estimated

that government-backed paramilitary groups killed at least 50,000 people, disappeared another 100,000, and perpetrated 626 village massa-
cres. The US government provided funds, training, and arms to the Salvadoran and Guatemalan governments. So as not to admit or undercut
US involvement, the Reagan administration adopted a policy that those
fleeing these countries were "economic migrants" fleeing poverty, not
government repression. See Coutin, *The Culture of Protest*.

15. Mathews, "The Sanctuary Movement Awaits Judgement."

16. Fife, "The Sanctuary Movement," 19–20.

17. Tomsho, *The American Sanctuary Movement*, 31.

18. Amy Frykholm, "Seeking Refuge," *Christian Century*, March 1,
2017, 32–34. See also Renny Golden and Michael McConnell, *Sanctuary: The New Underground Railroad* (Maryknoll, NY: Orbis, 1986). The
sanctuary movement was religiously diverse. As of 1987, 18 percent of
sanctuary congregations were Catholic, 7 percent were Presbyterian,
16 percent were Quakers, 19 percent were Unitarian, 10 percent were
Jewish, with the remaining 30 hailing from mainline Protestant traditions.
Many major denominations made official statements, including the Presbyterian Church, American Lutheran Church, American Baptist Church,
the Rabbinical Assembly, as well as Amnesty International, Americas
Watch, and more. "Denominational Breakdown," in Cunningham, *God
and Caesar*, 65.

19. Renny Golden and Michael McConnell, "Sanctuary: Choosing
Sides," *Christianity and Crisis*, February 21, 1983, 31–36.

20. McCorkle, United Press International, February 20, 1985.

21. Edward Havens, "Refugee Smuggling Case Nears End," United
Press International, March 24, 1986.

22. William Farmer, "A Statement on Sanctuary," *Perkins Journal* 38,
no. 3 (Spring 1985): 27.

23. Farmer, "A Statement on Sanctuary," 27.

24. "Sanctuary Trial," *Christian Century*, January 22, 1986, 64.

25. Fife, "The Sanctuary Movement," 23.

26. "Chief US Witness Testifies against 11 Who Aided Aliens," *New
York Times*, November 21, 1985.

27. Christina Medvescek, "Sanctuary Convictions: Law over Justice,"
Christian Century, June 4–11, 1986, 541–42.

28. "Chief US Witness Testifies against 11 Who Aided Aliens."

29. Edward Havens, United Press International, July 2, 1986.

30. McCorkle, United Press International, February 20, 1985.

31. "Despite Prosecutions, Sanctuary Movement Is Still Vital, Growing, Its Activists Insist," Associated Press, July 11, 1987.

32. As of early May 2021, it was reported that 22,500 children remained in US custody. Some of these children had entered the United States alone, but at least 5,000 had been separated from their parents by US authorities. Many of these parents were then deported without their children; 1,000 such children remained in US custody as of May 2021. See "Child Migrants: Massive Drop in Children Held by Border Officials," BBC News, May 5, 2021, https://www.bbc.com/news/world-us-canada-56405009.

33. Nelson Renteria, "Over 130 Migrants Killed after U.S. Deports Them to El Salvador, Rights Group Says," Reuters, February 4, 2020, https://www.reuters.com/article/us-usa-immigration-elsalvador/over-130-migrants-killed-after-u-s-deports-them-to-el-salvador-rights-group-says-idUSKBN1ZZ0G4.

34. Frykholm, "Seeking Refuge"; and Kimberly Winston and Amanda Hoover, "Sanctuary Churches, Cities, May Face Consequences from Federal Authorities," *Christian Century*, April 26, 2017, 13-14. The New Sanctuary Movement differs slightly from the original insofar as it not only seeks to protect migrants seeking entry to the United States but also seeks to prevent undocumented workers who have been working in the United States for decades from being deported.

35. Elie Wiesel, "The Refugee," *Cross Currents*, Winter 1984-1985, 386.

Contributors

Jacqueline A. Bussie is the executive director of the Collegeville Institute for Ecumenical and Cultural Research. She previously taught religion, theology, and interfaith studies classes at Concordia College in Moorhead, Minnesota. Her books include *The Laughter of the Oppressed* (2007), which won the national Trinity Prize, *Outlaw Christian: Finding Authentic Faith by Breaking the Rules* (Thomas Nelson, 2016), which won the 2017 Gold Medal Illumination Award for Christian Living, and *Love Without Limits: Jesus' Radical Vision for a Love with No Exceptions* (Fortress, 2018), which won the 2020 IAN Outstanding Religion Book of the Year Award.

Carolyn Renée Dupont is a professor in history at Eastern Kentucky University. Her research focuses on American religion and African American history. She is the author of *Mississippi Praying: Southern White Evangelicals and the Civil Rights Movement, 1945–1975* (New York University Press, 2013). She serves as the book review editor for the *Journal of Southern Religion.*

Mark R. Gornik served as the founding pastor of New Song in Baltimore and is the Director of City Seminary of New York (www

.cityseminaryny.org). He is the coauthor of *Stay in the City: How Christian Faith Is Flourishing in an Urban World* (Eerdmans, 2017) and author of the forthcoming *Sharing the Crust: A Story of Friendship and Love in a Neighborhood of God.*

Jane Hong is associate professor of history at Occidental College and the author of *Opening the Gates to Asia: A Transpacific History of How America Repealed Asian Exclusion* (University of North Carolina Press, 2019). She serves on the editorial board of the *Journal of American History* and has written for the *Washington Post* and *Los Angeles Times.* Hong is currently writing a history of how post-1965 Asian immigration has changed US evangelical institutions and politics (to be published by Oxford University Press).

Ann Hostetler is professor emerita at Goshen College, where she taught English and creative writing for over two decades. She is the author of *Safehold* (Dreamseeker Books, 2018) and *Empty Room with Light* (Dreamseeker Books, 2002), and editor of *A Cappella: Mennonite Voices in Poetry* (University of Iowa Press, 2003). Her scholarly articles have appeared in *PMLA*, the *Mennonite Quarterly Review, Emerson Studies Quarterly*, and elsewhere. Ann has also published poetry in *The American Scholar, Quiddity, Poet Lore,* and other literary journals. She edits the *Journal of Mennonite Writing* at mennonitewriting.org.

M. Therese Lysaught is a professor and associate director at the Institute of Pastoral Studies at Loyola University Chicago, where she specializes in Catholic moral theology and healthcare ethics and consults with healthcare systems on issues surrounding mission, theology, and ethics. She is an editor of *Gathered for the Journey: Moral Theology in Catholic Perspective* (Eerdmans, 2007) and *Catholic Bioethics and Social Justice: The Praxis of US Health Care in a Globalized World* (Liturgical Press Academic, 2018).

Charles Marsh is the Commonwealth Professor of Religious Studies and director of the Project on Lived Theology at the University of Virginia. Marsh's books include *God's Long Summer: Stories of Faith and Civil Rights* (Princeton, 1997), which won the 1998 Grawemeyer Award in Religion, *Strange Glory: A Life of Dietrich Bonhoeffer* (Knopf, 2014), which received the 2015 Christianity Today Book Award in History/Biography, and most recently, *Evangelical Anxiety: A Memoir* (HarperOne, 2022).

Mallory McDuff teaches environmental education at Warren Wilson College in Asheville, North Carolina, where she lives on campus with her two daughters. Her essays have appeared in *The New York Times*, *The Washington Post*, *Catapult*, *The Rumpus*, *Sojourners*, and more. She is the author of the books *Our Last Best Act: Planning for the End of Our Lives to Protect the People and Places We Love* (Broadleaf, 2021), *Sacred Acts: How Churches Are Working to Protect Earth's Climate* (New Society, 2012), and *Natural Saints: How People of Faith Are Working to Save God's Earth* (Oxford University Press, 2010), as well as coauthor of *Conservation Education and Outreach Techniques* (Oxford University Press, 2015).

Ansley L. Quiros is an associate professor of history at the University of North Alabama. Her award-winning first book, *God With Us: Lived Theology and the Freedom Struggle in Americus, Georgia, 1942–1976* (University of North Carolina Press, 2018), examines the struggle over race and Christian theology in Southwest Georgia. Her writing has also appeared in *The Washington Post* and *The Gospel Coalition*.

Daniel P. Rhodes is a founding board member of the Black Mountain School of Theology & Community and is Clinical Associate Professor of Contextual Education at the Institute of Pastoral Studies of Loyola University Chicago. His work focuses on the intersection of political theology, ecclesiology, and ethics. He copastored Emmaus Way in Durham with Tim Conder. Their collaboration produced the book *Organizing Church: Grassroots Practices for Embodying Change in Your Congregation, Your Community, and Our World* (Chalice, 2017). He is also coeditor, with Charles Marsh and Shea Tuttle, of *Can I Get a Witness? Thirteen Peacemakers, Community Builders, and Agitators for Faith and Justice* (Eerdmans, 2019).

Peter Slade is professor of the history of Christianity and Christian thought at Ashland University. Slade's first book, *Open Friendship in a Closed Society: Mission Mississippi and a Theology of Friendship* (Oxford University Press, 2009), is an interdisciplinary study of an ecumenical racial reconciliation initiative in Mississippi. He has been a coeditor of and contributor to two volumes with the Project on Lived Theology: *Lived Theology: New Perspectives on Method, Style, and Pedagogy* (Oxford University Press, 2016) and *Mobilizing for the Common Good: The Lived Theology of John M. Perkins* (University Press of Mississippi, 2013).

Jemar Tisby is the author of the *New York Times* bestselling book *The Color of Compromise: The Truth about the Church's Complicity in Racism* (Zondervan, 2019), and also *How to Fight Racism: Courageous Christianity and the Journey toward Racial Justice* (Zondervan, 2021). His latest book is *How to Fight Racism: Young Reader's Edition* (Zonderkidz, 2022). Jemar has been a cohost of the "Pass the Mic" podcast since its inception seven years ago. His writing has been featured in *The Washington Post, The Atlantic,* and the *New York Times,* among others. He is a frequent commentator on outlets such as NPR and CNN's New Day program. He speaks nationwide on the topics of racial justice, US history, and Christianity. Jemar earned his PhD in history, and he studies race, religion, and social movements in the twentieth century. You can follow his work through his newsletter, *Footnotes,* and on social media at @JemarTisby.

Shea Tuttle is the author of *Exactly as You Are: The Life and Faith of Mister Rogers* (Eerdmans, 2019), coauthor of *Phyllis Frye and the Fight for Transgender Rights* (Texas A&M University Press, 2022), and coeditor of *Can I Get a Witness? Thirteen Peacemakers, Community Builders, and Agitators for Faith and Justice* (Eerdmans, 2019).

Lauren F. Winner is an associate professor of Christian spirituality at Duke Divinity School and vicar of St. Paul's Episcopal Church in Louisburg, North Carolina. Her interests include Christian practice, the history of Christianity in America, and Jewish-Christian relations. Winner's books include *Girl Meets God: On the Path to a Spiritual Life* (Algonquin Books, 2002); *Mudhouse Sabbath: An Invitation to a Life of Spiritual Discipline* (Paraclete Press, 2007); *A Cheerful and Comfortable Faith: Anglican Religious Practice in the Elite Households of Eighteenth-Century Virginia* (Yale University Press, 2010); *Still: Notes on a Mid-Faith Crisis* (HarperOne, 2013); *Wearing God: Clothing, Laughter, Fire, and Other Overlooked Ways of Meeting God* (HarperOne, 2016); and *The Dangers of Christian Practice: On Wayward Gifts, Characteristic Damage, and Sin* (Yale University Press, 2018).

FURTHER READING

FLORENCE JORDAN

Jordan, Clarence. *Essential Writings*. Edited by Joyce Hollyday. Maryknoll, NY: Orbis Books, 2007.

K'Meyer, Tracy E. *Interracialism and Christian Community in the Postwar South: The Story of Koinonia Farm*. Charlottesville: University of Virginia Press, 1997.

Quiros, Ansley. *God with Us: Lived Theology and the Freedom Struggle in Americus, Georgia, 1942–1976*. Chapel Hill: University of North Carolina Press, 2018.

BRUCE KLUNDER

Sugrue, Thomas J. *Sweet Land of Liberty: The Forgotten Struggle for Civil Rights in the North*. New York: Random House, 2008.

Theoharis, Jeanne. *A More Beautiful and Terrible History: The Uses and Misuses of Civil Rights History*. Boston: Beacon Press, 2018.

Tisby, Jemar. *The Color of Compromise: The Truth about the American Church's Complicity in Racism*. Grand Rapids: Zondervan, 2019.

Tom Skinner

Emerson, Michael, and Christian Smith. *Divided by Faith: Evangelical Religion and the Problem of Race in America.* New York: Oxford University Press, 2000.

Skinner, Tom. *Black and Free.* Revised commemorative edition. Maitland, FL: Xulon Press, 2005.

Tisby, Jemar. *How to Fight Racism: Courageous Christianity and the Journey toward Racial Justice.* Grand Rapids: Zondervan, 2021.

Rachel Carson

Carson, Rachel. *The Sense of Wonder: A Celebration of Nature for Parents and Children.* New York: Harper & Row Publications, 1965.

Carson, Rachel. *Lost Woods: The Discovered Writings of Rachel Carson.* Edited by Linda Lear. Boston: Beacon Press, 1999.

Lepore, Jill. "The Right Way to Remember Rachel Carson." *The New Yorker*, March 19, 2018. https://www.newyorker.com/magazine/2018/03/26/the-right-way-to-remember-rachel-carson.

Allan Tibbels

Brown, Lawrence T. *The Black Butterfly: The Harmful Politics of Race and Space in America.* Baltimore: Johns Hopkins University Press, 2021.

Moore, Wes, with Erica L. Green. *Five Days: The Fiery Reckoning of an American City.* New York: One World, 2020.

Perkins, John. *A Quiet Revolution: The Christian Response to Human Need . . . A Strategy for Today.* Waco: Word Books, 1976.

Mary Paik Lee

Joshi, Khyati Y., and David K. Yoo, eds. *Envisioning Religion, Race, and Asian Americans.* Honolulu: University of Hawaii Press, 2020.

Lee, Mary Paik. *Quiet Odyssey: A Pioneer Korean Woman in America.* Seattle: University of Washington Press, 1990.

Yoo, David K. *Contentious Spirits: Religion in Korean American History, 1903–1945.* Honolulu: University of Hawaii Press, 2010.

Flannery O'Connor

O'Connor, Flannery. *A Good Man Is Hard to Find.* New York: Harcourt, Brace and Company, 1955.

O'Connor, Flannery. *Mystery and Manners: Occasional Prose.* Edited by Sally Fitzgerald and Robert Fitzgerald. New York: Farrar, Straus and Giroux, 1969.

O'Connor, Flannery. *A Prayer Journal.* Edited by W. A. Sessions. New York: Farrar, Straus and Giroux, 2013.

Pete Seeger

Dunaway, David King. *How Can I Keep from Singing? The Ballad of Pete Seeger.* 2nd ed. New York: Villard, 2008.

Seeger, Pete. *Pete Seeger: In His Own Words.* Edited by Rob Rosenthal and Sam Rosenthal. Boulder, CO: Paradigm Publishers, 2012.

Seeger, Pete, Len Chandler, and The Freedom Voices. *WNEW's Story of Selma.* LP, Folkways Records, 1965 (available on Spotify, YouTube Music, Amazon music, and other streaming services).

Toni Morrison

Bennett, Juda, Winnifred Brown-Glaude, Cassandra Jackson, and Piper Kendrix Williams. *The Toni Morrison Book Club*. Madison: University of Wisconsin Press, 2020.

Carrasco, David, Stephanie Paulsell, and Mara Willard, eds. *Goodness and the Literary Imagination: Harvard's 95th Ingersoll Lecture with Essays on Morrison's Moral and Religious Vision*. Charlottesville: University of Virginia Press, 2019.

Nittle, Nadra. *Toni Morrison's Spiritual Vision: Faith, Folktales, and Feminisms in Her Life and Literature*. Minneapolis: Fortress, 2021.

Jack Egan

Frisbie, Margery. *An Alley in Chicago: The Life and Legacy of Monsignor John Egan*. Franklin, WI: Sheed & Ward, 2002.

Johnson, Karen J. *One in Christ: Chicago Catholics and the Quest for Interracial Justice*. New York: Oxford University Press, 2018.

Satter, Beryl. *Family Properties: How the Struggle Over Race and Real Estate Transformed Chicago and Urban America*. New York: Picador, 2009.

Sarah Patton Boyle

Boyle, Sarah Patton. *The Desegregated Heart: A Virginian's Stand in Time of Transition*. Edited by Jennifer Ritterhouse. Charlottesville: University Press of Virginia, 2001.

Hobson, Fred. *But Now I See: The White Southern Racial Conversion Narrative*. Baton Rouge: LSU Press, 1999.

Shattuck, Gardiner H. *Episcopalians and Race: Civil War to Civil Rights*. Lexington: University of Kentucky Press, 2003.

Ramon Quiñones

Davidson, Miriam. *Convictions of the Heart: Jim Corbett and the Sanctuary Movement.* Tucson: University of Arizona Press, 1989.

Golden, Renny, and Michael McConnell. *Sanctuary: The New Underground Railroad.* Maryknoll, NY: Orbis Books, 1986.

Hinojosa, Victor. *A Journey toward Hope.* Houston, TX: Six Foot Press, 2020. (This is a children's book. Tambien disponable en Español: *Un jornada hacia la esperanza.*)

Luiselli, Valeria. *Tell Me How It Ends.* Minneapolis: Coffee House Press, 2017.

Nazario, Sonia. *Enrique's Journey.* New York: Random House, 2007.

INDEX

Page numbers in italics represent photographs.

, Samuel, 130–31

anto Chemical Company,

ɔ

.orley, Pat, 73–75

Morrison, Harold, 202

Morrison, Toni, 193–214, *194*;
Atelier Program, 311n25;
career, 202–3; childhood, 196–
97, 199; children, 202; education, 201–2; friendship with
Elaine Pagels, 207–8; influences, 203–4, 208; legacy, 195,
203, 211–12; lived theology
of, 205–7, 210–12; marriage
and divorce, 202; nuance and
ambiguity embraced by, 205;
public persona, 201, 204; religious formation and practice,
200–201, 205, 208–9; themes
explored by, 206–7, 210–13; at
Toni Morrison Society conference, 200. Works: *Beloved*,
203; *The Bluest Eye*, 195, 197,
203, 207; *Dreaming Emmett*,
213; *God Help the Child*, 213;
*Goodness and the Literary
Imagination*, 212; *Jazz*, 203,
208; *Love*, 203, 208; *The Origin
of Others*, 212; *Paradise*, 199,
203, 205, 208–11; "A Slow
Walk of Trees," 197; *Song of
Solomon*, 197, 203; *Sula*, 203;
Tar Baby, 203

Moss, Mr. and Mrs. Jonnie,
232–33

Mystery and Manners (O'Connor), 160

NAACP (National Association
for the Advancement of Colored People), 42–43

National Committee of Negro
Churchmen, 63–64

National Conference on Black
Power (1967), 68–69

Neblett, Charles, 186

Nelson, Claud, 18–19

Nelson, Elizabeth, 232

Newark uprising, 68

New Sanctuary Movement,
281–82, 322n34

New Song community, 111–13,
116

New Song Learning Center and
Academy, 114

Nicgorski, Darlene, 266, 277,
318n1

Nietzsche, Friedrich, x

Nixon, Hannah, 135

Nogales, Mexico, 263

Obama, Barack, 211, 213

O'Connor, Flannery, 141–66,
142; canceling of, 151, 153–54,
159, 164; death of, 145, 152–53;
education, 155–56; grace central for, 144–45, 155, 157–59,
162–65; letters, 146–49, 151–

...ation Church Commu-
Organization Project, 224
...gh, Willie, 17
ugliese, Ann Coe, 223

Quiet Odyssey (Lee), 122–23
Quiñones, Ramon Dagoberto,
259–82, *260*; appearance
of, 263–64; on immigration
policy, 264; and infiltration,
278, 280; joyful presence of,
263–64; refugees supported
by, 263–64, 267–73; "Sanctuary Trial," 261, 265, 275,
280–81

RAAN (Reformed African
American Network), 59, 81
"race tax," 225, 314n44
racism, anti-Asian: in California, 124, 126–28, 134;
COVID-19 and, 139; immi-
grant responses to, 125–26,
129–32; in US immigration
laws, 123, 124–25; among
white Christians, 129–31
racism, anti-Black: *vs.* Catholic
teaching, 312n18; in Chicago,
226, 314n45; internalization
of, 197–98; intrusions of
grace and, 165; of O'Connor,
146–52, 165; thug trope in, 37,
45–46, 51; viewed as individual problem, 73, 131, 198. *See
also under* white Christians

Radical Ambivalence (O'Donnell), 151
Ransom, John Crowe, 149
Rayburn, James, 280
Reagan administration, 320n14
Reagon, Bernice Johnson,
185–87, 190
Reagon, Cordell, 186
"Reclaiming Chicago," 236
redlining, 226–27
Reformed African American
Network (RAAN), 59, 81
refugees: Central American,
263, 267, 271, 276–77, 320n9;
children, 281, 322n32; "eco-
nomic," 267, 320n14; increase
in (1980s), 263; and US immi-
gration policy, 264, 266–67,
273, 320n9
Rehoboth Baptist Church,
20–22, 287n68
Reno, Donald, 281
"Revelation" (O'Connor),
143–45
Rhee, Syngman, 133–34
Ricks, Willie, 63
Ripatrazone, Nick, 212
Risner, William, 269–70, 275
Ritterhouse, Jennifer, 255
Roach, Peggy, 222, 229
Robeson, Paul, 175–76
Ross, Clyde, 229–31
Rothstein, Richard, 227
Russell, Richard, 152

...d systemic approach to rac-
sm, 57, 59–62, 70, 77–78, 80
Wiesel, Elie, 281–82
Wilkins, Ardelia, 197
Williams-Skinner, Barbara, 77
Willis, John Solomon, 197
Willis-Conger, Philip, 266,
318n1
Wilson, B. L., 244
Witness, a Black Christian
Collective, 81
Wofford, Chloe Ardelia. *See*
Morrison, Toni

Wofford, Ellah Ramah, 196,
200–201, 210
Wofford, George Carl, 196
Wofford, Lois, 196–98, 212
Woods, Joseph, 232
Words of Revolution (Skinner),
77–78
Workingman's Party, 124
Wright, Richard, 292n15, 312n11

Young, Andrew, 185, 187

Zinn, Howard, 171, 186